Threats and Alliances in th

Examining differing perceptions of threats and the subsequent alliance choices of two Arab states, Saudi Arabia and Syria, during three pivotal wars in the region – the Iran–Iraq War (1980–1988), the Lebanon War (2006) and the Gaza War (2009) – May Darwich analyses how ideational and material forces influence leaders' perceptions and policies in the Middle East.

Using these comparative case studies, Darwich advances our understanding of why, and the conditions under which, identity can play a predominant role in shaping the perception of threat in some cases, whilst material power is predominant in others. By engaging in significant debates about the role identity and material power play in shaping state behaviour in the Middle East, this study has significant implications for international relations theory and beyond.

MAY DARWICH is Lecturer in the Department of Politics and International Studies at the University of Birmingham. Her research focusing on bringing Middle East cases to debates within IR theory has appeared in internationally renowned journals, including *Foreign Policy Analysis*, *Journal of Global Security Studies*, *Democratization*, *Mediterranean Politics* and *Global Discourse*.

Threats and Alliances in the Middle East

Saudi and Syrian Policies in a
Turbulent Region

MAY DARWICH
University of Birmingham

CAMBRIDGE
UNIVERSITY PRESS

CAMBRIDGE
UNIVERSITY PRESS

University Printing House, Cambridge CB2 8BS, United Kingdom

One Liberty Plaza, 20th Floor, New York, NY 10006, USA

477 Williamstown Road, Port Melbourne, VIC 3207, Australia

314-321, 3rd Floor, Plot 3, Splendor Forum, Jasola District Centre, New Delhi - 110025, India

79 Anson Road, #06-04/06, Singapore 079906

Cambridge University Press is part of the University of Cambridge.

It furthers the University's mission by disseminating knowledge in the pursuit of
education, learning and research at the highest international levels of excellence.

www.cambridge.org
Information on this title: www.cambridge.org/9781108737630
DOI: 10.1017/9781108656689

First published 2019
First paperback edition 2020

A catalogue record for this publication is available from the British Library

Library of Congress Cataloging in Publication data
Names: Darwich, May, 1987- author.
Title: Threats and alliances in the Middle East : Saudi and Syrian policies in a turbulent
    region / May Darwich.
Description: Cambridge, United Kingdom ; New York, NY : Cambdridge University Press,
    2019. | Includes bibliographical references and index.
Identifiers: LCCN 2019014860| ISBN 9781108493628 (hardback) |
    ISBN 9781108737630 (pbk.)
Subjects: LCSH: Saudi Arabia–Foreign relations–Middle East. | Middle East–Foreign
    relations–Saudi Arabia. | Saudi Arabia–Foreign relations–20th century. | Saudi
    Arabia–Foreign relations–21st century. | Syria–Foreign relations–Middle East. | Middle
    East–Foreign relations–Syria. | Syria–Foreign relations–1971- | Middle East–Foreign
    relations–1979- | Iran-Iraq War, 1980-1988–Diplomatic history. | Lebanon War,
    2006–Diplomatic history. | Gaza War, 2008-2009–Diplomatic history. | International
    relations. | Threats.
Classification: LCC DS63.2.S33 D37 2019 | DDC 956.05/4–dc23
LC record available at https://lccn.loc.gov/2019014860

ISBN 978-1-108-49362-8 Hardback
ISBN 978-1-108-73763-0 Paperback

Contents

Figures and Tables

Figure

Tables

Acknowledgements

I have incurred a long list of debts while researching and writing this book. It is my honour to acknowledge all those who have influenced my work, both academically and personally. Without their support, this book would not have been possible. All faults remain only mine.

My sincere gratitude goes to my insightful and encouraging PhD supervisors. Their distinct gifts have complemented each other. Adham Saouli has been an invaluable mentor. His criticism and insistence on well-structured argument helped me develop my ideas and articulate them in clear and straightforward ways. During our discussions, he inspired me to make this dissertation into a work that satisfies my own interests and ambitions. Juliet Kaarbo has supported my work with both generous praise and invaluable advice. Her skill for providing genuinely constructive criticism, while preserving my passion and enthusiasm, is unique. Her professionalism and dedication make her an example that one can only aspire to emulate. For this, and for so much more, I am deeply grateful to both of them. I owe my passion for and fascination with IR theories to my master's degree supervisor, Dario Battistella, whose guidance and support made this work possible in the first place. I am also grateful to my PhD examiners, Morten Valbjørn and Ewan Stein, who gave me the confidence to take this project forward. I am also grateful to two anonymous reviewers who provided insightful comments that encouraged me to take both theoretical and empirical work in new directions.

I acknowledge with gratitude the Institute of Middle East Studies at the GIGA German Institute of Global and Area Studies in Germany, which provided me with an academic home and an intellectually nurturing and challenging environment. I would like to express my deep gratitude to André Bank, Maria Josua and Thomas Richter who provided support, inspiration and encouragement. At Durham University, my good fortune continued with amazing colleagues who encouraged and supported me through the final stages of this process. I am particularly grateful to Jutta Bakonyi and Ruth Wittlinger.

My heartfelt gratitude goes to all my friends and relatives who supported me through every stage of this long enterprise. I am particularly grateful to Eva Hoffman, Shamiran Mako, Francesca Batzella, Anouk Berthier, Zoey Reeve and Riham Hossam for their great friendship. I also would like to thank my cousins Noha and Ingi. I thank Aunt Rabha Baz and Uncle Ahmed Warda for being family beyond blood and borders. I am grateful to Aunt Soraya Baz, who passed away, for her tremendous love. I owe special gratitude to my sister Dina, who defeated my pessimism and always reminded me of the bright side during difficult times. Her love, enthusiasm and humour brought the sun out even during the darkest moments Middle East politics can bring.

My greatest and deepest gratitude is due to my parents, Mona and Ayman. All the words in the world would be insufficient to acknowledge how their unstinting love, sacrifice and selflessness contributed to this work. In societies where higher education has sadly become an unvalued privilege and where perseverance and ambition have become underappreciated values, they proved to be bastions of relentless encouragement and dedication. I am blessed by their existence. For being the sources of my ontological and physical security, I dedicate to them this humble effort as a small token of my endless adoration and gratitude.

Note on Transliteration and Translation

For Arab terminology, this book uses the system of translation adopted by the *International Journal of Middle East Studies (IJMES)*. The definite article *al* (the) that often precedes nouns and names is not capitalised, unless it is at the beginning of a sentence. Commonly used proper names and places have followed their standard English renderings, such as Al Saud, al-Assad, Gamal Abdel Nasser and Faisal. In addition, I have used accepted transliterations of common Arabic words like shari'a, Jihad and Ba'ath. In the Bibliography, the titles of all Arabic primary and secondary sources have been transliterated and then translated in squared brackets.

1 | Introduction
Debating Threat Perception

Iran is backing Assad. Gulf states are against Assad! Assad is against Muslim Brotherhood. Muslim Brotherhood and Obama are against General Sissi. But Gulf states are pro-Sissi! Which means they are against Muslim Brotherhood. Iran is pro-Hamas, but Hamas is backing Muslim Brotherhood! Obama is backing Muslim Brotherhood, yet Hamas is against the US! Gulf states are pro-US. But Turkey is with Gulf states against Assad; yet Turkey is pro-Muslim Brotherhood against General Sissi. And General Sissi is being backed by the Gulf states! Welcome to the Middle East and have a nice day.

K. N. Al-Sabah, *Financial Times*, 26 August 2013

This book examines a recurrent puzzle in the international relations of the Middle East. Leaders and regimes in the Middle East frequently make alliance decisions based on perception of threats emanating from both domestic and regional environments. When faced with both ideational and material sources of danger, regimes often diverge in their perceptions of what constitutes the most eminent threat. Whereas ideational forces shape leaders' threat perceptions in some cases, material forces override perceptions in other instances. This book addresses two questions: First, how do ideational and material forces shape regimes' threat perceptions? Second, why, and under which conditions, do ideational forces override material considerations in leaders' perception of threats, and vice versa?

On 22 September 1980, Saddam Hussein ordered the strike of air bases in Iran, thus launching the eight-year Iran–Iraq War. Following the Islamic Revolution in 1979, it became clear that the Ayatollahs were trying to export the revolution to Arab states of the Gulf. Though Saddam Hussein initiated the war, he obtained the support of Saudi Arabia, Jordan, Kuwait, Qatar, the United Arab Emirates (UAE), North Yemen, Tunisia and Morocco. Even Egypt that Saddam Hussein isolated regionally following the peace treaty with Israel (1979) supplied Iraq with Soviet military equipment. The support of Saddam Hussein in the Arab world was not unanimous, however. Syria and Libya gave military assistance to Iran in an attempt to balance Iraq's rising military ambitions in the region. This book focuses on the divergence in Arab leaders' alliance decisions based on the role of ideational and material forces in shaping their threat perceptions.

Throughout the 1970s, Iran and Iraq competed over hegemony in the Persian Gulf. Both countries transformed their military forces, thereby achieving a strategic parity where Iran was slightly superior. This balance of power was profoundly reversed by the Islamic Revolution in 1979. Viewing the army as Mohammad Reza Pahlavi Shah's most loyal institution, the Revolutionary Guards deliberately destroyed Iran's well-trained professional army, and hence altered the regional balance of power, ending Iran's regional supremacy. In the meantime, Saddam Hussein's regional military power increased significantly between 1975 and 1979, especially with a peak in the oil prices of 1973–74. Arab states, including Gulf states, were very much aware of Iran's declining military capabilities, as Ahmad Abdulaziz al-Jassim from the Kuwait Foreign Ministry pointed out:

In April 1980, an attempt was made on [the Iraqi Foreign Minister] Tariq 'Aziz life and there were some clashes along the Iran–Iraq border. At that time, Iran offered us to sell their Phantom airplanes to Kuwait. When we told them we were not interested, they asked us to relay the offer to the Saudis. They were not interested either. This showed us that Iran was not thinking of entering a war. (Quoted in Marschall 2003, 67)

Thus, it remains unclear why some Arab states consistently perceived a country ready to sell its air forces as a major source of danger, while Saddam Hussein's rising military ambitions were not perceived as such. An Arab collective regional balancing never materialised; instead, Arab states diverged in their perception of what constitutes the ultimate threat. Whereas Saudi Arabia, Egypt and Jordan perceived the threat of the message emanating from the Islamic Revolution in a militarily weakened Iran as paramount, Syria most feared Iraq's rising military power. This divergence of Arab regimes over the two protagonists of the Gulf – Iraq and Iran – raises provocative puzzles with direct relevance for understanding the role of ideational and material sources of threats in leaders' perception and alliance decisions. Iraq's military ambitions were a danger for all Arab regimes alike. Yet, they diverged in their perceptions of the regional balance of power. Similarly, the message of the Islamic Revolution that inspired resistance movements across the region constituted a challenge for all Arab regimes involved in supressing Islamic movements at home. The Gulf monarchies, Egypt, and Jordan, however, perceived such an ideational threat to be more pressing, whereas Syria and Libya considered Iraq's rising military power to be far more threatening. The apparent primacy of either ideational or material forces in states' threat perception constitutes one of the most intriguing puzzles for the study of threat perception in the international relations of the Middle East and beyond.

Syria and Saudi Arabia's divergence is particularly illustrative as both cases defy the existing literature on the role of ideational and material factors in the process of threat perception. Conventional neorealist approaches in International Relations (IR) argue that states sharing similar regional structures are likely to adopt converging foreign policies. Despite similar geographic proximity towards Iraq and convergent material interests in the stability in the Gulf, the Arab–Israeli conflict, and Lebanon, both Saudi Arabia and Syria differed in their reactions to Iran and Iraq.

In contrast to the assumption that identity convergence fosters cooperation, both Saudi Arabia and Syria perceived identity similarity as a source of fear. Despite the initial pan-Islamic message of the Islamic Revolution that conforms to the Saudi pan-Islamic identity narrative, Iran was perceived as more threatening than Iraq, a regime with a secular Ba'athist ideology. In that sense, Saudi Arabia, a monarchy that prides itself on its compliance with Islam, controverted the proper enactment of its pan-Islamic identity instead of embracing its principles; the pan-Islamic message of the revolution constituted the ultimate source of fear. In parallel, the Syrian regime, suppressing Islamist movements at home, allied with Iran against a seemingly like-minded secular Ba'athist regime in Iraq. This alliance violated the proper enactment of the regime's pan-Arab identity, according to which Arabs should unite against non-Arabs. In short, the Arab nationalist Syrian regime that championed a secular Ba'athist ideology supported non-Arab Iran – an Islamic regime bent on exporting its revolutionary theological doctrine – against a fellow Arab and Ba'athist regime in Iraq.

Furthermore, both cases challenge conventional wisdom on perceptual factors related to the effect of transnational ideologies and regimes' ultimate concern with domestic stability. This prerequisite for survival makes regimes more vulnerable towards revolutionary ideology aiming at destabilising their domestic rule. Although this argument explains the Saudi fear from the Islamic Revolution, the Syrian case poses a crucial challenge. Syria, a secular pan-Arab regime oppressing Islamist movements at home, should be equally threatened by the message of the Islamic Revolution. Yet, material considerations, such as the relative power distribution animated by Iraq's rising military ambitions, were prevalent in Syria's threat perception.

These puzzles raise questions with direct relevance to understanding the process of threat perception in the international relations of the Middle East and beyond. This book addresses the following primary question: Why, and under which conditions, do ideational forces dominate regimes' threat perception, and when do material forces override ideational ones in their perception of threat?

In the discipline of IR, threat perception has been a constituent element in the study of alliances.[1] Scholars studying the dynamics of alliance formation focus on two main phases in states' strategic calculus: (1) the perception or identification of a threat and (2) the decision about whether, and with whom, to ally in response to that perceived threat. Although threat perception has been amply studied within the alliance literature, the subject remains of the highest significance in terms of both theory development and policymaking. In academia, a widespread disagreement has dominated the debate on the factors that contribute to regimes' fear. Two explanatory camps stand out: one that identifies material factors as the primary driver in threat perception, and the other that privileges ideational forces. Together these two camps stake out the conceptual parameters of the study of alliance formation. This book sheds new lights on this debate by addressing the conditions that can explain when ideational forces will be predominant in states' fear of another and when material forces will be decisive.

On the one hand, realist scholars who have focused on material forces in shaping actors' threat perceptions have paid less attention

---

[1] I follow Walt (1987, 12) in defining an alliance as 'a formal or informal form of security cooperation between two or more sovereign states', but I extend the definition to include non-state actors.

to the role of ideational forces in this process. For example, Walt's (1987) neorealist-inspired balance-of-threat theory privileges material factors (aggregate power, geographic proximity, offensive capabilities). Although Walt adds 'aggressive intentions' as a source of threats, ideational factors remain secondary in his theory. Ideational factors are mere instruments in the hand of leaders to justify their material interest-driven foreign policies. By focusing on material factors and giving ideational factors a secondary role, neorealism offers viable explanations for some cases, but it cannot adequately account for others. For example, if neorealist explanations can offer a viable explanation for the Syrian alliance based on the prevalence of material factors in the balance-of-threat logic, they fall short of answering why Saudi Arabia supported a militarily ambitious Iraq against a militarily weakened Iran.

On the other hand, scholars favouring ideational forces in their analysis have considered material forces to be epiphenomena. Barnett (1996, 1998) offers an alternative constructivist explanation of threat perception and alliance choices based on the politics of identity. In *Dialogues in Arab Politics* (1998), Barnett argues that rivalry among Arab states and failure to achieve unity schemes is due to the dispute over definitions of Arab identity. In his account, regimes are in constant struggle to maintain domestic stability and legitimacy. Therefore, symbolic disputes over identity will be the main source of threats. While Barnett's constructivist approach rightly complements Walt's neorealism by showing the independent role of ideational forces in threat perception, he fails to specify the conditions under which ideational and normative considerations will outweigh material ones, and when the opposite will hold.

Other scholars present corrective explanations of both realism and constructivism by showing how ideology plays a crucial role in threat perception (Gause 2003; Haas 2012; Rubin 2014). They argue that ideologically oriented regimes with limited power capabilities can present a greater threat than shifts in the balance of power. These works argue that military capabilities are not always the primary determinant of threat perception, and domestic perceptual variables related to the salience of regime survival often affect foreign policy behaviour. Accordingly, decisions makers perceive ideational factors that threaten domestic stability and regime survival as the ultimate source of danger. These crucial insights shed light on why many Arab regimes felt threatened by the eruption of the Islamic Revolution despite Iran's declining military capabilities. Nevertheless, this scholarship does not account for the conditions under which such threat perception is triggered. The Syrian regime's threat perception was dominated instead by material considerations related to Iraq's rising military power. As is true for neorealism, ideational approaches offer invaluable insights for an elaborate understanding of alliance behaviour in the Middle East but remain insufficient in explaining the varying outcomes.

The modern Middle East abounds with examples demonstrating that dichotomised explanations, favouring either material or ideational forces, cannot account for some significant, yet apparently anomalous alliances in international relationship. Saudi and Syrian threat perceptions during subsequent regional wars raise similar questions about the role of ideational and material forces in threat perception and alliance decisions. The 2006 Lebanon War between Israel and Hezbollah constitutes another important episode. Although the war occurred between Israel and a non-state actor in Lebanon, its implications transcended the boundaries of the Lebanese–Israeli conflict and caused regional divisions. The Saudi Kingdom, conventionally portraying itself as the primary supporter of the cause against Israel, appeared to stand with Israel against a resistance movement. Consequently, it became puzzling why a non-state actor with limited capabilities – located, moreover, far from Saudi borders – was perceived as a threat. Meanwhile, Syria – a Ba'athist secular regime, oppressing Islamist movements at home – not only supported Hezbollah in order to balance Israel but also became more dependent on it for its survival.

Whereas some observers often depicted Saudi and Syrian alliances during the Iran–Iraq War and the 2006 Lebanon War in terms of sectarian affinities, with reference to the Sunni–Shiite divide in particular, the case of the 2009 Gaza War defies this sectarian lens; Hamas is an Islamic movement that finds its ideological origins in the Muslim Brotherhood belonging to a Sunni school of thought. Despite the identity convergence between Hamas and Saudi Arabia and their historical linkages related to the establishment of the group, the Kingdom perceived Hamas as a threat. Also, the Ba'ath regime, often depicted as Alawite (a strand of Shiism) in nature, perceived Hamas as an ally. The Gaza War provides uncontroversial evidence that threat perception is not driven by identity difference or sectarian divides. Whereas the Syrian regime oppressed the Muslim Brotherhood at home,[2] they supported an offshoot branch of the same group at the regional level to balance Israel's military superiority.

The puzzle of threat perception is not only related to historical events in the Middle East. Recent events pertaining to international relationships in the region challenge traditional explanations of threat perception. For instance, Egypt, often depicted as one of the few nation-states in the Arab world with exceptional ethnic and cultural homogeneity, perceived non-state actors with limited material capabilities – namely Hezbollah in Lebanon and Hamas in Gaza – as threats to Egypt's national interest. Meanwhile, Israel's military superiority is downplayed as a major source of threat in Egypt's official depictions of the regional balance of power. Furthermore, Iran, a geopolitically distant country, has constantly been identified as a threat to Egypt's national security (Rubin 2014, 98–100; Shama 2013, 111–52). Although Egypt has a predominantly Sunni population with exceptional ethnic homogeneity, the Sunni–Shiite debate has been instrumentally used to depict Iran as the most dangerous enemy during the Mubarak era but also during Mohamed Morsi's short-lived presidency (Saleh and Kraetzschmar 2015). Another example includes Saudi foreign policy towards Egypt following the 2011 Arab uprisings. The rise of the Muslim Brotherhood, a movement with a Sunni background, to power in Egypt was identified as a source of threat to Saudi decision-makers, despite shared elements in identity and the decline in Egyptian material capabilities during the Brotherhood rule (Darwich 2016). These examples pose several controversies in explaining the role of ideational and material forces in states decision-makers' threat perception.

These cases are not only provocative episodes in Middle East history, but they also yield theoretical and analytical questions for the study of threat perception in IR. They show that both ideational and material forces are crucial in explaining threat perception, and explanations giving primacy for one over the other often obscures the process of threat perception and alliance decisions. Despite the

---

[2] At the outbreak of the Islamic Revolution in Iran, the Muslim Brotherhood in Syria was inspired and hoped that the revolution in Iran would lead to a similar revolution in Syria to throw the al-Assad regime. This initial hope was followed by disappointment as the alliance and rapprochement between the Islamic Republic and the al-Assad regime became explicit. For more details on this episode, see Abd-Allah (1983, 179–87).

overwhelming importance of combining ideational and material forces in explaining Middle Eastern international relations, little consensus exists in either policymaking or academic circles around how and the conditions under which both ideational and material forces systematically shape processes of threat perception. This book attempts to unpack this often-overlooked phase and provides a comprehensive understanding of how and why some issues – rather than others – become the raw ingredients for leaders' perception of threats, which subsequently animate foreign policies. In what follows, I lay the foundations of the book by clarifying the broad outlines of the argument, why it matters, and how it contributes to the existing scholarship on threat perception in Middle East international relations.

Overview of the Argument

Leaders in the Middle East are in a relentless pursuit to preserve their regimes' survival, hinging upon both physical and identity security. They often face an unfavourable regional environment while fearing instability at home, what has been often termed as the 'logic of regime survival'. Leaders' perceptions in the Middle East are often at the origin of foreign policy decisions, and perceptions of threat are decisive in shaping states' conflictual and cooperative relationships with others. Furthermore, these perceptions are often transmitted and diffused to their societies through mass communication and media channels. The primary focus of this book is to examine the determinants of leaders' perceptions. In this regard, the major unit of analysis is the 'regime' (or leadership) rather than the 'state'. A closer look at the particularities of the state system in the Middle East reveals that statehood and sovereignty do not yet conform with the Westphalian notions of statehood.[3] Therefore, state power is often captured by a regime – a centralised authoritarian rule in the hands of a ruling elite or a leader – that absorbs state institutions.[4] Regimes (or leadership) are first and foremost concerned with their survival. They define what constitutes the 'national interest' and, hence, what constitutes a threat to it. In this context of states under formation and consolidation, the argument is

---

[3] For further details on the concept of sovereignty and statehood in the context of the Middle East, see Fawcett (2017) and Zartman (2017).

[4] For details about the basic components of regimes in the Middle East, see Owen (2012, chap. 3).

concerned with regimes' threat perception, often incarnated in their leaders or ruling elites.

In particular, I seek to explain why, and under which conditions, ideational forces create the ontological foundations for regimes' threat perceptions, and when material calculations override ideational constraints in periods of escalating tensions within and between states. My short answer is that both ideational and material forces are present in each process of threat perception. They interact, leading one or the other to become predominant in shaping the perception of threat. In some cases, leaders perceive ideational sources of threats as primary, while material sources of threats are of secondary importance. In other instances, material threats will evolve as the principal source of threats and ideational threats are perceived as secondary.

To explain the predominance of ideational or material factors in leaders' threat perception, two principal conditions are particularly relevant: the fluidity of regime identities and the range of policy options evolving from the relative power distribution. First, the fluidity of the regime identity relates to the likelihood of identity varying depending on the social context. States often hold multiple identities; different aspects of identity can become salient or likely to be activated in particular contexts. This fluidity of identity offers elites opportunities and constraints. Elites can choose aspects of their regime identity, attach new meanings to them, and use them as symbols to mobilise people. The degree of fluidity of identity is not similar across regimes. Some regimes can enjoy a higher degree of fluidity in their collective identity. In some societies, multiple identities co-exist, allowing the elites to activate and deactivate the various strands of identities. For example, Egypt has pan-Arab, pan-Islamic, Mediterranean, African and Egyptian nationalism strands of identities, providing the elites with relative flexibility in their foreign policy choices (Karawan 2002). In contrast, other states may be constrained by a fixed identity, where change and variation can put the cohesion of this collective entity at risk. For example, Saudi Arabia and other Gulf states illustrate these cases where the national identity is weak and sub-national identities – namely tribal, sectarian, and ethnic identities – are predominant. In these cases, regimes rely on pan-Islamism as the common element across different societal groups to provide an overarching identity to keep the society together. Regimes have very little ability to manoeuvre in facing threats to this overarching identity. Regimes with this type of fixed identity can perceive ideational threats as paramount due to their inability to activate other aspects of the threatened identity.

The second condition is the range of policy options evolving from the relative power distribution. Regimes often operate in an international environment, where the relative power distribution provides leaders with policy options to ensure the physical security of their regime. When faced with a military threat, leaders explore their options to ensure their physical survival. In some instances, the relative power distribution provides leaders with a clear structure where policy options are limited. In this situation, the structure leaves leaders with very little options in facing the threat. But, in other instance, regional and international structures do not come with clear prescriptions for leaders. In these situations, leaders are compelled to choose among multiple policy options to optimise their physical security.

Regimes facing various ideational and material sources of threats can diverge in their perceptions of which threat is more eminent based on the above two conditions. This book argues that when the distribution of military capabilities presents several policy options ensuring physical security but identity is fixed, leaders perceive threats to their identity as paramount. Hence, the predication of their identity narrative will dominate their perception of threat and will dictate the choice of the policy ensuring physical security. Material forces, on the other hand, are likely to dominate threat perception when identities are fluid and several identities co-exist and, in the meantime, the regimes face a distribution of military capabilities with limited policy options ensuring physical security. In this situation, leaders perceive threats to the regime's physical security as vital. Leaders perceive regime's identities as opportunities to reframe the narrative to conform to the exigencies of physical security.

This book differs from the previous literature in its characterisation of threat. Whereas previous work has dealt with threat perception as a discreet event that precedes alliance decisions, this book looks at threat perception as a process of interaction among regimes, between regimes and societies, and between regimes' material capabilities and identity narratives.[5] The book's argument, first, examines how both ideational and material forces shape regimes' fear. Second, it explores the conditions

---

[5] Similar conceptions of threat as a process can be found in Rubin (2014).

under which either ideational or material forces become predominant in the process of threat perception.

Ideational and Material Forces and How They Matter

I define 'material' factors as those related to 'the capabilities or resources mainly military, with which states influence one another' (Wivel 2005, 368). Particularly, I focus on the 'distribution of military capabilities' as the primary material factor influencing threat perception. This term refers to the real distribution of capabilities, to which states adjust or fail to adapt. This book agrees with structural realists that states construct their foreign policy with an eye towards constraints and opportunities that arise in the regional or international structure, which shapes a state's range of policy options. Nevertheless, states do not respond to structural exigencies in a natural manner. The literature emanating from political psychology and foreign policy analysis has enumerated several factors that hinder the structural realist model, such as leaders' misperceptions, the problem of rationality, domestic resources, and the clarity of the international system (e.g. Jervis 1976; Wohlforth 1993).

Hence, this book considers material forces to be structures that provide leaders with opportunities and constraints. The argument here focuses on the clarity of the relative power distribution (Ripsman, Taliaferro, and Lobell 2016, 21, 29). When states are faced with clear and eminent threats with little policy choice, states will behave as structural realists would expect and pursue a foreign policy decision that is dominated mainly by material concerns (Dueck 2005). Nonetheless, states are not always faced with stark choices. In some circumstances, when the international or regional environment does not present a clear structure, states have a range of policy options to choose from, rather than a clearly optimal policy dictated by the regional structure (Brawley 2009). Threat perceptions in these cases are more likely to be affected by ideational factors, which will guide leaders' perception through this unclear material structure.

'Ideational' factors include diverse elements such as culture, norms, values, beliefs, identity and ideology. The book focuses on 'identity'. Drawing on Jepperson et al. (1996, 59), identity refers to 'the image of individuality and distinctiveness (selfhood) held and projected by an actor'. Accordingly, state identity is the result of two primary

paths: current interactions between states (relational) and the characteristics that shape states' perception of the self (individual). The first
dimension of state identity is relational, according to which a state's
identity acquires meaning via its distinctiveness from others. The
second dimension of state identity is individual. Identity is about how
a state perceives itself. As Wendt (1999, 224) notes, identity is 'rooted
in the actor's self-understanding'. Regimes can base their actions upon
religion, as do Saudi Arabia or Iran, or on ideology, like the pan-Arab
regimes in Syria or Egypt under Gamal Abdel Nasser. This self-
perception relies on domestic sources, and it is corroborated by the
common belief that makes domestic groups aggregate their views
around a particular institution. The domestic sphere is a pool that
provides policymakers with a menu of identities. Accordingly, the
relational and domestic dimensions of state identity are not separable;
they interact and shape one another.

To examine how identity shapes threat perception, I build on the
assumption that regimes seek to affirm their self-identity and pursue
foreign policies that highlight their distinctiveness from others. An
ideational threat emerges when a set of ideas held and projected by
the other can challenge the regime's identity narrative at external and
domestic levels. These ideational challenges can be as important as
physical threats. Because the domestic and external spheres are inter-
connected, ideational challenges can pose an existential threat to the
state, jeopardising its narrative about the self vis-à-vis the other. If
leaders fail to maintain a consistent narrative about the regime's
identity and its raison d'être, domestic rifts can ensue. In short,
regime identity is threatened when the narrative about the state and
its distinctiveness is challenged. This challenge can lead to identity
insecurity, what some scholars termed as 'ontological insecurity'
(Mitzen 2006; Steele 2005). Mitzen (2006, 344) defines ontological
security as 'security not of the body but of the self, the subjective
sense of who one is, which enables and motivates action and choice'.
Accordingly, ontological insecurity can lead the weakening of the
regime narrative at the domestic levels. If the regime is unable to
formulate a narrative of state's raison d'être, societal groups can be
easily mobilised against the regime. Regime, therefore, perceive ideational threats as those endangering the distinctiveness, consistence,
and coherence of their identity narrative, in other words, their
ontological security. The resulting sense of insecurity usually leads

to policies, affirming and reinforcing the regime's self-identity, or in other words, its ontological security.

Ideational and Material Forces: When They Matter

States operate in a structure while facing ideational as well as material constraints and opportunities, which contribute to their assessment of threats. To specify when identities shape material considerations in threat perception and vice versa, I discern two primary conditions, the combination of which defines the direction of interplay. First is the fluidity of the regime identity, and second is the range of policies evolving from the relative power distribution.

First, the fluidity of the regime identity relates to the ability of leaders to 'activate' and 'deactivate' their identity narratives during certain social situations (Telhami and Barnett 2002b, 13–15). From this perspective, regime identity provides leaders with opportunities and constraints, influencing their perception of threat. Students of nationalism and identity politics have observed that states can hold multiples identities (Horowitz 1995; Laitin 1986; Young 1979). For example, Sadowski (2002, 13–138) explains how a Syrian officer can define himself in multiple ways: Arab, Ba'athi, Sunni versus non-Sunni, member of a sect, tribe, and/or family. Similarly, Karawan (2002, 156) argues that Egyptian foreign policy invoked various identities over time: Arab, Islamic, Middle Eastern, African and Mediterranean. These examples highlight the intrinsic character of identity, that is, fluidity. Several identities exist simultaneously in actors' definition of the self vis-à-vis others. A particular context renders one particular identity more significant than others, what scholars often refer to as 'the salience of identity'. If regime's self-identity is threatened by the emergence of a competing narrative at the structural level, leaders can reframe and invoke other images of their identities to preserve their stability and legitimacy. Nevertheless, identity can also be a constraint on state behaviour when it is fixed and inflexible. Saudi Arabia presents an example of this constraint, as the regime identity is inextricably related to a strict Salafi-Wahhabi interpretation of Islam. In short, I consider an identity to be fixed if a single identity is dominant and leaders cannot invoke other narratives. An identity is fluid when states have several identities and leaders tend to activate and deactivate these narratives.

The second condition relates to the clarity of the relative power distribution. States operate in an international environment, where the relative power distribution provides states with policy options in ensuring their physical security. When faced with a military threat, leaders explore their options to ensure their physical survival and their security policies. In some instance, the relative power distribution provides the leader with a clear structure where policy options are limited. But, in other instances, regional and international structures do not come with clear prescriptions for states. In these situations, leaders are likely to choose among multiple policy options to optimise their physical security.

The book shows that when the distribution of military capabilities presents several policy options ensuring physical security whereas identity is fixed, leaders perceive threats to their identity as more salient. Accordingly, regimes aim to reinforce their self-identity by framing their preferred course of action in those identity terms. Material forces, on the other hand, are likely to dominate threat perception when identities are fluid, and several identities co-exist and, in the meantime, the regimes face a distribution of military capabilities with limited policy options ensuring physical security. In this situation, leaders perceive threats to their physical security as more prominent. Henceforth, the regime identity undergoes a process of adaptation to conform to material security needs. More specifically, the material interest is likely to determine which identity narrative is selected.

The plausibility of this theoretical argument is illustrated through a comparison of Saudi and Syrian threat perceptions and alliance choices during three wars: the Iran–Iraq War (1980–88), the 2006 Lebanon War, and the 2009 Gaza War. The Saudi case illustrates a situation where the regime identity is fixed, based on a rigid interpretation of Islam. During several episodes of regional conflicts, Saudi leaders faced a relatively unclear relative power distribution with multiple policy options in the pursuit of physical security. In this context, threats to regime identity dominated leaders' threat perception and delineated the realm of choices that the political elite regarded as serving the physical security of their regimes. On the other side of this spectrum, the case of Syria illustrates a situation where the regime identity was fluid, including multiple narratives, such as pan-Arabism and Syrian nationalism. The relative power distribution presented high material constraints, which left Syrian leaders with limited policy options to ensure physical security. Perceiving threats to their physical security, Syrian leaders engaged in a process of regime identity reinterpretation to accommodate the material constraints. This book thus shows that threat perception is not only a mere event preceding alliance decisions but a complex phenomenon involving material capabilities and identity politics, at the intersection of both domestic and international levels.

The prevalence of either ideational or material forces in leaders' perceptions of threats leads to different foreign policy behaviour. If leaders perceive threats to their physical security to be vital, they attempt to activate aspects of their identity to mobilise the people behind their chosen strategies to cope with the perceived threat. In this path, elites use mass communication through media channels, such as television, radio and newspapers to disseminate and diffuse their threat perceptions to their societies. Through these narratives, elites play a role in the diffusion of identity narratives that support their pursuit of physical security. In the opposite case, if leaders perceive threats to their identity as eminent, they will choose to mobilise their material sources and choose the policy options that ensure the cohesion of the regime and society around the regime identity. In this case, leaders pursue policy options that reinforces their existing identity narratives.

Why Study Saudi and Syria Threat Perceptions?

The book employs inter- and intra-case comparisons to illustrate the plausibility of the previously discussed theoretical argument. The main cases are Saudi and Syrian threat perceptions during the Iran–Iraq War (1980–88), the 2006 Lebanon War, and the 2009 Gaza War. Saudi and Syrian cases were selected for an in-depth analysis based on variations in the dependent variable[6]; both cases diverged in every threat perception and alliance decision. I also examine both states' threat perceptions through intra-case comparisons, which focus on the changes in threat perception and state policies through three different wars. The dynamics of threat perception are also subject to inter-case variations as Syrian and Saudi threat perceptions are compared during each war.

Beyond providing a valuable opportunity for theory development, the examination of Syrian and Saudi threat perceptions raises questions with direct relevance to understanding current and future events

---

[6] For further details about this strategy of case selection, see Van Evera (1997, 77).

in the Middle East. Why did Saudi Arabia – a pan-Islamic regime – fear the rise of other Islamist movements in the region, such as Hamas and Hezbollah? Why has Syria, a secular Ba'athist regime suppressing Islamists at the domestic level, supported similar movements at the regional level? Recent changes in the political landscape of the region as a result of the 2011 Arab uprisings make answers to these questions more relevant than ever to the understanding of regional dynamics. The case of Saudi threat perception vis-à-vis Hamas and Hezbollah can inform our understanding of its subsequent threat perception of the rise of the Muslim Brotherhood to power in Egypt in 2012 or towards the Islamic State in Iraq and Syria (ISIS). Also, examining the dynamics of Syrian threat perception and foreign policy bears far-reaching implications for understanding the current regional coalitions as a result of the Syria crisis. In addition, the cases of Syria and Saudi Arabia are of intrinsic importance. Both states have been incredibly important for regional stability and security in several spheres: the Arab–Israeli conflict, Lebanon and the Persian Gulf. Saudi and Syrian threat perceptions, and their consequent foreign policy behaviour, have had a tremendous impact on regional politics and will do so for years to come.

Furthermore, with the rise of sectarianism in Middle East politics, policy debates on the role of identity in conflict became divided into two clusters. The first treats sectarian identities as the source of conflict and violence in the region (the primoridalist approach) (e.g. Abdo 2017). Relying on divisions within Islam, some scholars have portrayed Syrian foreign policy as driven by *Shiite politik* based on the 'Alawite identity of the ruling elite (Agha and Khalidi 1995; Bronson 2000; Hussein 2012; Susser 2007). This narrow approach does not unpack Syria's alignment with the Sunni Palestinian movement Hamas; nor does it account for the incompatible interests and policies implemented by Syria and Iran regarding many issues, such as the US-led invasion of Iraq in 2003 (Lawson 2007; Ma'oz 2007b; Saad-Gorayeb 2007). Similarly, Saudi foreign policy during the Iran–Iraq War was portrayed as a 'Sunni' state facing a Shiite revolution in Iran (Fürtig 2002; Goldberg 1990; Ulrichsen 2013; Yamani 2008). The second cluster considers sectarianism as a mere instrument in the hands of leaders to justify their interest-based decisions (the rationalist approach) (Okruhlik 2003; Wehrey et al. 2009). By adopting the concept of ontological security in examining self–other relations, the book suggests a different starting point in examining sectarianism – that is, that states have a stake in maintaining these sectarian divisions to fulfil ontological security needs and establish an identity narrative that ensures difference and distinctiveness, which ultimately contributes to identity security.

Beyond these policy-relevant insights, this study contributes to the long tradition of studying Arab states' foreign policies. By far, single-country foreign policy analysis predominates in the tradition of studying Arab regimes' behaviour, while comparisons remain overlooked and underdeveloped in the field. Whereas the existing literature presents insightful analyses into the foreign policies of Syria and Saudi Arabia, they are presented as part of single-country analyses (Hinnebusch and Ehteshami 2002; Korany and Dessouki 2008; Telhami and Barnett 2002a). Moreover, these studies remain generic and do not aim to study particular periods or important events, such as wars. For example, the Syrian–Iranian alliance is often examined as an 'odd' case that is not comparable to any other alliance in the region (Agha and Khalidi 1995; Goodarzi 2006; Hirschfeld 1986). Similarly, Saudi foreign policy analysis is rarely compared to other foreign policies.[7] Examining Syrian and Saudi alliance choices through a comparative perspective should lead to an in-depth understanding of regional political dynamics in the Middle East, while situating these within major IR debates. By studying these alliances as part of a pattern, and from a comparative perspective, I show that the received historical consensus, which exists around these cases, can be understood differently.

Contributions of the Argument and Its Relationships with Existing Explanations

International Relations scholars have long given threat perception a central role in theories of war, alliances, conflict, cooperation and conflict resolution. The arguments about how states' decision-makers assess threats are subject of wide debate. In the realist tradition, threat was often equated to military power, and neorealist scholars often assumed equality between objective measures of power at the structural level and threat assessment (e.g. Mearsheimer 2001; Waltz 1979).

---

[7] For an exception, cf. Hinnebusch (2015).

Limiting their explanations to a single understanding of threat, neorealists regard state behaviour driven by ideational factors as irrelevant and irrational (Feaver et al. 2000, 165–9; Kitchen 2010, 121–3). In the last decades, scholars started looking at subjective dimensions of threats, such as 'intentions' as a source of threat perception that is independent of military capabilities (e.g. Walt 1985).[8] To account for this difference between objective and subjective sources of threats, some scholars grounded in political psychology explored the variance between what leaders perceive as threatening and what the evidence of intentions and military capabilities suggests (e.g. Jervis 1976). With the cultural turn in international relations in the last three decades, other scholars begun to look seriously at socio-cultural sources of threat perception. Accordingly, identity and domestic societal factors influence how a state's decision-makers perceive threats (Barnett 1996; Herrmann 2013; Hopf 2002). This debate over the sources of threat perception has shaped the study of threat perception in the international relations of the Middle East.

Scholars of Middle East politics have applied and adapted these theoretical approaches to empirical questions related to different aspects of threat assessment. This book contributes to the scholarly literature on threat perception and alliance formation in Middle Eastern international relations. The book both complements and challenges three theoretical strands – namely neorealism, constructivism and regime security approaches. I argue that these theoretical formulations are not well suited to explain the interaction of ideational and material forces in threat perception, as they rely predominantly on one factor or the other.

First, my argument both complements and challenges neorealist arguments about threat perception in the Middle East. Due to the high degree of militarisation and the recurrence of interstate conflicts in the Middle East, generations of scholars have been content to view the Middle East through the lens of anarchy and power politics, while considering identities to be mere instruments of policy legitimation. From a neorealist perspective, shifts in the relative power distribution alone can drive threat perception and alliance formation. Balance of power theory and the security dilemma exemplify such structural, material approaches to threat perception (Waltz 1979). States moving

---

[8] For an overview of this literature, see Stein (2013).

to increase their capabilities will lead to insecurity of others regardless of intentions and ideational factors. Stephen Walt's *The Origins of Alliances* presents a refinement of the neorealist heavy focus on the capabilities as the determinant of threat. He proposes the balance of threat theory, according to which states assess threats based on aggregate power, geographic proximity, offensive power and aggressive intentions. Walt introduces a cognitive dimension in his neorealist explanation, considering the perception of 'aggressive intention' as an independent source of threat. Nevertheless, Walt argues that ideology is a secondary factor and a mere instrument in the hands of Arab leaders to legitimise decisions based on material factors. This book refines the balance of threat theory by developing an argument about the conditions under which ideational forces override material ones, and vice versa. Researching the conditions under which ideational and material forces override foreign policy decision have received little attention in the literature (cf. Risse et al. 1999).

Second, the book complements constructivist explanations of threat perception in the Middle East by providing a firmer foundation for the role of identity in shaping leaders' threat perceptions. Constructivism challenges the neorealist assumption about the deterministic relationship between material power and threats and argues that threats are social constructions. Accordingly, threats are inextricably related to a state's identity and its perception of the significant other. This does not mean that constructivism has discarded the material factors in shaping actors' behaviour. Rather, constructivists argue that leaders' ideas about the material forces are more important than the material forces themselves (Adler 1997; Onuf 1989; Wendt 1992, 1999). In the same vein, the literature on securitisation theory suggests that non-military issues can be framed into threats through identity narratives (e.g. Buzan, Wæver, and Wilde 1998; Waever 1995). On the one hand, scholars considered the Middle East with its multi-layered identity politics as a rich pool to test constructivist hypotheses (Barnett 1996, 1998; Lynch 1999, 2002). On the other hand, constructivism has allowed a refreshing interpretation of Arab politics that takes into account the particularity of the Middle East without lapsing into culturally reductionist arguments.[9] In his seminal work *Dialogues in Arab Politics*, Michael Barnett (1998) offers an important critique to

---

[9] Unlike, for example, Ajami (1992, 2009) and Salem (1994).

Walt's account of regional alliances. While examining the rise and fall of pan-Arabism in Arab politics, Barnett illustrates how non-material factors, namely identity, shaped conflict and cooperation among Arab regimes. He argues that rivalry and conflict among Arab regimes was the result of a symbolic struggle among Arab leaders over the definition of Arabism, which was inextricably related to regime's legitimacy and survival at the domestic level.

Even though constructivism has actively the role of ideational forces in international relations, it hardly accounts for the interaction between ideational and material forces.[10] Constructivist work on Middle East politics not only highlights the centrality of identity issues and ideational structures in shaping state behaviour, but it emphasises them to the exclusion of material factors. By looking at material structures as the result of an actor's perception, constructivism conflates actors' material and ideational needs. For instance, Barnett's constructivist account failed to specify when strategic considerations will outweigh symbolic and normative ones, or when the opposite will hold (Gause 1999, 21). As Barnett (1996, 446) states, 'sometimes identity politics will figure centrally: at other times a strategic logic might provide an exhaustive explanation. There is no theoretical or empirical justification, however, for assuming the primacy of one over another'. This conflation of identity and material interests in constructivism has overshadowed the myriad mechanisms of interaction between ideational and material forces.

The book shares important areas of similarities with and differences from the constructivist explanations of threat perception. On the one hand, the book's argument shows the centrality of identity narratives in shaping threat perceptions in some instances. The book, however, takes a different stance by arguing that the pursuit of physical security is distinct from identity security. By separating these two distinct conceptions of security, the book moves beyond the constructivist literature, according to which identity and interests are co-constituted. By adopting an ontological security approach to examine the role of identity in threat perception, the book argues that states' decision-makers pursue both material and ideational security needs. Based on this clear separation between ideational and material spheres, this

---

[10] For more details on this criticism, see Risse et al. (1999) and Meyer and Strickmann (2011).

book provides clear conditions for the primacy of ideational or material forces in the process of threat perception. Furthermore, by including the literature on ontological security and self–other relations, the argument adds a new depth to the constructivist approach. It shows that the characteristics of identity narratives, such as fluidity, can shape threat perception.

Furthermore, the book contributes to the constructivist debate over the role of identity in conflict and cooperation. On the one hand, some scholars argue that a shared identity can limit the perception of threats. Accordingly, if two states share the same identity, threat perception should diminish regardless of the material balance of power (Haas 2003; Hopf 2002; Horowitz 1985; Huntington 1993; Rousseau and Rocio 2007; Wendt 1999). On the other hand, other scholars argue that identity similarity can lead to rivalry and conflict (e.g. Barnett 1996; Kienle 1990). The book extends and refines Barnett's argument on identity similarity as a source of rivalry. Through adoption of an ontological security conception, the book shows why and how identity similarity can lead to identity risks and perception of threats. Whereas the existing literature explains such risks in terms of regime legitimacy, the argument here shows that similarity is a risk as actors have an ontological need to assert distinctiveness and difference.

A question that can provide some challenge to the ontological security approach: 'What is the added value of drawing on the concept of ontological security rather than identity in the constructivist approach?' Although ontological security is tied to the concept of 'identity', it is not synonymous with identity. Instead, ontological security specifies that some dynamics are articulate and more visible, which would not be otherwise. For example, the constructivist approach relies on how identity is shaping interests. Ontological security goes further to show that actors behave in particular ways congruent with their identity because they are acting from a need. Those identities provide some sort of continuity and stability. This sort of need for distinctiveness and stability has not been thematised in the constructivist approach within IR of the Middle East, and ontological security can be a good starting point for that.

Third, the book extends and refines crucial insights offered by the scholarship on regime security. Middle East scholars have criticised both neorealist and constructivist attempts for de-emphasizing regional particularities and complexities (e.g. Halliday 2005; Hinnebusch 2015;

Noble 2004).[11] They have criticised these approaches for disavowing the role of domestic environment in affecting state's foreign policies. They have opted instead for a modified IR Theory applied to the Middle East that includes domestic factors which influence leaders' perception of threat, such as ideology (Gause 2003; Rubin 2014), economic capabilities (Barnett and Levy 1991, 1992; Brand 1994, 1999; Lawson 1996), state-society relations (Gause 1990; Salloukh 2004) and legitimacy (Telhami 1999).

From this perspective, the prerequisite of regime survival replaces state security as the unit of analysis. Scholarship on regime security argues that transnational ideologies can present greater and more immediate threats than shifts in the military balance of power. Mark Haas (2012) in *The Clash of Ideologies* explains how ideologies, as independent factors, are likely to shape leaders' perception of threats. Gause (2003) presents a middle ground by combining the elements of threats underlined by Walt (1987) and the importance of transnational identities highlighted by Barnett (1996) to explain alliance decisions in the Gulf. He argues that Arab states overwhelmingly perceived ideational threats – which emanated from abroad and targeted the domestic stability of Arab ruling regimes – as more salient than material threats. Rubin's (2014) *Islam in the Balance* is another attempt to analyse how ideas and political ideology are more threatening to regime security than changes in the relative power distribution. He examines threat perceptions and policies of two Arab, Muslim-majority states – Egypt and Saudi Arabia – in response to the Islamic Revolution in Iran (1979) and the Islamic state in Sudan (1989). Along similar lines, Rubin (2014, 108) argues that sectarian framing can be seen as a strategy of 'ideational balancing', whereby elites manipulate narratives with the purpose of mobilising the masses around the threat of a sectarian other. Wehrey (2013) illustrates how the ruling elites in the Gulf have used sectarianism to prevent the emergence of broad-based opposition movements. In other words, stocking sectarianism is a strategy to maintain control over societies and strengthen the legitimacy of the ruling elites.

---

[11] Other classic works of Middle Eastern international relations provide a reading of inter-Arab politics as driven by domestic considerations, where foreign policy has been portrayed as a crucial tool in the hands of leaders seeking to preserve their hold on power (Bar-Simon-Tov 1983; Kerr 1971; Mufti 1996; Seale 1986; York 1988).

This book extends these insights on regime security by presenting a more comprehensive account of how both ideational and material threats shape threat perception. It builds on the assumption that leaders driven by regime survival logic are the primary unit of analysis in the international relations of the Middle East. But it also problematises the concept of 'regime security' beyond the legitimacy issue. It argues that regime security can be tied to other dynamics of identity, such as fluidity, distinctiveness and consistency. Through the lens of ontological security, this book examines sectarianism as serving actors' need of distinctiveness and their security-as-being. From this perspective, ontological security is not synonymous with discourses as instruments to serve legitimacy and domestic survival. Instead, ontological security is the 'presence of a stable self-understanding, which can include positive, neutral, and negative components' and a consistent identity and narrative (Mitzen and Larson 2017). Therefore, sectarianism provides stability and continuity in identity narratives for some actors in an uncertain environment, and actors become attached to this sort of stability and distinctiveness. This dynamic is best captured by ontological security. Whereas the instrumentalist argument of regime security approaches treats sectarianism as a rationalist strategy consciously employed by elites for survival, ontological security makes the dynamics attached to the endeavour of maintaining sectarian narratives more visible, such as the need for stability, consistency and distinctiveness, which would not be otherwise apparent drawing on instrumentalism alone. In other words, elites know that it is in their interest to promote behaviour and identity narratives that maintain sectarianism, and yet do not entirely understand *why*. Elites may be aware that some identities can be sources of threats to the stability of their identity, but they are not fully conscious of the reason for their discomfort. More importantly, they are unconscious If why sectarian narratives can provide more stability over other sources of identity, and that is where ontological security aims contribute.

Plan of the Book

The five remaining chapters of the book are organised as follows. Chapter 2 develops a theoretical framework for explaining how ideational and material forces shape states' threat perceptions as well as the conditions for their interplay. In this chapter, I develop the conception of security as both physical and ontological, in which the interaction of ideational and material forces can be analysed. The chapter shows that in some cases, ideational sources of threat are perceived as predominant, and, in other cases, material sources of threats are so perceived. As an explanation of this variation, the chapter outlines the conditions of the interplay between ideational and material forces, based on the fluidity of the regime identity – assessed through mutability of the regime identity narrative – and the clarity of the relative power distribution – assessed through the multiplicity of available policy options to ensure physical security. The chapter also includes a research design section that discusses methods and case selection criteria.

The book then explores the plausibility of this framework empirically by examining a number of cases that have been at the heart of historical and theoretical work on the international relations of the Middle East. Chapters 3, 4 and 5 apply the theoretical framework to a comparative study of Syrian and Saudi threat perceptions during three major wars in the region: the Iran–Iraq War (1980–88), the 2006 Lebanon War, and the 2009 Gaza War. Beyond their intrinsic importance, these events have been chosen to allow variation on the dependent variable of the study, i.e., threat perception. During these regional wars, Saudi and Syrian perceptions of threat presented diametrically extreme, opposite cases. The aim of these chapters is to show – through primary and secondary sources – how the perceived historical consensus that does exist can be understood in a very different way when we look through different theoretical lenses. The case study chapters are written to be comparable within and across cases. The empirical chapters present counterintuitive findings on some key debates within IR Theory. Furthermore, each chapter deals with alternative explanations of those empirical cases within the scholarship on Middle East politics and then offers an interpretation of events based on the book's theoretical argument.

Chapter 3 examines Saudi and Syrian threat perceptions during the Iran–Iraq War (1980–88). This chapter explores why and under which conditions Saudi Arabia and Syria diverged in their perceptions of threats emanating from both Iran and Iraq, despite their shared vulnerability towards the message of the Islamic Revolution and their geographical proximity to a militarily rising Iraq. The Saudi case illustrates a situation where state identity is immutable, while the distribution of military capabilities presented the leadership with multiple options. The exigencies of Saudi identity based on Wahhabism and pan-Islamism alongside the lack of a strong Saudi national identity delineated the realm of choices in pursuing physical security. Due to the lack of multiplicity in regime identities, ideational sources of threats became predominant. The Syrian case illustrates a situation in which the regime identity included multiple narratives and the distribution of military capabilities imposed threats emerging from the military capabilities of both Iraq and Israel. These material constraints left the Syrian leadership with limited policy options to ensure the state's physical security. Rather than shaping the perception of material power, leaders forced a reframing and reinterpretation of the regime's identity to accommodate the material constraints. To render possible its alliance with Iran against a fellow Arab regime in Iraq, the Syrian regime reframed its pan-Arab identity narrative by re-interpreting Arabness as the struggle against Israel instead of as unity among Arabs.

Chapter 4 examines Saudi and Syrian threat perceptions during the 2006 Lebanon War. The Saudi Kingdom, portraying itself as the primary supporter of the Arab cause against Israel, blamed and condemned Hezbollah for instigating the conflict. The chapter examines the question of why a non-state actor with limited capabilities, located far from the Saudi borders, came to be perceived as a threat. Syria, a regime oppressing Islamist movements at the domestic level, supported Hezbollah, within the security calculus which perceived Israel as the ultimate threat. Whereas Hezbollah constituted a source of identity instability for the Saudi Kingdom and, hence, endangered its ontological security, Israel's military supremacy constituted the primary source of danger to the physical security of the Syrian regime. In this situation, the alliance with Hezbollah became crucial for the Syrian regime, whose leaders capitalised on Hezbollah's popularity by including some Islamic elements in the regime narratives. Chapter 4 examines the conditions under which ideational and material forces interplayed in the process of threat perception. It argues that this variation is related to the fluidity of identity of Saudi and Syrian regimes as well as their policy options in facing material sources of threats.

Chapter 5 examines Saudi and Syrian threat perceptions during the 2009 Gaza War, where the Saudi Kingdom perceived Hamas as a threat and the Syrian regime perceived it as a strategic ally. Although Hamas is a non-state actor that generated threat perceptions similar to those towards Hezbollah in the Saudi regime, this case provides novel insights into the role of sectarianism in shaping threat perceptions. Hamas in the context of the Gaza War presents a least-likely case study – or a crucial case study – that provides stronger evidence for the book's overarching argument and increases the confidence in the validity of the theoretical framework. Saudi and Syrian regimes' threat perception during the 2009 Gaza War diverged from prior theoretical suggestions. As opposed to Hezbollah, Hamas is a political Islam movement that finds its ideological origins in the Muslim Brotherhood – belonging to a Sunni school of thought. Considering the nature of the Hamas identity narrative, it was expected that Saudi Arabia would find in Hamas an ally based on identity convergence and history of cooperation, and Syria was expected to find it as a potential threat considering that the al-Assad regime had been oppressing an offshoot of the same group at the domestic level. Despite the identity convergence between Hamas and Saudi Arabia, the Kingdom perceived Hamas as a threat. Also, the Ba'ath regime, often depicted as Alawite in nature and oppressing the Brotherhood at the domestic level, regarded Hamas as an ally. The comparison in this chapter has wider implications for the role of identity in Middle Eastern international relations. The interplay of ideational and material forces in Saudi and Syrian threat perception, as well as the following alliance choices, provides uncontroversial evidence that sectarian identities per se do not drive threat perception. Instead, sectarianism can be a source of ontological security.

In Chapter 6, the conclusion returns to the main theoretical and empirical puzzles discussed in this introductory chapter. It synthesises the results of how the ebb and flow between material and ideational sources of threats in the cases of both Saudi Arabia and Syria led to divergent perceptions and alliance choices. This concluding chapter summarises the findings within and across cases and highlights the contribution of this argument to the threat perception research programme within IR literature as well the international relations of the Middle East. Furthermore, the conclusion broadens the analytical lens by discussing how the book's theoretical framework is applicable to other case studies, such as Saudi threat perceptions towards the Muslim Brotherhood in Egypt and the Islamic State of Iraq and Syria. The chapter also explores how this book's argument can be extended to inform other states' threat perceptions in the Middle East, such as Egypt and Jordan.

2 | Why and When States Perceive Threats

A Theoretical Framework

> Of course, we can always construct a theory or a generalisation if we wish as long as we remember that it serves the limited and heuristic purpose of throwing light on a small number of features of the phenomenon at the expense of obscuring all others.
>
> James Tully, *An Approach to Political Philosophy* (1993, 276)

This chapter develops a theoretical framework that presents the conditions under which ideational and material forces systematically shape regimes' threat perception and alliance choices. This theoretical framework presents a fusion of realist assumptions – the centrality of the relative power distribution in the quest for physical security and survival – with the premises of ontological security. Responding to fundamental existential questions of being, ontological security is intimately connected with identity; its pursuit, therefore, requires a state to reinforce its distinctiveness and differentiation from the other while pursuing a coherent and consistent identity narrative at the domestic level. The central claim is that ideational and material forces are in constant interaction in shaping leaders' threat perceptions. In some cases, material sources of threats affect the discursive formation of regime identity. In other cases, regime identity provides leaders with opportunities and constraints by making some policy choices plausible or not. The framework further specifies the conditions under which ideational and material forces become predominant in regimes' threat perception. Two principal conditions are particularly relevant: the clarity of the regional power distribution and the fluidity of the regime identity narrative.

Before proceeding to the framework, I define three key terms: 'threat', 'perception' and 'regime–state nexus'. Threats can be defined 'in the passive sense [as] an anticipation of impending danger rather than in its active sense of an undertaking by one actor to impose a sanction on another' (Cohen 1978, 95). If 'A threatens B', we focus on

B's conditions. Similarly, social psychologists have defined threat as 'the *outcome* of A's (intended future) activities as perceived (imagined) by B' (Baldwin 1971, 72 emphasis in original). Perception is defined as 'the process of apprehending by means of the senses and recognising and interpreting what is processed' (Stein 2013, 366). Even in the case of concrete objective evidence of danger, if a threat is not perceived, there will be no defensive reaction or alliance. Similarly, a threat might be perceived even if the intention to harm is absent or if there is no objective evidence of its presence (Cohen 1978, 93).

This book focuses on threats perceived by leadership in the Middle East. Before addressing this topic, I start by discussing the analytical distinction between states and regimes, which has important implications for the question of threat perception. The literature on democratic transition has made the distinction between state, regime and government. A regime can be defined as 'the formal and informal organisation of the centre of political power, and its relations with the broader society. A regime determines who has access to political power, and how those who are in power deal with who are not' (Fishman 1990, 428). Another definition would be 'that nexus of alliances within and without the formal bureaucratic and public sectors that the leaders form in order to gain power and keep it' (Waterbury 1983, xiii). Accordingly, regimes present a form of political organisation that is more stable than a government but less permanent than the state. The state, however, is the most permanent structure of political domination, including coercive capacities and abilities to control society.[1] Although the distinction has been useful in examining cases in southern Europe and Latin America, the cases of the Middle East present a challenge to this distinction.[2]

The history of state formation in the Middle East is inextricably intertwined with regime power and dominance (Anderson 1986, 1987; Ayubi 1996; Owen 2004).[3] As Longva (2000, 193) puts it, a Saudi notion of belonging 'to a land or an 'imagined community' is unthinkable because the country itself is appropriated to the ruling family

---

[1] My understanding of the state follows Skocpol's thesis (1979).

[2] On Latin American cases, see Cardoso (1980), and on southern European cases, see Stephan (1986).

[3] All authors writing about Third World security have constantly made the distinction between state and regime security (Ayoob 1995; Buzan 1991, chap. 2; Job 1992)

whose name it bears'. The same observation applies to the Hashemite Kingdom of Jordan. In other words, state apparatuses in the Middle East have been co-opted, penetrated and captured by authoritarian regimes. As Anderson (1987, 7) describes states in the Middle East, 'a stable government administration and a military which controls the use of force are the *sine qua non* of statehood'.[4] Brand (1994, 24) makes a similar analytical distinction between national security as 'defined in terms of territorial integrity and core values' and regime security as 'the maintenance of power by the same leaders of ruling coalition, depending upon the complexity of the country'. Along these lines, this book focuses on the threat perception of the elite in power, which becomes diffused and transmitted through state apparatuses. Also, writing about 'regime identity', I signify these narratives promoted by the elite in power and transmitted through the bureaucratic body in the state.

The chapter consists of four sections. First, I explore the overarching eclectic approach of the proposed theoretical framework. My aim is not to put forward a grand theoretical model for the study of threat perception. Instead, I present a framework that theorises the conditions under which either ideational or material forces become predominant in the process of threat perception. Second, I explore how ideational and material forces shape threat perception. Third, I outline the conditions under which either ideational or material forces dominate threat perception, which is the core argument of the book. The chapter finally moves to a discussion of the research design and the selection criteria for the case studies.

Analytical Eclecticism: Building an Integrated Framework of Analysis

The puzzle of threat perception cannot be solved with either material or ideational explanations, nor can it be addressed from within either uniquely domestic or regional contexts. In order to advance to a position that gives weight to both ideational and material structures, and also to systemic and domestic levels of analysis, the present theoretical framework is grounded in 'analytical eclecticism' (Sil 2000; Sil and Katzenstein 2012). 'Analytic eclecticism' is defined as 'any

---

[4] Scholars of authoritarianism in the Middle East have often made the link between state capacity and regime strength (e.g. Koehler 2017).

approach that seeks to extricate, translate, and selectively integrate analytic elements – concepts, logics, mechanisms, and interpretations – of theories or narratives that have been developed within separate paradigms but that address related aspects of substantive problems that have both scholarly and practical significance' (Sil and Katzenstein 2012, 10). Another definition would be 'a process according to which theorists construct coherent analytical frameworks by evaluating, synthesising, and reflecting on insights from disparate paradigms' (Makinda 2000, 206). That is possibly what Walt (1998, 30) envisioned when he wrote that 'no single approach can capture all the complexity of contemporary world politics'. From this perspective, I argue that developing an eclectic framework allows the analysis to deal with complex empirical puzzles without imposing any a priori theoretical contour. Jervis depicts this approach as 'engaging with the "isms" without being confined by them' (quoted in Sil and Katzenstein 2010, 67).

The theoretical framework developed next attempts to reveal how different factors hang together in the process of threat perception. Incorporating insights from ideational and material approaches allows for the exploitation of their respective strengths and creates new avenues for investigating the dynamics of threat perception. Accordingly, the argument in this book goes beyond a flexible eclectic approach that only combines causal insights from separate paradigms; it presents a synthesis based on a multi-theoretical framework. Hellman (2003, 149) speaks of a 'pragmatic fusion and synthesis' in solving complex empirical puzzles. Similarly, Moravcsik (2003) offers an exceptional view of 'synthesis' in IR theory. He presents a dissenting view of theories as instruments subjected to testing and synthesis. He argues that elements from different theoretical paradigms do not need to share the whole set of ontological assumptions; only some fundamental coherence while downplaying epistemic principles can lead to fruitful synthesis. Following Moravcsik's understanding, this book presents a multi-theoretical framework combining ideational and material elements from 'ontological security' and 'realism', sharing some ontological foundational assumptions. Both approaches recognise the presence of ideational and material elements in IR phenomenon. Although each approach is biased towards one element or the other, both fundamentally agree on the presence of both elements.

This theoretical approach is not without pitfalls. Some scholars argue that developing a balanced inquiry combining ideational and material components is fundamentally prevented by theoretical obstacles, based on Kuhn's (1970, 148) thesis about the 'incommensurability of paradigms'.[5] I argue that existing theoretical debates in IR do not represent a compelling barrier to a balanced inquiry (e.g. Barkin 2010). The ontological debate is about the nature of the social world; is there an objective reality in the world or is it a subjective creation? In IR theory, the objective position is frequently connected to realism and the 'subjective' view is connected to constructivism. These extreme positions or one-sidedness are not, however, reflected in realism or constructivism. Although realists and constructivists conduct their analysis based on privileging one side or the other, they fundamentally agree on the presence of both elements in IR.

Another caveat to this eclectic approach can be found in Hollis and Smith's (1990) claim that a synthesis between material and ideational forces is impossible, as there will always be 'two stories to tell'. One story is based on the objective material dimension of the social phenomenon, and the other underpins a normative subjective dimension.[6] One way to overcome this epistemological caveat is to treat identity as a causal factor that is analytically independent of material factors. Although state identity sometimes shapes material interests, it may be the case that states uphold particular identity narratives because it is in their interest to do so. In addition, states can maintain identities that contradict their interests, and it is for this reason that identities and interests should remain conceptually and analytically distinct. As Hinnebusch (2003b, 362) articulates it,

Systemic material and normative structure as well as states interests and identity, are autonomous of each other, but stability depends on a correspondence between them ... They can be in conflict, but where this is so, in time either norms and identity will likely stimulate revolts against material power structures perceived to be illegitimate or they will be altered to conform to material interests and constraints.

---

[5] The 'incommensurability of paradigms' implies that arguments from different paradigms cannot be combined or matched with one another. This is because they deploy different concepts and conceptual systems, ask different questions, and select different facts.

[6] Kratochwill and Ruggie (1986) share similar scepticism.

These eclectic and synthetic approaches have been evident in the study of Middle East international relations, especially in the research of Hinnebusch (2003a, 2005b, 2013) and Gause (2003), even though they do not explicitly refer to it as 'analytical eclecticism'.[7] The impact of these earlier works should not be dismissed, as they represent the first step in encouraging others to pursue eclectic explanations. These previous works do not, however, specify the conditions under which factors interplay; if one element in the argument does not explain state behaviour, another probably will. This book builds upon these previous efforts to deal with ideational and material forces as analytically and conceptually distinct while examining their various interactions.

Ideational and Material Forces: How They Shape Threat Perception

A good starting point is to define 'ideational' and 'material' factors and their corresponding layers of security. Despite its prominence in mainstream IR literature, material forces as a source of threat remain imprecisely defined. Material forces are intimately related to physical security, which suggests concerns about the physical survival of the regime. In other words, some threats are purely physical and put the survival of the regime at stake. In this context, I understand 'material' factors as those related to 'the capabilities or resources, mainly military, with which states influence one another' (Wivel 2005, 368). This definition of material factors might be extended to include economic power, which is inextricably related to military capabilities. Here, I focus on 'relative power distribution' as the primary material factor influencing threat perception. This term refers to the real distribution

---

[7] Several existing approaches have sought to combine ideational and material factors in the study of world politics more broadly by adopting theoretical and methodological pluralism. Notable attempts include the International Society approach or the English School (Buzan 2004; Buzan and Gonzalez-Pelaez 2009), Cox's neogramiscianism based on the notion of historical structures (Cox 1996; Sørensen 2008), the Historical Sociology approach (Hinnebusch 2010b; Hobden and Hobson 2002), and a few works in foreign policy analysis (FPA) (Nau 2002; Risse et al. 1999). Other scholars have borrowed realist insights about the relevance of capabilities, their distribution among state actors, and the role of threat perception, and have incorporated these within a constructivist framework (Meyer and Strickmann 2011; Rousseau 2006). Similarly, neoclassical realists have combined ideational domestic variables – such as elites' perceptions – with material systemic factors (Glenn 2009; Kitchen 2010; Wohlforth 1993).

of capabilities, to which states adjust or fail to adapt. Despite its significance in generating 'fear', relative power distribution alone is insufficient to measure material power. For this reason, I draw a connection between a state's military power and its ability to use it based on the logic of the offence–defence balance, which is defined as 'a state's ability to perform the military missions that are required to successfully attack, deter, or defend' (Glaser and Kaufmann 1998, 48).[8] According to this conception of security, changes in the relative power distribution trigger 'fear'. Based on objectified sources of physical harm, states identify their friends and enemies.

Ideational factors include diverse elements such as culture, norms, values, beliefs, identity and ideology. As scholars deal with these elements in different ways, definitions can be overlapping or even contradictory. That is what Abdelal et al. (2006, 695) identify as 'definitional anarchy'. As Finnemore (1996, 16) highlights, 'one analyst's norm might be another's institution and a third scholar's identity'. Among many ideational forces, my focus here is on 'identity', which deserves a thorough discussion. Although identity is central to social sciences and is at the heart of constructivism within IR, it is a difficult concept to define.

In this theoretical framework, I focus on 'identity' as part of the ontological security realm. This layer of security signifies another motivation for state behaviour, which is the pursuit of a stable definition of the self that is distinct and different from the other. According to Jepperson et al. (1996, 59), identity refers to 'the image of individuality and distinctiveness (selfhood) held and projected by an actor'. In other words, actors have an intricate need to have a distinctive and consistent sense of self and to have that sense affirmed by others. Some IR scholars have aimed to transfer the concept of 'ontological security' – coined by the psychiatrist R. D. Laing and only recently introduced to IR theory – from the individual to the state level.[9] The concept was further developed in Giddens' structuration theory (1984,

---

[8] In some cases, states have considerable military power that cannot be used efficiently. For example, the Saudi Kingdom has grown as the most important importer of military hardware in the region. Nevertheless, the lack of personnel makes the relative power distribution an insufficient lens for assessing the Kingdom's capabilities (Cronin 2014, 236–9).

[9] Cf. Zarakol (2010), Huysmans (1998), McSweeney (1999), Mitzen (2006), and Steele (2005, 2008).

1991). He defines ontological security as 'the confidence that most human beings have in the continuity of their self-identity and in the constancy of the surrounding social and material environments of action' (1991, 92). This sense of self is reflected in agents' behaviour. As Mitzen argues, 'ontological security is security not of the body but the self, the subjective sense of who one is, which enables and motivates action and choice' (2006, 344). Accordingly, agents choose a course of action that conforms to their self-identity.

The ontological security lens offers explanations for foreign policy behaviour driven by ideational sources of threats. From this perspective, alongside realist accounts – according to which security and survival are achieved through the accumulation of military capabilities – actors also engage in ontological security–seeking behaviour that affirms their self-identity as distinct from the other, which provides them with 'a sense of continuity and order in events' (Giddens 1991, 243). Hence, ontological security involves the ability to 'experience oneself as a whole ... in order to realise a sense of agency' (Mitzen 2006, 342). In other words, actors need to feel secure in who they are, as they see themselves and as they want to be seen by others. This claim suggests that 'insecurity' means that individuals are confused about who they are and uncomfortable with their identity in social interactions with others (Steele 2005, 525).

The sources of ontological security are a subject of contention among scholars. Some scholars have looked at the sources of ontological security as endogenous. Steele (2008) argues that ontological security is couched in a state's intrinsic narrative about the self. From this perspective, the sense of self enables the state to process its environment and build sustainable relationships with others. However, other scholars argue that a state's sense of self is based on social interaction with others. As Mitzen (2006, 354) argues, state identity is 'constituted and sustained by social relationships rather than being intrinsic'. In this interpretation, the sense of self is only reinforced and distinguished through sustainable interactions with others.

Drawing on this debate, Zarakol (2010, 19) has sought a middle ground by arguing that both are 'partly right'. According to Kinvall (2004, 749), 'internalised self-notions can never be separated from self–other representations and are always responsive to new inter-personal relationships'. Building on this compromise, I argue that the exogenous and endogenous sources of ontological security are inextricably related. The sense of self acquires meaning not only through the actor's distinctive individual characteristics embedded in actor's reflexive understanding of the self, but also through the uniqueness of this narrative from that of the other (Nabers 2009, 195). For example, the Islamic element in Saudi state identity evolved from domestic historical and sociological origins, which highlights the intrinsic aspect of identity. That being said, this Islamic element has been framed and reframed through interaction with other states in the Middle East and with the international environment.

It appears, therefore, that identity is also about how a state perceives itself, which represents the second dimension. According to Wendt (1999, 224), state identity is 'rooted in the actor's self-understanding'. Self-identity does not originate in interaction with others. Instead, actors extract their self-identity from their own characters. For example, states might base their actions on religion, as in Saudi Arabia or Iran, or on a secular ideology, as in the pan-Arab regimes in Syria or Egypt under Nasser. This self-perception mostly relies on domestic sources and is corroborated by the common belief shared by domestic groups aggregating their views around a particular institution. The domestic sphere is, therefore, a pool that provides policy-makers with a 'menu of identities' (Telhami and Barnett 2002b). Accordingly, the relational and domestic dimensions of state identity and its ensuing ontological security are not separable; rather, they interact with and shape each other. With these two dimensions, the concept of 'identity' and its corresponding realm of ontological security function as a crucial link between external and domestic structures. For example, the emergence of Arab nationalism was a response to both domestic (aimed at uniting and mobilising societies) and external factors (against colonialism) (Mufti 1996).

When do states feel ontologically insecure? Because the sources of ontological security are both endogenous and exogenous, insecurity can emerge from the self and from interaction with others. In the first case, actors can become ontologically insecure if contradictions emerge within their identity narrative, or if they choose a course of action that is incongruent with their narrative of the self. This insecurity leads to instability and disruptions, as the actor's self-definition comes under question. Such insecurity can lead to shame, what Steel (2008, 13) defined as 'state anxiety over the ability to reconcile past (or prospective) actions with the biographical narrative states use to justify their behaviour'. For example, Japan and Turkey's reluctance to apologise for historical crimes comes from an anxiety to reconcile their current identity narrative with past actions (Zarakol 2010).

At the same time, the sources of insecurity can be exogenous. As the very basis of identity construction is differentiation and uniqueness from others, any disturbance in the self-versus-other distinction leads to agents' uncertainty about their own identity. Therefore, if the discursive constructions of the 'self' and the 'other' become increasingly similar, agents become ontologically insecure; they perceive the very basis of their self-identity to be eliminated. In contrast to the conventional wisdom that similar identities lead to convergence and cooperation, cultural and identity similarities can lead to divergence and conflict. Based on social identity theory, Brewer (1991) postulates that the need for distinctiveness is met through comparisons. Consequently, similarity constitutes a threat to one's need for differentiation or distinctiveness. As Currie notes, 'one's individuality is more threatened by similarity rather than difference' (2004, 86).

If changes in the relative power distribution trigger physical insecurity and fear, what triggers an actor's ontological insecurity? If continuity and order in the self-versus-other relationships are the primary sources of ontological security, 'critical situations' that disrupt actors' distinctiveness can pose risks to their sense of self. Giddens defines 'critical situations' as 'circumstances of a radical disjuncture of an unpredictable kind which affect substantial numbers of individuals' (1984, 61). These unpredictable situations constitute an identity threat, as 'agents perceive that something can be done to eliminate them' (Steele 2008, 12). According to the indigenous and exogenous understanding of ontological security, these critical situations can emerge from incongruence between the action and narrative of an actor's self-identity but can also emerge during the interaction with others.

However, what is the worst scenario in a case of ontological insecurity? Can it ultimately lead to the elimination of actors just as physical insecurity does? According to Rumelili (2015, 60), 'concerns about instability and uncertainty of being can easily be politically mobilised and manipulated into concerns about survival'. In an extreme case, ontological insecurity can ultimately lead to physical insecurity. If leaders fail to maintain a consistent narrative about the state's self-identity and its *raison d'être*, domestic rifts can ensue. In

Table 1 *States of ontological and physical security*[10]

	Physical Security	Physical Insecurity
Ontological Security	States experience stability and certainty in being/ do not experience concern about physical danger.	States experience stability about being and consistent identity narrative/ experience concern about physical harm.
Ontological Insecurity	States experience instability and uncertainty about their being (identity risks)/ do not experience concern about physical harm.	States experience instability and uncertainty in their being/ experience concerns about physical harm.

Source: Author

other words, ontological insecurity can lead to questioning the self-identity of actors.

The ontological security literature stresses that ontological and physical security are distinct, because they are characterised by different dynamics and process. Although the two types of insecurities are inherently separate, I argue that they are interrelated and affect one another. The next section explores this linkage between the two in the process of threat perception. While the ontological and physical security spheres have different dynamics, they constitute two interrelated layers. Based on this dual conception of security, I argue that, in some instances, states suffer from ontological insecurity while their physical security remains intact, and that the opposite can occur in other instances (see Table 1). Under certain conditions, threats to identity, and the ensuring ontological insecurity, can shape how regimes perceive material forces. Under other conditions, a change in the material factors can lead to gradual changes in the regime identity.

Ideational and Material Forces: When They Matter

States operate within a structure and face both ideational and material constraints and opportunities which contribute to their assessment of threats. The argument here is built on the assumption that ontological

[10] A similar conception of security can be found in Rumelili (2015).

and physical security are distinct types. Whereas physical security is associated with military threats to the state, ontological security is associated with those dynamics and processes that centre around the reproduction of identity narratives and the maintenance of a system of certitude. I do not subscribe to the argument positing that identity politics and material interests – and their corresponding layers of security – are opposed or mutually exclusive. Instead, in every situation, states will experience two dimensions of security: ontological and physical. Physical and ontological security are often reconcilable. In some cases, the exigencies of ontological security predominate states' threat perception. Decision-makers, therefore, constrain the state's strategic options to those that are consistent with perceived ontological security needs. In other cases, the prerequisite of physical survival is the primary driving force, and elites shape identity or narratives to make the preferred strategies acceptable.

Over the last few years, the scholarship on ontological security has expanded to focus on this process of reconciliation between ontological and material security needs. Lupovici (2012), for example, discusses the problem that Israel faces when confronting the threat of Palestinian militants. While Israel has an identity narrative based on three elements – that is, Jewish, democratic and security provider – the exigencies of its physical survival make it act in contradiction with these narratives, which creates what Lupovici characterises as 'ontological dissonance'. To reconcile these two spheres of security, Israel adopted a strategy of avoidance, where an individual can avoid grappling with these contradictions. One illustration of this strategy is the wall. Another example of such reconciliation is presented by Selden and Strome (2016) who examine the case of India's alliance with the United States in the post-Cold War era. During the Cold War, India embraced an identity of non-alignment and wariness of the United States. Following the end of the Cold War, India's economic and military interests shifted, which required an alliance with the United States to balance China. Following this change in policy option, the narrative in Indian identity changed from non-alignment towards democracy to stronger relations with the United States. In both of these cases, elites have manipulated the societal foundation of ontological security to make some policy choices acceptable.

Other examples included states sacrificing their physical security to conform to the exigencies of their ontological security. Mitzen's (2006) work on the security dilemma shows how states continue conflicts even when their material interests do not require it. Instead, their ontological security emanating from the stables routines of the security dilemma explain the perpetuation of conflict. Steele (2008) also examines why a state would fight a war when its material interests do not demand it, or vice versa. He examines the case of Belgium's participation in World War II despite its inability to match Germany and the case of Great Britain's non-intervention during the American Civil War when its interests required an intervention. Both cases, Steele argues, can be explained by ontological security; both the states' strategic options were constrained by perceived ontological security needs.

The task ahead is, therefore, to explain systematically why and when ideational forces create the ontological foundations for leaders' threat perceptions in the Middle East, and when material calculations override ideational constraints in periods of escalating tensions within and between states. Two conditions are primarily relevant to explain why ideational and material forces become predominant in states' threat perception: the clarity of the regional power distribution and the fluidity of the regime identity.

First, the fluidity of the regime identity relates to the likelihood of identity varying depending on the social context. States often hold multiple identities; different aspects of identity can become salient or likely to be activated in particular contexts. This fluidity makes identity a structure offering elites with opportunities and constraints. Elites can choose aspects of their state identity, attach new meanings to them and use them as symbols to mobilise people. The degree of fluidity of identity is not similar across states. Some states can enjoy a higher degree of fluidity in their collective identity; other states may suffer from a fixed identity, where change and variation can put the cohesion of this collective entity at risk. In some cases, state identity can be multi-layered, malleable, that is, easy to change and manipulate around the politics of the day. In other cases, identities can be fixed and rigid, and this rigidity can be related to the inability of the state of outstrip older, more deeply entrenched elements of identity. Hence, states with fixed identity can perceive ideational threats as paramount due their inability to activate other aspects of the threatened identity.

In the Middle East, few states have some level of ambiguity and malleability in their identity narrative due to the history of state formation. Jordan's collective identity, for example, is constituted of four elements: (1) family and lineage, (2) civic identity, (3) pan-Arabism and (4) religion. This eclectic nature of identity resulted in what Frisch (2002) characterises as 'fuzzy nationalism', which is driven by security concerns. Sadowski (2002, 13–138) contemplates how the Syrian identity is multi-layered including elements of Arabism, Ba'athism, religious sectarianism, tribalism, and family and lineage. Karawan (2002) also shows how Egypt's collective identity has included several strands of identity, such as pan-Arabism, pan-Islamism, Mediterranean identity, Africanism and Egyptian national-ism, which provided the elites with opportunities to frame and reframe identity narratives around the exigencies of the state's material secur-ity. Such notions of identity flexibility and fluidity have also been used beyond Middle East cases. Even in modern states with a long history of statehood, identity fluidity and multiplicity have shaped, for example, Britain's identity and foreign policy. As Cohen (1995) argues that British identity has sustained a degree of malleability and fuzziness.

In other situations, state identity can be inflexible and less multi-layered, which can be the result of more entrenched historical processes. State identity in the Gulf illustrates this process. Due to the weakness of state institutions and a weak national identity, leaders often rely on Islam as a transnational identity that ties all tribes and societal groups. From this perspective, the religious dimension is somehow fixed and does not allow leaders freedom of manoeuvre or fuzziness to adapt the regime identity narratives to the exigencies of physical security.

Second is the range of policy options evolving from the relative power distribution. States operate in an international environment, where the relative power distribution provides states with policy options in ensuring their physical security. The international system does not always provide states with clear signals about threats and opportunities. In extreme cases, states can be faced with a clear and eminent danger, and they can easily discern the threat and determine how to counter it given the resources at their disposal. One example is Saddam Hussein's invasion of Kuwait (1990–1), which presented a very clear threat to the stability of the region. Most situations are not as clear-cut, leaving great ambiguity over the nature of threats and the appropriate response to them. For example, the rise of Iran's nuclear capabilities in the last decade requires the United States and other regional actors to respond in a military risk-taking behaviour. As the system rarely provides clear information to states to guide their policies, then states often have a range of policies from which to choose.

When faced with a military threat, leaders explore their options to ensure their physical survival. In some instances, the relative power distribution provides leaders with a clear structure where policy options are limited. But, in other instance, regional and international structures do not come with clear prescriptions for states. In these situations, leaders have to choose among multiple policy options to optimise their physical security. This logic has been identified and operationalised by neoclassical realist scholars, in what they termed the 'clarity' of the international system (Ripsman, Taliaferro, and Lobell 2016, 46–52). This clarity has several components, one of which is whether some policy options stand out to face the threat, or states are faced with several policy options. The clarity of options is rare in international politics. In some situations, the policy to face the threat can be clear and easily discernible. In 2007, Israel faced a situation with an undeclared nuclear facility in al-Kibar, Syria. The Syrian regime was isolated at the international level, and the United States was supportive of an Israeli action. The option of a preventive military strike on the reactor was a clear logical policy option for Israel to face this threat (Agence France-Presse 2018). In other situations, states are faced with several options to face threats with no obvious optimal policy response. For example, the Syrian crisis following the 2011 uprisings has presented the Saudi Kingdom with sources of threats, but the regional structure also presented the Kingdom with several policy options to face the situation without a clear optimal choice. States facing ideational and material threats can diverge in their perceptions based on these two conditions: fluidity of identity and the clarity of policy options. Accordingly, states face one of these four situations (see Table 2).

(1) The first situation is when state identity is fixed, and meanwhile the distribution of military capabilities comes with a clear policy option to ensure state's physical security. In this situation, regime identity is clear and relatively stable and often acts as a constraining factor in foreign policy decision, and alliance decisions in particular. In the meantime, state's physical security is endangered, and regime identity is a constraining factor. This situation corresponds to a case in

Table 2 *The conditions of the interplay between ideational and material forces*

	Ontological Security	
Physical Security	Fixed Identity (rigid identity)	Fluid Identity (multi-layered identity)
Single policy option	(1) Fixed identity and limited policy options. The direction can go both ways.	(3) Leaders have multiple identities but limited policy options. Threats to material forces override identity constraints (the case of Syria)
Multiple policy options (more than one)	(4) Leaders have a fixed identity but have several policy options in navigating the relative power distribution. Threats to identity override the constraints of the relative power distribution (the case of Saudi Arabia)	(2) Leaders have multiple identities and perceive multiple policy options to redress the relative power distribution. Leaders have the options to either face threats to identity or material forces.

which actors experience the fear of harm while also experiencing a clear, rigid sense of being. In this situation, it is hard to tell analytically which logic will dominate. That is an ambiguous situation in which one cannot know how states will attempt to restore their security and how they will prioritise between the two security spheres. An example of this such a situation is illustrated through the case of Hezbollah and its involvement in the Syrian crisis since 2013. The al-Assad regime is the vital conduit between Iran and Hezbollah, which allowed Iranian financial and military support to reach Lebanon. From this perspective, Hezbollah's involvement in the war to support the survival of the al-Assad regime is the only policy option to maintain the group's physical survival. In the meantime, this strategy contradicts Hezbollah's Islamic identity centred around the resistance against Israel. Hezbollah's deep involvement in the Syrian crisis was framed by its leader Hassan Nasrallah as a resistance strategy but this time towards the Islamist non-state actors, often portrayed as *takfiris,* in Syria (Boserup et al. 2017). This fixity in identity as well as limited policy options for physical survival put Hezbollah in an acute position of a potential ontological dissonance, where the actions contradict the identity. Although Hezbollah remains the dominant political actor in Lebanon, its popular legitimacy at the domestic level has declined and its appeal to the Arab public opinion have waned after its involvement in Syria (Drake 2013; Lob 2014). This case shows that in rare situations, actors can face situations of both fixed identity narrative and limited policy options, which could lead to a costly outcome.

(2) The second situation is when the relative power distribution provides the regime with multiple policy choices in its pursuit of state's physical security, and the regime also holds multiple identities. This situation provides elites with freedom of manoeuvre in pursuing physical and identity security. It is, however, difficult to predetermine which factor identity narrative will connect with a particular policy option and which connection will prevail. Egypt alliance shift after the 1973 war illustrates this situation. Egypt has a multi-layered identity that allowed its adaptation to the choices made by leaders. At the time, Egypt had several policy options to preserve its physical security, either allying with the United States or with the USSR to exercise further leverage during its bargain with Israel. Egypt's foreign policy choice was often attributed to the personal characteristics of Anwar al-Sadat's leadership and his belief system (Karawan 1994).

(3) The third possibility is a situation in which state identity is fixed and the distribution of military capabilities presents multiple policy options, which can lead to debates and divides among the ruling elite about the most suitable policy to adopt. In this situation, regimes are likely to perceive threats to their identity as more eminent. They will, therefore, attempt to reinforce their identity security. The relative power distribution offers actors the opportunity to adjust their policies related to the physical survival to the dictate of the identity. This situation may arise following revolutions in which the other is not physically threatening but its new

identity may threaten the stability of the self. Also, the resolution of protracted conflicts can challenge the previously shaped conflictual identities. The cases of Turkey and Japan apologising for past crimes is an example of such situation. In the Middle East, one can think of the rise of the Muslim Brotherhood to power in Egypt as a source of instability to the Saudi identity narrative based on its image as the leader of the Sunni world (Darwich 2016). The 2011 uprisings left Egypt militarily and economically weak, but the rise of a new Brotherhood regime constituted a source of instability to the regime narrative of the Kingdom. In some extreme situations, states have a stake in engaging or remaining in a conflict to serve the stability of their identity (Mitzen 2006). The Arab–Israeli conflict also follows this logic. For example, Palestinians and Israelis remain in the conflict as their identities shaped around the conflict provide actors with certainty and continuity (Lupovici 2012).

In situations in which the exigencies of identities predominate threat perception, the state will react with policies aiming at restoring identity stability. These policies are situated in the context of alliance politics, and regimes often adopt reactive mechanisms. First, states seek to reframe their identity narrative and frame the other in a demonising manner. Ontological insecurity leads actors to engage in practices that mark the other as being not only different but also inferior and threatening (Campbell 1992, 135–6). Second, states attempt to force a new, stable self–other distinction, or in other words reinvent their identity narrative. The new self–other distinction has a *negative* dimension, as the actor aims to discredit the other. This ontological insecurity dimension affects the physical security dimension. The framing of the other as an existential threat affects regime choices of friends and enemies. In other words, this perception of the relative power distribution and states' choice of allies become subjugated to this self–other distinction, which originally arise to restore the actor's ontological security.

(4) The fourth situation occurs when regimes have a fluid identity, where multiple identity narratives co-exist, whereas the power distribution comes with a single policy option to ensure the state's physical security. In this situation, regimes perceive threats to their physical security as more eminent. In this case, the material interest is likely to determine which identity is selected and carries the day

within the regime narrative. Regime identity, therefore, undergoes reframing and adjustment to accommodate these material constraints. This is a situation where actors maintain a fluid identity that offers regimes with various opportunities and a flexibility of manoeuvre. However, the regime faces danger to the physical survival of the state. In these situations, regimes are consistently faced with limited policy options in facing the threat of material nature. Regime identity, in this instance, is constantly framed and reframed to serve the purposes of physical survival. Syria provides an illustration for this path. The Ba'athist regime has constantly faced a constraining relative power distribution, where the regime had very few policy options, often balancing Israel. In the meantime, the regime possessed multiple identity narratives – such as Arab, Ba'athist, Levantine, Mediterranean Syrian, tribal and ethnic – which allowed the regime some flexibility in adapting its regime identity narrative to face material threats to the state's physical survival.

When regimes are in such situations of ontological security and physical insecurity, they are likely to react with policies to redress the state's physical security. Hence, their identity narratives become subjugated to the exigencies of relative power distribution. Accordingly, regimes choose their enemies and friends based on their material interest, and reframe their identity narrative to be congruent with their choice of allies. Accordingly, a new self–other emerges where the other is identified as an enemy based on its capabilities and intentions to cause harm. In short, regime move to reframe this self–other distinction based on the relative power distribution in the realm of physical security.

Research Design and Methods

The aforementioned conceptual framework is deployed to examine the persistently divergent Saudi and Syrian threat perceptions during three major wars in the Middle East: the Iran–Iraq War (1980–98), the 2006 Lebanon War, and the 2009 Gaza War. This book employs inter- and intra-case comparisons. Table 3 shows that inter-case comparisons will focus on comparing Syrian and Saudi threat perceptions in each war. Intra-case comparisons will focus on looking at each Syrian and Saudi threat perception over time to discern a pattern.

Table 3 *Inter- and intra-case comparisons of Syrian and Saudi threat perceptions*

		Inter-Case Comparison <---------------------->	
		Saudi Arabia	Syria
Intra-Case Comparison ∧ ⋮ ∨	Iran–Iraq War (1980–88)	Iran	Iraq
	Lebanon War (2006)	Hezbollah	Israel
	Gaza War (2009)	Hamas	Israel

The choice of inter-case comparison between Syria and Saudi Arabia followed three criteria: (1) the intrinsic importance of the cases, (2) both cases present two extremes cases,[11] and (3) divergence of outcomes from predictions made by various theoretical explanations.

Although both capitals, Damascus and Riyadh, have generally conveyed the impression of coordination and a kind of alliance – or at least an entente – in various spheres, they have differed on almost every alliance choice during major wars in the region, especially since the Iranian Revolution (1979).[12] These diametrically opposite decisions present one of the most intriguing puzzles in modern Middle East politics. The intrinsic importance of Saudi and Syrian threat perceptions, as well as the ensuing alliance decisions, stems from their significant role in shaping wider regional dynamics.

Substantive importance and fascination cannot, however, be the only criteria for selecting a case study. As the primary goal of this research is to infer an explanation of the interplay between ideational and material factors shaping threat perception, Syria and Saudi Arabia constitute extreme cases.[13] Saudi Arabia and Syria portray extreme cases that manifest the predominance of ideational or material forces in the process of threat perception. The Syrian case demonstrates a situation of ontological security and physical insecurity, in which the exigencies

---

[11] These case-selection criteria were in the list identified by Van Evera (1997, 77–8).

[12] Syria and Saudi Arabia shared common interests in the Arab–Israeli conflict and in Lebanon (Sunayama 2007).

[13] Extreme cases are usually selected because the study variable is very high, making the causes behind it much easier to identify (Van Evera 1997, 79–81).

of regime's physical survival have shaped the regime's identity framing. The Saudi case, however, represents a case of ontological insecurity and physical security, where Saudi foreign policy choices were aimed at restoring the regime's identity security.

These cases are further intriguing because both cases diverge from the predictions made on the bases of various theoretical lenses. Realist-based explanations underscore the geopolitically shaped balance of power as the origin of Syria's alliances. Due to the failure of the Syria–Iraq rapprochement in 1978 and the collapse of the Syria–Egypt axis after the Camp David accords (1978), the Iranian Revolution was a 'gift' for Syria to overcome its isolation and create a new geopolitical situation in which it would play a dominant role in the Middle East (Hirschfeld 1986). However, realist explanations fall short of explaining why Saudi Arabia supported a military ambitious Iraq against a military weakened Iran.

As the Saudi case diverged from realist predictions, Syria constitutes a deviation from regime security approaches. Regime security explanations are based on a critique of realism's preoccupation with external threats to state security (Ayoob 1995; Buzan 1991; David 1991; Job 1992). They explain foreign policy choices in terms of regimes' evaluation of the overlapping domestic and regional threats affecting its stability and survival (Dawisha 1990; Gause 2002). According to this approach, external threats are often related to domestic ones, as foreign opponents instrumentalise transnational identities to destabilise the Saudi Kingdom through subversion.[14] From this perspective, the Kingdom feared an Islamic spill-over, which can stir the subversion of the Shiite minority in the Eastern Province, which manifested in November 1979, February 1980, and November 1980 (Kostiner 1987; Long 1990). According to this explanation, Syria, a secular pan-Arab authoritarian regime suppressing Islamist movements at home, should have been equally threatened by the message of the Islamic Revolution. Therefore, the Syrian choice to ally with Iran was considered as an 'odd' case (Byman 2006; Goodarzi 2006; Lawson 2007). In short, both realism and regime security approach account

---

[14] This was the major dilemma facing the Kingdom during the rise of pan-Arabism of Nasser in the 1950s and the Islamic Revolution in Iran (1979). For an excellent comparison between both threats, see cf. Nahas (1985).

only for either the Saudi or the Syrian case but does not provide a comprehensive explanation of their divergence.

The choice of intra-case comparison is based on the selection of major wars in the region, where both Syria and Saudi Arabia undertook divergent alliance decisions based on disparate threat perceptions. The first case is the Iran–Iraq War (1980–88), and the most paradoxical, divergence between Saudi and Syrian alliance choices in the Middle East. In 1979, the Islamic Revolution in Iran and the Iraqi invasion of Iran were the subject of disagreement among Damascus and Riyadh. Whereas the Syrian regime perceived rising Iraq as a viable military threat and the Islamic Republic as a potential ally necessary to balance Saddam Hussein and Israel, the Saudi regime's perception of the situation was drastically different. For the Kingdom, the message emanating from the Islamic Revolution constituted the ultimate threat. Accordingly, the royal family ignored Saddam Hussein's regional ambitions. This divergence is even more paradoxical when seen against the background of the two states' identities. A secular Ba'athist regime in Syria, claiming to be an ardent supporter of the Arab cause, allied with a non-Arab Islamic theocracy that rejects the concept of the nation-state and promotes the overthrow of secular regimes. On the other hand, despite its claim of Islamic universalism and the rejection of pan-Arabism defended by the socialist republics in the region, Saudi Arabia allied with a secular socialist Ba'athist regime in Iraq.

The second and third cases are the 2006 Lebanon War and the 2009 Gaza War. Saudi Arabia and Syria joined opposing camps, which created a regional division between the so-called moderate axis (Saudi Arabia, Egypt, and Jordan) and the resistance axis (Syria, Iran, Hezbollah and Hamas). Both wars constitute episodes in the Arab–Israeli conflict. Despite shared interests in Lebanon and the Palestinian territories as well as converging ideational narratives supporting the Arab cause, both Saudi Arabia and Syria diverged during these wars. Whereas Syria considered Hezbollah in 2006 and Hamas in 2009 to be allies in fending off Israeli superiority, Saudi Arabia perceived their identity narratives as more threatening. This is an even more puzzling case considering that Saudi Arabia was Hamas' chief funder between 2000 and 2004.[15]

---

[15] For an overview on the development in the relations between Hamas and Saudi Arabia, see Stratfor (2015) and O'Brien (2003).

Although both wars reflect similar conflictual dynamics in the region, the case of Hamas in the context of the 2009 Gaza War is a *crucial case study*, or, in other terms, a least-likely case study that increases the confidence in the validity of the theoretical framework. A least-likely case study is one that, 'on all dimensions except the dimension of theoretical interest, is predicted not to achieve a certain outcome, and yet does. It is, therefore, used to confirm a theory' (Gerring and Seawright 2007, 115). This least-likely case is often used as the most difficult test for a theoretical argument, and hence provides the strongest evidence.[16] The analyses of the Iran–Iraq War and the 2006 Lebanon War establish that sectarian identities *per se* were not the driving force behind Saudi perceptions of Iran and Hezbollah as threats, and that identity similarity based on Islamism provided the ultimate threat for Saudi ontological security. Moreover, the two cases also argue that Syria's alliance with Iran and Hezbollah and the al-Assad regime's threat perception is based on material sources of threats. The 2009 Gaza War is a critical case that provides a harder test for this argument. Saudi and Syrian regimes' threat perception during the 2009 Gaza War diverged from prior theoretical suggestions made by regime security approaches and conventional approaches to the study of sectarianism in the international relations of the Middle East.

First, in contrast to the Islamic Republic in Iran and Hezbollah, Hamas is a political Islam movement that finds its ideological origins in the Muslim Brotherhood – belonging to a Sunni school of thought. Considering the nature of Hamas identity narrative, it was expected of Saudi Arabia to find in Hamas an ally based on identity convergence and history of cooperation. From a regime security approach, the Saudi Kingdom would find in supporting Hamas an opportunity to bolster its regime stability at the domestic level and confirm its identity narrative based on supporting Sunni Islam in the region and beyond. From a similar perspective, Syria was expected to perceive Hamas as a potential threat, considering that the al-Assad regime had been oppressing an offshoot of the same group at the domestic level. The rise to power of a similar group in Gaza while garnering support across the Arab world might have inspired and empowered the Brotherhood

---

[16] For a discussion on the least-likely case study or the crucial case study, see Eckstein (1975), Levy (2008) and George and Bennett (2005).

opposition in Syria. Yet, the Kingdom perceived Hamas as a threat as similarity threatened the ontological security of its identity narrative and stability. Also, the Ba'ath regime, often depicted as Alawite in nature oppressing the Brotherhood at the domestic level, regarded Hamas as an ally and reinforced its pan-Arab identity narrative as Israel remained the ultimate source of material threat.

Second, the comparison in this chapter has wider implications for the role of identity in Middle Eastern international relations. The interplay of ideational and material forces in Saudi and Syrian threat perceptions, as well as the following alliance choices, provides uncontroversial evidence that sectarian identities *per se* do not drive threat perception. Instead, the argument provides evidence that sectarianism can be a source of ontological security. The al-Assad regime and Hezbollah are often depicted as driven by a 'Shiite' identity. An examination of Syrian alliance with Hamas provides further evidence that challenges simplistic essentialist explanations of alliances in the Middle East. As opposed to Hezbollah, Hamas is a movement that finds its ideological origins in the Muslim Brotherhood belonging to a Sunni school of thought. Despite the identity convergence between Hamas and Saudi Arabia, the Kingdom perceived Hamas as a threat due to similarity in identity. The Saudi Kingdom promoted sectarian identity as a source of distinctiveness and ontological security. In short, the Gaza War, as a crucial case study, provides strong evidence that threat perception is not driven by sectarian identities *per se* and that ontological security presents an alternative lens to the rise of sectarianism in the Middle East beyond essentialist and instrumentalist approaches.

This is book has excluded the alliance decisions of Syria and Saudi Arabia during the Iraqi invasion of Kuwait (1990–91). In this case, both Saudi Arabia and Syria converged in their alliance decisions and joined the US-led coalition aimed at compelling Saddam Hussein to withdraw from Kuwait. The exclusion of this event from the book can seem to be eschewing the comparative and the variation in the dependent variable. Instead, this case is excluded based on the non-compliance with the scope condition of the inquiry of the book. Whereas the main research question of this book is concerned with threat perception in the context of alliance decisions, states can decide on alliance decisions based on factors other than threat perception, such as bandwagoning for profit (Schweller 1994). Whereas the Saudi Kingdom has joined the US-led coalition as Saddam Hussein threatened the physical security of the Kingdom, the Syrian regime joined the US-coalition for 'profit'. This profit included economic aid from the United States and the Gulf countries (Kienle 1994).

In this book, intra- and inter-case comparisons follow the method of 'structured, focused comparison' (George 1979; George and Bennett 2005, 67–9). In ascertaining the process of threat perception across the case studies, I utilise three research methods: congruence procedure, longitudinal analysis, and process-tracing. As the study is theory-driven, the empirical cases are used to illustrate and to develop the theoretical framework. Congruence procedure is used to test whether there is a strong correlation between the argument's predictions and leaders' perceptions of threat; (Van Evera 1997, 61–3) also argues that congruence procedure enables to observe variables in intra-case comparisons and then determine whether these variables co-vary as predicted by the theoretical argument. For example, if threat perception is driven by identity threats, there should be no evidence of objective military threat. Similarly, in the case of a military threat, there should be relative military imbalance. This does not mean that there is causation. But building correlation is one step towards proving causality.

Longitudinal analysis allows close examination of the timing of changes in both the independent variables (state identity and military capabilities) and dependent variables (threat perception). Does the change in the dependent variables follow a change in the independent variable? For example, did the Syrian decision to ally with Iran in 1979 follow a change in the relative power distribution? Also, events that lead to the disruption of self-identity should be followed by important changes in identity narratives. Here, a longitudinal analysis shows how identity narratives have changed over time, either as a response to ontological insecurity or physical insecurity. In addition, process-tracing allows us to trace the events to establish the relations between variables. Van Evera (1997, 64) describes it as exploring 'the chain of events or the decision-making process by which initial case conditions are translated into case outcomes'. In other words, process-tracing allows the analyses to show what is inside actors' heads by examining speeches, pronouncements and statements that explain why leaders make the choices they do.

It is true that, given the closed and secretive nature of the decision-making processes of both the Syrian Ba'athist regime and the Saudi Kingdom, inaccessibility to primary sources and interviews with current government officials in Damascus and Riyadh remains the chief obstacle to a complete and accurate picture of the inner workings of these authoritarian regimes. This book does not seek to reconstruct events but rather to evaluate theoretical explanations to present a different interpretation of events based on the proposed theoretical framework. The successive chapters offer empirical evidence to substantiate and develop this framework. The book is based on an exhaustive survey and analysis of the available secondary sources in Arabic, English, and French, most notably Middle Eastern and Western newspapers and, more importantly, numerous books and articles published by historians (both from the region and Western countries). These secondary data are supplemented with primary sources, such as speeches, official government statements and memoires.

3 | The Iran–Iraq War (1980–1988)

Saudi Arabia wants to balance us out with Iran, and balance us with Syria, and balance us with Jordan. And Jordan wants to balance us with Syria, and wants to balance us with Saudi Arabia, and wants to balance us – we are a priority weight balance over all … All of this is a soap opera. We know all of this and we are disturbed.

Saddam Hussein (1979) (quoted in Woods, Palkki and Stout 2011, 131–2)

As rivals often share mutual enemies and allies back opposite sides in the same conflict, Saddam Hussein's quote underlines an evident fact: Iraq was a source of fear to its Arab neighbours. Nevertheless, a collective regional balancing never materialised; instead, Arab polarisation and divergence prevailed. The alliances formed in the wake of the Iran–Iraq War (1980–88) proved enduring in moulding events and reshaping the political landscape of the Middle East for decades. Whereas Saudi Arabia identified Iraq as a friend and Iran as an enemy, Syria considered Iraq as a source of danger and Iran as a reliable ally.

This chapter argues that this divergent outcome can be unravelled by paying attention to the interaction between identity and material power, and the conditions under which they dominate threat perception and alliance choices. The analysis in this chapter focuses on the period leading to the outbreak of the Iran–Iraq War. It focuses on threat perceptions of Saudi Arabia and Syria and their alliance decisions since the outbreak of the Iranian Revolution through the first few months of the war. Although alliances and threat perceptions have developed through the course of this eight-year war, the analysis is limited here to the alliances formed at the outbreak of the war.[1] In 1979, the Islamic Revolution altered Iran's regime identity and

---

[1] For further details about the different stages in the war and the different regional dynamics, see Goodarzi (2006) and Ulrichsen (2013a).

emerged as a source of ontological insecurity for Iran's neighbours in the region. Moreover, the Revolution altered the regional power distribution, creating physical insecurity for others in the region. In the Saudi case, the emergence of an Islamic government in Iran claiming to play a pan-Islamic role constituted a source of identity risk for the Kingdom. At the same time, the change in the relative power distribution left the Saudi elite in a state of confusion and uncertainty with several options. To restore its identity security, the Saudi Kingdom discredited the Islamic Republic and reinvented a distinct identity framing based on a sectarian self–other distinction, namely a Sunni–Shiite discourse. This new self–other distinction shaped the Saudi elite's perception of their physical security. In the Saudi case, the material considerations became subjugated to the exigencies of identity stability and security.

In contrast, the change in the material configuration led to the isolation of the Syrian regime, which feared its Iraqi neighbour. Unlike the Saudi case, Iran's altered regime identity did not disturb Syrian identity security as the Ba'ath regime maintained a distinct identity based on pan-Arabism, according to which the self was defined as opposed to an 'Israeli other'. In this state of ontological security and physical insecurity, the Syrian identification of material dangers predominated its threat perception and alliance decisions. This particular configuration shaped the regime's identity, which was changed and reinterpreted to accommodate the material constraints. Such a causal path was conditioned by the fluidity of the regime identity and the limited policy options. The fluidity of Syria's identity enabled the regime to adopt a broader pan-Arab narrative based not on the Arab dimension but on animosity towards Israel. This is the context in which Syria widened its definition of 'us' to include the Islamic Republic.

This chapter is structured as follows. In the first section, I contextualise Saudi and Syrian alliance choices in the regional developments of 1979–80. Second, I examine Saudi threat perception and explore the strategic position of the Kingdom in the relative power distribution. I then discuss how the Iranian Revolution disrupted the stability of the Saudi regime identity and led to a case of ontological insecurity. Third, I explore Syrian threat perception. Here, I discuss Syria's regional position in the relative power distribution, which led to the regime's physical insecurity. I then demonstrate how identity and the self–other distinction responded to the physical needs of the Syrian regime.

The Islamic Revolution, the Iran–Iraq War, and Regional Reactions

Political shocks – such as wars, revolutions or economic crises – are often a catalyst for ideational and material discontinuities.[2] The Islamic Revolution in Iran (1979) was one such exogenous shock that moulded regional events significantly for decades, as it brought about substantial changes to the normative and geopolitical order in the Middle East.

From an ontological security perspective, this external shock may be considered a 'critical situation'. The revolution altered Iran's identity and, hence, its relations with others. As an actor's identity has a strong relational dimension, based on the self–other distinction, changes in any others' identity may lead to changes in the identity of the self. The revolution altered the state identity of Iran from a monarchy ruled by the Shah to a populist Islamic Republic governed by Ayatollah Rouhallah Khomeini's Islamic worldview. The key to understanding Khomeini's world order is the idea of *vilayat-e faqīh*[3] (the rule of the leading jurisprudent), according to which the government or the rulership (*vilayat*) belongs to God, to the Prophet, to the infallible imams, and, by extension, to the pious *faqīh*. The rule of the *faqīh* is temporal until the Twelfth Imam (*al-Mahdi*) appears. Khomeini called on all rulers in Muslim countries to return to 'true and unique Islam'. The new ideology posited that, being the only 'Government of God', Iran had a role in spreading justice around the Islamic world. This drastic change in Iran's identity could not be contained within its borders since it affected others' identity security and stability, as the latter remained inextricably tied to the consistent distinction of the self vis-à-vis the other (Iran in this case).

The Islamic Revolution emerged around the idea of building an 'Islamic community' that would transcend sectarian and national boundaries. Khomeini believed that Muslim countries should unite (*tawḥīd*) in order to successfully counter Western influence. He saw nationalism as a source of disunity and disintegration between Muslim

---

[2] Political shocks are considered to be 'rare moments' in history leading to dramatic changes in states' policies. For examples, on 'shocks', cf. Legro (2005), Goldstone (1993), Ikenberry (2000) and Walt (1996).

[3] For more details on the religious foundations of this system, cf. Al-Labbad (2005).

countries. Therefore, Khomeini's ideology may be regarded as 'pan-Islamic' (Menshari 1990). In September 1980, he declared:

Nationalism that results in the creation of enmity between Muslims and splits the ranks of the believers is against Islam and the interests of the Muslims. It is a stratagem concocted by the foreigners who are disturbed by the spread of Islam . . . More saddening and dangerous than nationalism is the creation of dissension between Sunnis and Shi'is and diffusion of mischievous propaganda amongst brother Muslims. (Khomeini 1981, 304)

Accordingly, the Islamic Republic pursued a foreign policy strategy that appealed to both Arabs and Muslims. Palestine constituted a central theme in Khomeini's ideology from the earliest days of the Islamic Revolution (Ramazani 1986, 151–4). Iran consistently emphasised its commitment to the Palestinian cause. Khomeini identified the Israeli–Palestinian conflict as the issue that would allow him to expand the appeal of his revolution beyond his Shiite sect and rally Muslims behind Iran. On 18 February 1979, Yasser Arafat, leader of the PLO, was received in Teheran as the first foreign visitor after the revolution. The Teheran radio reported that Arafat received a pledge from Khomeini that the Iranian would 'turn to the issue of victory over Israel' after Iran had consolidated its achievements (Markham 1979). Shortly after he came to power, Khomeini established the yearly 'Jerusalem Day' in support for the Palestinians and named the elite expeditionary unit of the Islamic Revolutionary Guard Corps (IRGC) after the holy city of Jerusalem(Ghattas 2017). In his speeches, Khomeini often stressed Iran's support for 'his beloved Palestine' (Khomeini 1980). Furthermore, Khomeini stressed that 'Selfishness, servitude, and the surrender of some Arab governments to direct foreign influence has prevented tens of millions of Arabs from freeing Palestine from the yoke of Israeli occupation and usurpation' (Takeyh 2009, 62).

This pan-Islamist narrative was accompanied by increasing financial support to Hamas, the Palestinian Islamic Jihad and Hezbollah in Lebanon. The Iranians thus presented themselves as the leader of Islam in the region and as the epitome of virtue in the Arab–Israeli conflict. As pan-Islamism constituted the basic tenet of Khomeini's theory of an Islamic state, some regional actors found the stability of their identity disrupted, which negatively affected their ontological security. Some Arab actors discovered that it was difficult to establish clear and distinctive boundaries between themselves and the 'Persian' other.

The Islamic Revolution was pivotal in altering the material power configuration in the Middle East. Indeed, it destroyed the US–Iranian partnership and distorted alliance patterns in the region. The relative power distribution was transformed from a situation of Iranian regional hegemony to one of power parity between Iran and Iraq. Throughout the 1970s, Iran enjoyed a considerable supremacy in the region. This hegemony was observable in the size of its armed forces, which was nearly double that of Iraq, and through its yearly military spending, which ranked the highest in the region (Gause 2003, 285). The Shah exerted hegemony over the Persian Gulf and played a dominant role in the Middle East. The military balance between Iran and Iraq was estimated roughly two-to-one in Iran's favour due to its three-to-one manpower advantage and its predominant arsenal (Cashman and Robinson 2007, 279).

The Iranian Revolution altered this equilibrium. Ayatollah Khomeini's first act after seizing power on 11 February 1979 was to deliberately destroy the Shah's well-trained professional military, which was regarded as disloyal to the Islamic regime. Approximately 5,000 of the most experienced officers, mostly trained in the United States or Israel, were executed; thousands more were imprisoned or exiled (Segal 1988, 952–3). By some estimates, 30–59 per cent of the highest-ranking officers, mainly majors and colonels, were killed. The size of Iran's army in 1980 was about half of what it has been in 1979 (down from approximately 415,000 men to 240,000 men). Military spending fell from 15 per cent of GNP to 7.3 per cent (Cashman and Robinson 2007, 279). In short, Iran set about destroying its military capacity to threaten its neighbours or to even defend itself. In the meantime, Iraq, which was supported by the Soviet Union and profiting from the oil windfall of 1973–74, increased its own military capabilities throughout the 1970s. By 1980, its military had doubled in size (to 242,000 men). Its military spending jumped from 14 per cent of GNP in 1972 to 21 per cent in 1980. As a result, the military balance tilted towards parity between Iran and Iraq (Gause 2009, 51–4).[4]

These material and normative changes caused by the Iranian Revolution set up the context for the outbreak of the Iran–Iraq War. The change in the material balance of power provided Saddam Hussein

---

[4] For more details, cf. Chubin and Tripp (1988), Cordesman (1994) and The International Institute for Strategic Studies (1980).

with the opportunity to launch what he thought would be a short victory against his weakened rival. It soon became apparent that Hussein's misperception of the situation led both countries into a costly eight-year war, during which Saudi Arabia and Syria joined opposing camps. The former supported Iraq while the latter allied with Iran. Despite their professed neutrality, the southern Gulf states (Kuwait, Saudi Arabia, and, to a lesser degree, the United Arab Emirates and Oman) openly provided financial and military support to Iraq. The financial assistance, including oil and non-oil support, amounted to approximately US$25 billion from Saudi Arabia alone (Ulrichsen 2013, 115).[5] In addition, Jordan also openly supported Saddam Hussein. King Hussein of Jordan provided Iraq with military hardware and economic aid. He also negotiated credit and loans from Western countries to purchase weapons on behalf of Iraq. Despite Egypt's ousting from the Arab League in March 1979, it sold advanced weapons to the Iraqi army in 1981.

Syria, and to a lesser extent Libya, opposed this main trend in the Arab world and thereby prevented Iraq from claiming an 'Arab' war against the 'Persian' neighbour. On 7 October 1980, Syria became the first Arab state to side officially with Iran. Syria criticised Iraq for attacking a potential ally of the Arabs, especially in their struggle with Israel. Alongside this verbal support, Damascus provided Iranian armed forces with war materiel and made its airfield available for Iranian strikes in the west of Iraq (Goodarzi 2006; Kienle 1990; Marschall 1992; Stanely 1990).[6] This Arab polarisation over the Islamic Revolution and the Iran–Iraq War led to an unprecedented deterioration in inter-Arab relations, as it exacerbated older conflicts between Arab regimes.

Saudi Arabia and the Quest for Distinctiveness

On the eve of the Iran–Iraq War, Saudi Arabia supported an aspiring Iraq against a militarily weakened Iran. The external shock of the Islamic Revolution and the resulting change in the regional power distribution created a state of uncertainty that made the Saudis unable

---

[5] For more details on the financial and military assistance provided by the Gulf states in support of Iraq, cf. Quandt (1981a), Lotfian (1997), Nonneman (2004, 1986), Adib-Moghaddam (2006) and Ulrichsen (2013a).

[6] This fact was denied by Syrian leaders (Baraka 2011).

to identify the most eminent source of danger. Amid this initial confusion and disarray, the ideational message of the Iranian Revolution challenged the stability of the Saudi regime identity. Seeking to distinguish their state identity from Iran's pan-Islamic appeal, the Saudi elite framed the Iranian other in a demonising manner. Moreover, the Saudis narrowed down their regime identity from pan-Islamism to Sunni Islam and, thereby, established a new identity narrative based on a different 'us-them' distinction. The new self–other shaped elite's perception of the relative power distribution and guided their policy preference. This section is divided into two parts. First, I present the Kingdom's position in the new relative power distribution, which demonstrates a case of physical security. I then explore the case of Saudi ontological insecurity, which influenced the elite's perception of the Kingdom's physical security and shaped its alliance decision.

The Relative Power Distribution: 'A Structure without an Instruction Sheet'[7]

Although the Saudi support of Iraq seemed assertive at the outbreak of the war, the decision was preceded by a long period of uncertainty among Saudi ruling elites approximately from January 1979 to September 1980 (Altoraifi 2012, 128–31; Safran 1988, chaps. 12, 14). Before 1979, Saudi Arabia was successful in pursuing separate and incompatible strategies in different areas – namely, the Gulf, the Arab–Israeli conflict, and the partnership with the United States. The Islamic Revolution in Iran coincided with other crises: the signing of the Egyptian–Israeli peace treaty, the Soviet invasion of Afghanistan, and strains in the Saudi–US partnership. Embroiled in disarray and uncertainty, the royal elite was compelled to make strategic choices in order to adapt to these critical changes. Nevertheless, the new relative power distribution did not come with evident sources of danger to the Kingdom's physical security. Throughout 1979, this ambiguity in the relative power distribution provided the Saudis with multiple policy options in pursuing their physical security. This section examines three areas relevant to the Saudi physical security: the Gulf, the Arab–Israeli sphere, and the Saudi–US partnership.

---

[7] This title is based on Blyth (2003).

Physical security in the Gulf is of primary concern in Saudi foreign policy. Before 1979, the major sources of instability in the Gulf were communist infiltration and the Ba'athist regime in Iraq, whose pan-Arab identity constituted a source of threat to the stability of the Kingdom's identity. Based on these concerns, Saudi Arabia relied on the United States to ensure the Kingdom's physical security. This security arrangement was part of the so-called twin pillar strategy, according to which the United States ensured the stability of the Gulf through the build-up of two regional powers, Iran and Saudi Arabia. It was in this framework that the Shah's regime emerged as a military hegemon in the Middle East (Ramazani 1979, 822).

In 1975, the Algiers agreement was signed to settle the long-standing dispute between Iran and Iraq.[8] The settlement marked an Iraqi turn towards moderation in its relations with its Arab neighbours (Niblock 2006, 50). This change transformed the strategic configuration in the Gulf as it led to the emergence of the Riyadh–Teheran–Baghdad tri-angle (1975–79), which allowed Saudi Arabia more room to man-oeuvre in pursuing its physical security in the region. The agreement enabled the Kingdom to play Iraq off against Iran, while consolidating its own influence over smaller Gulf countries (Safran 1988, chap. 10). From this perspective, the Saudis managed to use Iraq's opposition to impede the Shah from consolidating the Iranian hegemony in the Gulf. At the same time, Iran's opposition to Iraqi aspirations of domination constituted substantial gains for the Saudis.[9]

Although this triangle brought many gains to the Kingdom, the Islamic Revolution turned the post-1975 strategic configuration upside down. With the fall of the Shah in Iran, Saudi Arabia lost a friendly regime with which it shared many norms, such as preserving the status quo in the region and a dominant US role in safeguarding stability in the Gulf. Moreover, Saddam Hussein took advantage of the sudden absence of a military-predominant Iran at the regional level to assert Iraq's own role in the Gulf. After the withdrawal of Egypt from the Arab–Israeli conflict, Hussein positioned Iraq as the champion of the Arab cause and the only regional power capable of saving Arab states from any regional threat, including the spread of the Islamic

---

[8] For more details on this agreement, cf. Sirriyeh (1985).
[9] For a detailed account of Saudi–Iranian relations prior to the Islamic Revolution, cf. Badeeb (1993).

Revolution. While Iraq asserted itself as an ambitious power aspiring to a leading role in the region, the new regime in Iran was caught up in revolutionary chaos. Iran was weakened and had neither the time nor the capability to contain Saddam Hussein's regional ambitions. The relative power distribution portrayed the weakness of Iran's capability in standing as a threat to the Kingdom's physical security.

It is worth noting that the decline in Iran's military capabilities did not usher in an Iraqi hegemony in the region. Instead, the change in the relative power distribution revealed an emerging parity between Iran and Iraq. The Iranian Revolution and the subsequent change in the regional configuration did not directly affect the physical security of the Kingdom. Saudi Arabia initially sought to keep the balance between Iraq and Iran by appeasing Iran without provoking Iraq. In case one became too dangerous, the Saudi elite hoped to play one against the other (Ehteshami 2002). The emerging power parity in the Gulf was too ambiguous for the Saudis to identify their optimal policy option. For example, and despite the Shiite demonstrations in the Eastern Province in Saudi Arabia and other Gulf countries, King Khalid sent a letter of congratulations to Khomeini when the Islamic Republic was founded by a referendum on 30 March 1979:

We always welcome the establishment of an Islamic government in any country, and we believe that the establishment of such a government in Iran will lead to a greater measure of understanding and to closer ties. After all, this is consistent with our constant call for adopting the Islamic *shari'a* as the basis of government. (Quoted in Samore 1983a, 423–4)

The fall of the Shah and the changes in the Persian Gulf coincided with other developments in the Arab–Israeli area, where the Kingdom faced additional uncertainty. Before 1967, the Saudi involvement in the Arab–Israeli conflict was limited to the Palestinian question (Piscatori 1983, 37–8). Like the majority of Arabs, the Saudis resented Israel. Zionism was considered a primary concern for the security and stability of the Saudi regime. In addition, the repeated Arab defeats and the Israeli occupation of Jerusalem made the Arab–Israeli conflict a foreign policy concern for the Kingdom. The Riyadh–Cairo–Damascus trilateral axis thus emerged, with the purpose of maintaining a military balance against Israel. King Faisal developed a partnership with Egypt and mediated the tensions with Syria (Sunayama 2007, 37). Beyond this diplomatic role, the Kingdom's involvement was mainly financial (Safran 1988, 261–4; Taylor 1982, 49).

The short-lived Arab reconciliation over the issue of balancing Israel during the Yom Kippur War (1973) was quickly replaced by inter-Arab polarisation, which began to surface following King Faisal's death. The Camp David Accords (1978) and the subsequent Egyptian–Israeli peace treaty (1979) constituted a real challenge to the Kingdom since the Saudis were forced to take sides. Despite Saudi efforts to maintain Arab cohesion, especially through the triangular axis, the alliance finally collapsed. Consequently, Egypt's withdrawal from the conflict created a military imbalance in favour of Israel. While sympathising with the Egyptian initiative, Saudi Arabia could not afford the costs of taking such a position publicly. As an alternative, Saudi Arabia mediated between Damascus and another powerful Arab state, namely Iraq (Kienle 1990, 100). A strong Arab opposition front was formed and threatened any party that would not actively penalise Egypt. The Saudis were torn between two options: (1) to espouse the US-oriented strategy of endorsing the Egyptian–Israeli peace treaty while confronting the Damascus–Baghdad axis, as well as the Islamic Republic, or (2) to join the Damascus–Baghdad axis in confronting Egypt while risking the US connection. Serious strains emerged in the Saudi–US partnership when Washington proposed to link the protection of the Kingdom to Saudi support for the Egyptian–Israeli peace treaty (Safran 1988, 231). In short, the events in the Arab–Israeli sphere created a confusing situation for the royal elite. Nevertheless, the Arab–Israeli imbalance created by the withdrawal of Egypt did not endanger the physical security of the Kingdom. The conservative, oil-rich Kingdom is not a frontline state in the conflict with Israel and has no territorial quarrel with it. Unlike other Arab states – such as Egypt, Syria, Jordan and Iraq – Saudi Arabia's involvement in the conflict was limited to financial and diplomatic means rather than military ones (Bahgat 2009b).

Alongside the Gulf and the Arab–Israeli conflict, the partnership with the United States constituted the third pillar in Saudi foreign policy. Throughout 1979, this partnership seemed to undergo some changes, which contributed to Saudi confusion and uncertainty about the relative power distribution. Since the Kingdom's creation in 1932, Saudi Arabia relied on its partnership with Great Britain then with the United States as a safeguard to its physical security. This partnership was always a source of tension and embarrassment to the Saudi royal family in both Arab and Islamic worlds. Saudi elites were, however, successful in maintaining a balance between preserving the US connection and preserving its status in the Arab world. Nevertheless, the Iranian Revolution and the signing of the US-sponsored Egyptian–Israeli peace treaty created acute tensions in this partnership.

In the Gulf, losing the Shah undermined the US reliability as a security asset (Lippman 2004, 209; Safran 1988, 275). As Safran (1988, 354) explained,

It provided clear confirmation of a point the Saudis already suspected: that in its dealing with the Gulf countries, Saudi Arabia included, the United States was prompted only by its interest in oil and would work with any regime that would serve that interest. American's refusal in September 1979 to provide asylum to the shah only underscored that point.

Accordingly, Saudi Arabia attempted to rely on regional cooperation to address regional security concerns. Since the 1978 Baghdad Arab summit, reconciliation between Saudi Arabia and Iraq seemed to be possible (Goodarzi 2006, 27–8). Following the failure of the Baghdad–Damascus axis, Saudi Arabia and Iraq signed a mutual security pact in February 1979 (Nonneman 1986, 14, 2004, 173). Nevertheless, this pact did not indicate a firm tilt towards Iraq. Instead, it reflected Saudi Arabia's ambiguous stance on the issue. At the same time, the Saudi minister of interior declared that this cooperation concerned only civil defence, police, and extradition (Ramazani 1986, 73). However, relying on a wider Arab consensus either in the Arab–Israeli sphere or the Gulf seemed futile as the Syrian–Iraqi axis quickly dissolved leaving the Saudi leadership in an even more puzzling situation.[10]

At the outbreak of the Iran–Iraq War, Saudi Arabia had to take a firm position, especially after the split in the Syrian–Iraqi axis. While the new regional configuration did not generate evident physical security threats to the Kingdom, the position to be taken still had far-reaching implications. Throughout 1979, the regional structure remained ambiguous for the Saudi elite, who wavered between two options. The first was balancing Iraq's military ascent by supporting a weakened Iran, while befriending the nationalist Arab camp – namely Syria and the Palestinian Liberation Organisation (PLO) – in the

---

[10] For a detailed account of this ephemeral rapprochement, cf. Baram (1986) and Kienle (1990).

Arab–Israeli sphere. This choice would mean scuppering the long-term strategic relationship with the United States and incurring the hostility of Iraq. It would also involve improving Saudi relationship with Moscow at the expense of the Kingdom's relationship with Washington. The second option was supporting Iraq and sacrificing Saudi Arabia's traditional strategy of maintaining a balance of power between Iran and Iraq in the Gulf. This option would mean accepting Iraq's regional hegemony and depending more on the United States for security. The choice would imply Saudi support for the Egyptian–Israeli peace treaty and would engender the hostility of Syria and Iran.

The absence of a precise source of danger and the ambiguity of the regional structure throughout 1979 triggered acute tensions within the royal elite, which was divided between those for supporting Iraq and those for befriending Iran. A conservative faction, led by King Khalid and Prince Abdullah, favoured befriending Syria and welcoming the Islamic fervour of the new Iranian regime. This faction was supported by a younger generation in the family led by Saud bin Faisal that advocated for the strengthening of Saudi ties with the nationalist Arab Camp and for the improvement of relations with Moscow at the expense of the reliance on the United States (Abir 1993, 127–8; Samore 1983a, 416–22). In fact, Saud bin Faisal explicitly referred to the Soviet role in the Middle East as 'positive' (Quandt 1981b, 69; Sunayama 2007, 57). The opposing faction – led by Crown Prince Fahd and Sultan, who relied on the influential power of the Sudairi clan in the family[11] – advocated a pro-US stance stemming from a deep hostility to the Soviets. Fahd's pro-US moderate foreign policy and modernist project were partly discredited and blamed for the 1979 siege of Grand Mosque of Mecca[12] as well as the Shiite uprisings in the Eastern

---

[11] This is most powerful clans of the Al Saud family, derived from the patronymic of Fahd's mother – Hussa bint Ahmad Al Sudairi – who was married to King Abdel-'Aziz. This marriage resulted in seven sons: Fahd, Sultan, Abdel-Rahman, Nayef, Turki, Salman and Ahmed. The seven sons of Hussa al-Sudairi constituted the largest bloc of full brothers forming a strong alliance within the House of Al Saud.

[12] In 1979, a group of Sunni dissidents seised the Grand Mosque in Mecca for three weeks condemning the rule of Al Saud. In fact, these events had no direct connection to the Iranian Revolution. It was only the timing that made these actions even more challenging to the regime's stability (Gause 1991, 2009, 48). For more details on this incident, see Trofimov (2008) and Hegghammer and Lacroix (2007a).

Province (Abir 1988, 145–7). This divergence between the Saudi elite resulted in the defeat of Crown Prince Fahd and his self-exile in Spain[13] when his brothers took over his responsibilities.

Fahd's temporary withdrawal left room for the Khalid–Abdullah faction to impose its own vision. This conservative coalition within the royal family temporarily reoriented many of the Kingdom's policies away from those pursued by Fahd and the Sudairis. In the Arab–Israeli sphere, Saudi Arabia now supported the radical Arab countries, in clear contradiction with the Saudi traditional policy. At the Arab summit in Baghdad (1978), Saudi Arabia agreed to the exclusion of Egypt from the Arab League and the imposition of a boycott, based on a total rejection of the Camp David Accords and of US policy in the Middle East. As part of the new regional emphasis of this coalition, Khalid and Abdullah led the first Saudi efforts to accommodate Khomeini. The Saudi newspaper *Al-Rai al-Am* said that Saudi Arabia even warned against any actions that would undermine the 'courageous stance taken by Iran in support of the Arab nation and its struggle against Zionism'(Ghattas 2017). As Prince Abdullah explicitly declared,

The new regime in Iran has removed all obstacles and reservation in the way of cooperation between Saudi Arabia and the Islamic Republic of Iran. Islam is the organiser of our relations. Muslim interests are the goal of our activities and the holy Koran is the constitution of both countries ... For this reason I am very optimistic about the future of relations between us and the Islamic republic of Iran. Our cooperation will have an Islamic dynamism against which no obstacles facing the Muslims can stand ... the material potentials – money and oil – possessed by the Islamic Republic of Iran and Saudi Arabia, and by the Islamic and Arab worlds will be utilised and directed by an Islamic spirit – a spirit which is superior to all hollow secular pomp such as authority, dominance, or self-interests. The fact is that we are very relieved by the Islamic Republic of Iran's policy for making Islam and not heavy armaments, the organiser of cooperation, a base for dialogue and the introduction to a prosperous and dignified future. (Samore 1983a, 423–4)

Amid this acute disagreement, Saudi royal family members exercised a high degree of self-restraint in dealing with their differences. In the face of rumours swirling around the Kingdom and in the media, King

---

[13] There are no consensual explanations for the reasons behind this self-exile (Samore 1983a, 417–18).

Khalid and Prince Abdullah denied any weakening in the unity of the royal family. In an interview with the Gulf News Agency on April 21, Prince Abdullah stated the following: 'We have lived with one another for a long time. We have inherited concepts and a way of life and family ties which we have all established on profound religious and solid ethical bases. We have been brought up in this country on these bases for successive generations. In our firm Islamic beliefs, estrangement among blood relatives is considered an unforgivable sin'. Like Khalid and Abdullah, Fahd denied all allegations of divisions within the royal family, especially between himself and Abdullah (Samore 1983a, 425–7). Safran (1988, 238) notes: 'although the leadership did not visibly split again, the policies pursued showed all the marks of an intermittent tug of war, punctuated by improvisations, compromises, and zigzags'.[14] Mordechai Abir (1988, 146) went further in asserting that 'The more radical among the new elite hoped and even believed that the end of the Saud's regime was rapidly approaching'.

Although this confusion and policy debate within the Saudi royal family might appear to be inherent to the ritual foreign policymaking process, this serious dispute between senior princes underlined an intrinsic contradiction in the Saudi regime's identity. Riyadh was hitherto successful in maintaining an exceptional balance between its 'special relationship' with the United States and its pan-Islamic identity, which was challenged by the Islamic Revolution in Iran (Samore 1983b, 372). The pan-Islamic dimension in the Saudi identity has been reinforced and consolidated during the 1950s–60s and shaped the Kingdom's foreign policy. This prevalence of the ideas is explained by two parallel processes. Firstly, this pan-Islamic element embedded in the Saudi regime identity provided guidance through the relative power distribution in the region. Secondly, pan-Islamism provided an efficient glue to reintegrate the fragmented ruling elite. In the absence of other elements of nationalism, these dynamics show the mechanisms behind the fixity of the regime identity in the Saudi Kingdom.

During the summer of 1979, however, the family dispute had been contained and a compromise was achieved based on a combination of nationalist and pragmatic strategies. On the one hand, a consensus was

[14] The Al Saud house has been known for stability due to efficient mechanisms in solving intra-family conflicts and tensions. For more details on these mechanisms, see Stenslie (2011) and Herb (1999).

achieved in the Arab sphere confirming the break with Egyptian President al-Sadat, while working to preserve the Arab credentials by preserving the front with Baghdad against Iran. On the other hand, Saudis favoured to strengthen cooperation with the United States in areas of mutual interests such as energy policy and security ties. This enabled a compromise between a nationalist tilt on the regional level and dependence over the United States. By mid-1979, Fahd was back resuming his previous responsibilities. This compromise shows that family consensus was resumed by re-embracing the traditional ideas guaranteeing a consensus and, hence, survival of the regime.

These internal tensions demonstrated that Al Saud faced an uncertain and ambiguous relative power distribution, and, hence, that an Iranian military threat to the Kingdom was not imminent, as it took almost one year to decide between the two available options. Instead, these tensions underlined an intrinsic contradiction in the Saudi regime's identity. The ontological security of the Kingdom was endangered by the new identity of the Islamic Republic. To restore its identity security, the Kingdom reframed its identity, which eventually influenced its perception of the relative power distribution and its threat perception.

The Regime Identity: From Pan-Islamism to Sunni Islam

Whereas the Islamic Revolution in Iran and the subsequent regional material configuration did not endanger the Kingdom's physical security, the new identity of the Islamic Republic caused Saudi ontological insecurity. The Saudi regime identity was based on pan-Islamism, which provided the Kingdom with the source of distinctiveness in the region. Ironically, its claim to be the protagonist of 'true' Islam in the world sowed the seeds of its vulnerability to other emerging Islamic models in the region. In 1979, the Islamic Revolution in Iran constituted a 'critical situation' that endangered the stability of the Saudi regime identity. The Kingdom feared that it would lose its unique Islamic credentials once the revolution adopted a similar pan-Islamic identity. In other words, the distinction according to which the Kingdom had consolidated its own identity vis-à-vis the other states in the region became irrelevant. Seeking to re-establish its ontological security, the Saudi state narrowed its regime identity from pan-Islamism to Sunni Islam. Based on the prominence accorded to the Sunni version of

Islam, Iran was identified as a Shiite 'other', which was framed in demonising terms. This new emerging self–other distinction defined not only the Saudi identity but also determined its identification of enemies and friends, which inextricably related to its physical security.

Before examining the Saudi Kingdom's ontological insecurity, I will briefly explore what 'Saudi state identity' means. As opposed to Arab states, where nationalism was based on ethnic elements – such as Arabism – combined with territorial affinities related to the struggle against colonialism, the Saudi Kingdom was not formed on the basis of a 'national' identity. The nature of the Saudi society – composed of diverse clans, tribes and Bedouins – did not allow the emergence of a state around a collective national identity. The Arabian Peninsula was rarely unified until the forces of Al Saud succeeded in unifying the country in the early twentieth century (Kostiner 1990). Modern Saudi Arabia came into existence as a result of the Al Saud's attempt to establish an Islamic monarchy on the Arabian Peninsula. The unification of the Arabian Peninsula was the outcome of a long-standing alliance between Muhammed Ibn Abd al-Wahhab (the eponym of Wahhabism) and the Al Saud.[15]

Two elements constituted the identity of the newly established regime: religion and the loyalty to the royal family. These two basic tenets were identified by King 'Abdul Aziz (known as Ibn Saud): 'Two things are essential to our State and our people ... religion and the rights inherited from our fathers' (quoted in Nevo 1998, 35). The role played by the Al Saud in unifying the country provided a source of loyalty to the ruling family. Gulf states, including Saudi Arabia, used oil wealth to consolidate their legitimacy among various societal groups (Davis 1991, 24). Nevertheless, these new states, the Saudi

---

[15] Wahhabism refers to the Saudi variant of the Sunni tradition. The word 'Wahhabism' is derived from the teachings of the Muslim scholar, Muhammad Ibn Abd al-Wahhab, who lived on the Arabian Peninsula in the eighteenth century (1703–92). Ibn 'Abdul Wahhab founded a religious movement that aimed to reverse what he perceived as the moral decline of the Islamic society on the Arabian Peninsula. Based on an alliance between Muhammed Ibn Abd al-Wahhab and Muhammed Ibn Saud, the founder of the first Saudi state, Wahhabism provided the ruling family with legitimacy and a powerful tool with which to unite various tribes and regions. It is worth noting that the term 'Wahhabism' is a pejorative term. The Wahhabis call themselves *Muwahidun* (monotheists). Despite the imperfection of the term 'Wahhabism', I retain it, as it is widely used.

Kingdom including, lacked a distinct identity that could stand in contrast to the patriotism developing in the neighbouring Arab states.[16] Since the Kingdom contains within its borders two of the three holy cities in Islam – Mecca and Medina – its identity came to be based on an appropriation of Islamic symbols; 'our constitution is the Quran and the application of *shari'a'*. As Nevo (1998, 35) states, 'religion has played a prominent role not only in moulding the individual's private and collective identities but also in consolidating [the] national values'.[17] According to a survey conducted in 2003, Saudis consider religion the most important element of their identity; territorial nationalism comes second (Thompson 2014, 233).

Islam, and its Wahhabi interpretation in particular, enabled the regime to distinguish itself from other regional actors.[18] For decades, the Kingdom relied on Islam to provide it with a unique identity in the region, separate from the secular pan-Arab ideology that swept the region during the 1950s and 1960s under the charismatic leadership of Egyptian President Nasser (Piscatori 1983). Pan-Arabism refers to the political project of unifying all Arabs under a single state. In an attempt to discredit pan-Arabism, the Kingdom emphasised the imagery of the pan-Islamic *umma*[19] and crowned itself the defender of the faith in the region. This pan-Islamic narrative, which prescribed solidarity among Muslims, was often identified by King Faisal (1964–75) as the inherent *raison d'être* of the Saudi state (Sindi 1986). With the demise of the pan-Arab project, the pan-Islamic discourse gained leverage among the Arab masses. Saudi Arabia portrayed itself as the representative of the Muslim world and prided itself on being the only Islamic state to rule according to *shari'a*.

While the ideal of Islamic unity and solidarity is encapsulated in the Quranic notion of *umma*, pan-Islamism became an integral component of Saudi regime identity and foreign policy only in the 1960s and 1970s under King Faisal. To promote this identity narrative, King

---

[16] On the lack of a national Saudi identity, see the article of the leading Saudi columnist Hamid Al-Din (2014).

[17] For further details on the role of Wahhabism in the formation of the Saudi state, cf. Ayoob and Kosebalaban (2008).

[18] This does not mean that the state identity was an amalgamation of diverse groups in the society. Instead, the Al Saud monopolised the state's identity narrative.

[19] *Umma* is used to refer to all Muslims as one community bound by religion.

Faisal established a number of national and supranational institutions that worked to promote cooperation and solidarity in the Muslim world (Hegghammer 2010, 17–18). The Organisation of Islamic Conference (OIC) was established between 1969 and 1972 as an intergovernmental organisation with influence in the diplomatic sphere. In 1962, the Kingdom funded the foundation of the Muslim World League (MLW), which is a non-governmental institution involved in cultural, educational and charitable activities. The support of the Palestinian cause came as the most significant manifestation of pan-Islamism in Saudi regime identity. The Kingdom funded the Palestinian struggle against Israel and directed most of its foreign aid budgets to the conflict, which became consistently framed in pan-Islamic terms (Ochsenwald 1981, 276).

Since the very beginning of the Palestinian issue, and following the 1967 defeat, the Saudi Kingdom was very keen to play an important role in supporting the Palestinians, which was characterised in a press release by Saudi Ministry of Foreign Affairs as 'an Arab and Islamic duty' (Saudi Ministry of Foreign Affairs 2016). In Khartoum Arab summit following the defeat, the Saudi Kingdom presented financial aid to the Palestinians. In 1978 Baghdad Arab summit, the Kingdom announced a total financial aid of US$197,300,000 in ten years starting from 1979 until 1989. Furthermore, during the 1988 Algiers Arab summit, the Kingdom allocated a monthly financial aid of US$6 million (Saudi Ministry of Foreign Affairs 2016). Furthermore, the Saudi government launched several domestic initiatives to raise funds for the Palestinian cause. In December 1967, King Faisal established the 'Popular Committee for Aiding the Mujahidin of Palestine'.[20] The committee organised several fundraising campaigns and provided moral and material support to the Palestinian people (Hegghammer 2010, 21). In addition, the Kingdom provided financial and logistical aid to the resistance movement (Fatah) and the PLO since 1969 (Niblock 2006, 59–60).

The Saudi support for the Palestinian resistance was constantly framed and justified with reference to religion, and this narrative was strongly supported by the Saudi *ulama*. The Grand Mufti Sheikh

---

[20] For more details on this committee, see Jamus (2001).

Abdul Aziz bin Baz,[21] in a mid-1960s publication,[22] proclaimed: 'It is known in Islam that the call to Arab nationalism, or any other form of nationalism, is false and a grave mistake. It is an assault on Islam and its followers' (quoted in Al-Yassini 1983, 13). In late 1968, the Popular Committee asked Great Mufti Muhammed bin Ibrahim for a fatwa on whether *zakah* (alms) money collected in Saudi Arabia could be used to fund the Palestinian cause. On 3 December 1968, the Mufti issued a fatwa authorising 'the use of part of the *zakah*, on the condition that it's the Government which supervises its expenditure, ... to purchase weapons for the fighters who are fighting the Jewish enemies of God' (Hegghammer 2010, 20). The pan-Islamic appeal enabled the Saudis to re-establish a distinguishable state identity in a region dominated by pan-Arabism. After the 1967 Arab defeat and the demise of pan-Arabism, Saudi Arabia was able to crown itself the defender of the faith in the region, with a particular focus on an Islamic framing of Arab issues, such as the Palestine cause.

Whereas the Saudis embraced a pan-Islamic identity, the Shah opted to construct an identity for the Iranian state that appealed to Iranian nationalism permeated with liberal Western values. These two very distinct identity narratives did not deter Saudi Arabia and Iran from developing an entente over issues of shared interests, such as the security of the Gulf, the alliance with the United States, and containing communism and pan-Arabism in the region.

Just when Saudi Arabia had consolidated its distinct identity as the sole Islamic model in the region, the Islamic Revolution broke out in Iran in 1979 and undermined the Saudi's self-identity by altering the representation of the other. The Islamic Revolution downplayed Persian nationalism and promoted Islamic universalism. The revolution aimed to transcend its national context and called for Muslim unity and solidarity (Buchta 2002). The new identity of the Islamic Republic portrayed Iran as the vanguard of revolutionary and anti-imperialist Islam and the legitimate leader of the Muslim *umma*. It thus explicitly converged with the Saudi worldview, which was also based on

---

[21] Ibn Baz, one of the most prestigious Islamic scholars, was the grand mufti for the Kingdom from 1993 until his death in 1999.

[22] From Abdul Aziz bin Baz's indicative title *Naqd al-Qawmiyya al-'Arabiyya 'alā Daw' al-'Islām wa al-Wāqi'*[A Critique of Arab Nationalism Based on Islam and Reality].

solidarity among Muslims, and, hence, competed with the Saudi claim to distinctive leadership.

Iranian foreign policy became subordinated to the new norms of the Islamic state encapsulated in the slogan *na sharghi na gharbi, jomhuri-ye eslami* (neither Eastern nor Western; only the Islamic Republic). With this detachment from the Cold War rationale, the Islamic Republic radically moved from preserving the *status quo* under the patronage of the United States to a revisionist role in the region. According to Khomeini, Muslims formed a single community (*umma*), and the existing borders were the result of imperialism and domination. He argued that Islam was one and that Muslims should henceforth unite: 'Muslims must become a single hand. They must become a united hand, remain united, become one; they must not think themselves separate from us' (quoted in Halliday 2002, 31). This claim remained a core concern for Iran and was reflected in the country's new constitution, which proclaimed solidarity among Muslims transcending all sectarian divisions. Accordingly, the Islamic Republic pursued a foreign policy strategy that appealed to Arabs specifically and all Muslims generally. Iran consistently emphasised its commitment to the Palestinian cause. This pan-Islamist narrative was accompanied by increasing financial support to Hamas, the Palestinian Islamic Jihad and Hezbollah in Lebanon. The Iranians thus presented themselves as the leader of Islam in the region and the epitome of virtue in the Arab–Israeli conflict, a narrative similar to the one embedded in Saudi regime identity. In other words, Iran presented an alternative to Saudi regime's monopoly over the Palestinian cause.

Pan-Islamism should serve as a common denominator between the Iranian Republic and the Kingdom of Saudi Arabia. Ironically, its implications were divisive. The Kingdom saw the foundations of its state identity eroded. As a Saudi official explained this tension,

Iran's biggest struggle is with Saudi Arabia, not with the United States. Iran wants to challenge the Saudi version of Islam, that is the division of politics and religion. Saudi Arabia wants to help Muslims by sending scholars, for instance to China, and by inviting students. We educate them about religion without political propaganda. In Senegal, for example, Saudi Arabia invests money in order to improve the living conditions of the people without influencing them politically. Iran, on the other hand, pays imams to reach the masses. They want to turn the people into fanatics and preach how evil Saudi Arabia and the United States are. (Quoted in Marschall 2003, 48)

The Saudi regional position as the leader of pan-Islamism was now challenged by another pan-Islamic movement driven by revolutionary, idealistic, anti-imperialist and anti-monarchic values (Adib-Moghaddam 2006, 28–30). The distinctiveness the Saudi state claimed to have in relation to other actors was endangered by the rise of a pan-Islamist ideology in Iran. Saudi anxiety was magnified by the Iranian Revolution's efforts to discredit the Kingdom's version of Islam. Turki bin Faisal Al Saud[23] has offered an interesting perspective on the anxiety the Saudis experienced:

Saudi Arabia is the Custodian of the Two Holy Mosques,[24] and the Birthplace of Islam, and as such it is the eminent leader of the wider Muslim world. Iran portrays itself as the leader not just of the minority Shiite world, but of all Muslim revolutionaries interested in standing up to the West. (Al Saud 2013, 38)

This challenge to the distinctiveness of Saudi identity was also related to the domestic dimension of its identity narrative. The first event in this respect was Juhaymān al-'Utaybī's siege of the Mecca Mosque on 20 November 1979. Employing a discourse grounded in the Wahhabi tradition, Juhaymān accused the regime of deviating from Islamic values (Al-Rasheed 2006, 105).[25] Moreover, he accused the *ulama* of interpreting the Quran in ways that served the non-Islamic policies of the ruling family (Nevo 1998, 42). Almost simultaneously, the Shiites in the Eastern Province of the Saudi Kingdom staged protests on 28 November 1979. The regime claimed that its small Shiite community – estimated at approximately 350,000 in 1986 – was subject to Iranian influence (Goldberg 1986, 230). Scholars of regime security approach argue that these domestic problems might have posed a threat to the Saudi regime and led the elite to reframe their identity. I, however, argue that the domestic dimension on its own could not have posed an identity risk to the regime. There is no compelling evidence that Iran was involved in Saudi internal affairs. Khomeini's speeches inspired a small number of Shiite clerics in Saudi

---

[23] Turki al-Faisal is a member of the Saudi royal family. From 1977 to 2001, Prince Turki was the director of *al-mukhābarāt al ʿāma* (the Saudi general intelligence service).

[24] This title was introduced in 1986 in reaction to Iranian demands to place Mecca and Medina under international rule.

[25] For more details on Al-'Utaybī's movement, cf. Hegghammer and Lacroix (2007b) and Kechichian (1990).

Arabia (Ibrahim 2006, 117). Nevertheless, this community was small, and its influence on the stability of the Saudi regime was far from significant. From an ontological security perspective, I argue that the domestic dimension became relevant only because the narrative of self-identity is inextricably related to the interaction with the other, which was disrupted following the critical situation created by the Islamic Revolution. The domestic dissent only magnified the shakiness of the regime's identity narrative and its ontological insecurity.

These circumstances drove the Saudi rulers to reinvent their state's identity. To re-establish a sense of self vis-à-vis the changing representation of the Iranian 'other', they needed to separate their narrative from generic pan-Islamic rhetoric. The Saudis thus narrowed their identity to privilege the Sunni tradition, known for its rejection of the Shiites as a legitimate Islamic community. Seeking to distinguish the Saudi version of Islam from the Iranian one, the Kingdom reinvigorated a sectarian discourse. Sunni Islam was broadly introduced into Saudi foreign policy not as a source of legitimacy but as a component of Saudi regime identity distinguishing the Kingdom from the Islamic Republic.

The reduction of the Saudi pan-Islamic identity to a Sunni Islamic one created a new self-versus-other distinctiveness couched in sectarian terms (Sunni versus Shiite). Henceforth, the Kingdom adopted an anti-Shiite discourse designed to discredit the pan-Islamic narrative of the Iranian Revolution. In pursuing this endeavour, the regime strengthened the power of the *ulama* (as representatives of the state religion) and promoted the Kingdom's conservative Sunni image. It also reinforced a stricter Wahhabi code of conduct, granting the *ulama*, such as Ibn Baz, more control over social and religious life (Steinberg 2005, 28–9). This was manifested in the strengthening of the religious strands in the educational system. All of this resulted in the state becoming more closely associated not only with Islamic symbols but also with a Sunni approach that rejected Shiite symbols (Niblock 2006, 55). Moreover, the Kingdom's rulers aimed to consolidate the Kingdom's image as the eminent leader of the Muslim world by using the title of 'the custodian of the two holy sites' – Mecca and Medina.

In addition to creating this new distinction, the Kingdom counter-framed the Islamic Republic to demonise the latter's claims.[26] The

---

[26] Counter-framing dynamics of the sectarian other has also been observed in the work of Wehrey (2013), Rubin (2014) and Gause (2014a).

Saudi clerical establishment produced an abundant flow of anti-Shiite publications to blunt the pan-Islamic appeal of the Islamic Revolution.[27] Sectarian language became explicit. From the perspective of the Sunni *ulama*, the Shiite propensity for saint worship, shrine and grave cults, and veneration of imams were abhorrent acts of polytheism (*shirk*). Indeed, Sunni-Wahhabi scholars pronounced Shiites to be 'the incarnation of infidelity, and ... polytheists', making it the duty of believers 'to manifest enmity to the polytheists [who] were perceived as unbelievers (*kufar*), and were therefore liable to the severest sanctions, including that of holy war (Jihad)' (Goldberg 1986, 232). In short, this Saudi counter-framing of Shi'ism placed the Iranian regime outside of the Muslim community, describing them as defectors (*rafidda*). It is important to note here that the Saudi anti-Shiite discourse is not entirely novel (Jones 2007). Since its foundation, the Kingdom has announced its rejection of Shiism based on fatwas issued by Sheikh Taqiyy al-Din bin Taymiyyah, who considered Shiites to be heretics. He also accused Shiites of blasphemy. Accordingly, Muhammed Ibn Abd al-Wahhab, the founder of Wahhabism, denounced all Shiites as unbelievers (Mouzahem 2013). Nevertheless, the Islamic Revolution in Iran and the Saudi need for identity distinctiveness led to an intensified anti-Shiite narrative.

In short, based on the Saudi quest for distinctiveness, and ontological security, the representation of the 'Saudi-Sunni self' was contrasted with the 'Iranian-Shiite other' in Saudi foreign policy. The discourse of exclusion – based on religious otherness and framed by a religious narrative – highlighted Saudi Arabia's religious uniqueness, which was necessary to forge a distinct regime identity narrative. In other words, sectarianism was simply a strategy for re-establishing the Kingdom's distinctiveness and, thus, its ontological security.

The previous interpretation of the Saudi regime identity highlighted how the establishment of an Islamic Republic in Iran with a revolutionary pan-Islamic discourse undermined the very distinct identity of the Saudi Kingdom. In its ceaseless quest for distinctiveness, the Saudis narrowed their identity and reinvented a new self–other narrative based on sectarian distinction. The new self–other provided the elite with guidance in navigating a confusing and ambiguous relative power distribution. Henceforth, their alliance decision emerged from this

---

[27] For an overview, cf. Algar (2002).

self–other distinction. This situation of ontological insecurity and physical security explains the Saudi decision to support Saddam Hussein against the Islamic Republic over the eight years of the Iran–Iraq War. As the Saudi regime identity was fixed and lacked the fluidity to be reinvented, the physical security of the Kingdom was not under acute threat. Instead, the Kingdom wavered among several policy options to ensure its physical security. These two conditions created the context for the predominance of ideational factors in Saudi threat perception.

Syria: Demystifying Rationalism

If Saudi Arabia faced a situation of ontological insecurity and physical security, the Syrian regime was an illustration of a critical physical insecurity, where the regime was faced with limited options to ensure its survival. This insecurity defined not only Syria's choice of allies but also the framing of its identity narrative. Whereas the Islamic Revolution endangered the distinctiveness of the Saudi identity, the Syrian identity adjusted and adapted to the exigencies of the regime's physical security needs. This section examines why and how an Arab nationalist Syrian regime that claims a secular Ba'athist ideology supported non-Arab Iran – an Islamic regime bent on exporting its revolutionary theological doctrine – against a fellow Arab and Ba'athist regime, Iraq. Syria's physical insecurity was reinforced by the rise of a more hostile Ba'athist ideology under Saddam Hussein, which attempted to create domestic instability and weaken the rule of al-Assad regime in Syria.

'We did not want Iran to be defeated as we were aware of Saddam Hussein's plans' (Baraka 2011). With these words, former Syrian Vice President Abd al-Halim Khaddam[28] explicated the Syrian position in 1979. Exposed to an Israeli military supremacy on its western borders, Syria could not endure an Iraqi military victory on its east. Just at the moment when Syria was in need of a regional ally, a regime change in Iran provided an opportunity to balance Iraq and Israel. In these circumstances, the Syrian regime reframed its identity to embrace an alliance with a non-Arab state. The Syrian regime's self–other

---

[28] Abd al-Halim Khaddam was Syria's foreign minister from 1970 until 1984 and then vice president of foreign affairs until 2005. In December 2005, he went to exile in France. Since then, he has conducted several interviews with Arab newspapers and satellite channels about his relationship to Hafiz al-Assad and Syria's relationship with Lebanon, Iraq and Iran.

distinction was based on pan-Arabism, which distinguishes between Arabs and non-Arabs. This identity framing underwent a change wherein the self–other distinction became based on the animosity towards Israel and the championing of the Palestinian cause at the expense of the Arab Ba'athist component. In other words, Syria's physical insecurity guided the regime's identity narrative. The reframing of Syrian identity narrative was also reinforced by an ontological dissonance due to the similarity with Ba'athist vocation in Iraq under Saddam Hussein. This process has often been described in the literature as the redefinition of Arab nationalism in Syrian terms (Chalala 1988; Maltzahn 2013; Sadowski 2002). Such reframing in the Syrian identity was allowed by the nature of the regime identity that was multi-layered and malleable. This chapter argues that the predominance of material considerations in Syria's foreign behaviour is enabled by the fluidity of its regime identity. To elucidate this argument, I first unpack Syria's physical insecurity, which was caused by Iraq and Israel's military supremacies. In this context, Syria faced very limited policy options to ensure its physical survival. I then lay out the fluidity of the regime identity, which underwent a reframing from pan-Arabism to a more state-centric conception accommodating the dictates of the relative power distribution and avoiding ontological dissonance due to the rise of a Ba'athist ideology in Iraq.

The Strategic Balance of Power: Limited Options

Syria has conventionally faced unfavourable geostrategic conditions. It is unprotected by natural boundaries and has, hence, remained vulnerable to its Arab (especially Iraq either under both the monarchy and the Ba'ath party) and non-Arab neighbours (Israel and Turkey). Syria's relatively small size and its limited manpower made the quest for alliances the predominant preoccupation of al-Assad's regime and the preferred foreign policy choice when faced with regional threats. To keep the balance against Israel, for instance, Syria sought alliances with Arab regimes: Egypt from 1958 to 1961 (United Arab Republic), Egypt from 1966 to 1975,[29] Iraq from 1965 to 1971, and Saudi Arabia from 1971 to 1975, and Iraq from 1978 to 1979.[30]

---

[29] A defence agreement between Egypt and Syria was signed in 1966 (The International Institute for Strategic Studies 1979).
[30] For a summary of inter-Arab alliances, cf. Taylor (1982, 123–4).

Throughout the 1970s, al-Assad was successful in balancing Israel's military capabilities. Following the 1967 defeat, al-Assad improved Syria's relationship with its Arab neighbours. He sought a military alliance with Egypt, which he considered to be an indispensable actor in the case of war. In addition, he terminated Syria's isolation from the oil-rich Gulf monarchies and concluded a détente with Iraq (Salloukh 2000, 400–1). During the Yom Kippur War (1973), the emergence of the Riyadh–Cairo–Damascus axis exemplified al-Assad's new pragmatic approach. While al-Assad allied with al-Sadat to combine Egypt and Syria's capabilities in a coordinated attack on Israel, the Saudi Kingdom used the oil weapon to pressure Western powers (Sunayama 2007, 37–9). In 1979, al-Assad's strategy to maintain Syria's regional alliances collapsed. Two regional developments endangered Syria's physical security and led to its isolation: the Egyptian–Israeli peace treaty and Iraq's military ascent following the Islamic Revolution in Iran.

The withdrawal of Egypt from the Arab–Israeli conflict constituted the most acute challenge to the Syrian regime, as it became exposed to Israel's military supremacy. Although the Egyptian–Syrian alliance was fruitful during Yom Kippur War in 1973, it was severely tested by post-war diplomacy. Despite the constraints of pan-Arabism, al-Sadat showed a willingness to enter bilateral negotiations with Israel under US auspices. Syria's fears of isolation increased when Egypt and Israel signed the first American-mediated disengagement agreement in January 1974. In September 1975, al-Sadat signed the second disengagement agreement, known as the Sinai II Agreement. The subsequent direct talks between Egypt and Israel led to the signing of the Camp David Accords in September 1978 and to the Egyptian–Israeli peace treaty in March 1979. In one move, this treaty removed the Arab world's strongest actor and Syria's primary ally from the Arab–Israeli theatre and left the Syrian regime severely exposed (Drysdale and Hinnebusch 1991, 63–4; Ehteshami 1996, 50). In March 1978, Syria's fears of Israeli military supremacy materialised when Israel invaded Lebanon and occupied a stretch of South Lebanon all the way to the Litany River. Lacking a strategic depth, Damascus was close to the dreaded scenario: an Israeli attack against Syria through al-Beqaa Valley and on the Golan Heights (Seale 1989, 310–12).

From 1977 to 1979, al-Assad attempted to restore the balance against Israel through three strategies: (1) increasing its military build-up with more reliance on the Soviet Union, (2) mobilising an Arab opposition front to isolate Egypt and (3) finding other Arab partners to counterbalance Israel's military capabilities. However, these efforts were unsuccessful.

The breakdown of the Egyptian–Syrian alliance convinced the Syrian elite that self-reliance in defence was a fundamental requirement of the new balance-of-power equation. Therefore, the Syrian regime triggered a huge military build-up, known as the 'strategic parity' policy (Eisenstadt 1992; Khalidi and Agha 1991). Syria's conscripted forces grew from 50,000 in 1967 to 227,500 in 1979 (The International Institute for Strategic Studies 1979, 42). More than 20 per cent of GDP was devoted to this military build-up. Defence expenditure increased from US$1.12 billion in 1978 to US$2.04 billion (The International Institute for Strategic Studies 1979, 39, 42, 45). However, the Syrian regime was unable to achieve parity with Israel. In 1978, Israel had a total armed force of 164,000 soldiers with a potential of mobilising up to 400,000 in 24 hours (Kandil 2008, 428–9). The expansion of the military forces under al-Assad and the supply of a modern arsenal weapons placed a heavy burden on the Syrian economy and transformed Syria into a major recipient of Arab and Soviet military aid. By the late 1980s, Syria's debt to the Soviet Union amounted to US$10 billion (Ehteshami 1996, 55).

Alongside this internal balancing strategy, Syria attempted to mobilise an Arab front to counterbalance Israel's military preponderance. After al-Sadat's visit to Jerusalem, Syria, South Yemen, Algeria, Libya and, the PLO formed the Steadfastness and Confrontation Front (*Jabhat al-Ṣumūd wa al-Taṣadī*). They were later joined by Iraq and Saudi Arabia. Initially, the front attempted to convince Egypt to give up its negotiations with Israel. Following the Baghdad summit of November 1978, a delegation was dispatched to Cairo headed by Lebanese Prime Minister Salim al-Huss. The delegation offered al-Sadat US$5 billion annually for ten years in return for not signing the peace treaty with Israel. However, al-Sadat refused to meet the delegation (Salloukh 2000, 433). Accordingly, the front moved to isolate Egypt and apply sanctions. The coalition had the potential to act as the most important inter-Arab force in the Arab–Israeli sphere. Nevertheless, this Arab quasi-consensus was short-lived as polarisation emerged. In short, the Steadfastness and Confrontation Front turned out to be ineffective in realising Damascus' intentions in building a front to counterbalance Israel.

When Damascus observed this ineffectiveness in building an Arab consensus against Israel, it set its sight on Baghdad as the primary regional partner that could fill the vacuum caused by Egypt's exit from the Arab camp. Given its military capabilities and geographic location, Iraq was the only Arab state capable of counterbalancing Israel. In the first half of 1979, Syria's critical vulnerability and Iraq's regional ambitions brought about what Kienle (1990, 135) termed the 'marriage contre nature' between the two states. Nevertheless, the rapprochement was short-lived. On 28 July 1979, Baghdad announced that a conspiracy against the regime has been discovered and accused Syria of domestic interference. Damascus swiftly denied any involvement in Iraqi internal affairs and dispatched Abd al-Halim Khaddam and Hikmat al-Shihabi[31] to resolve the issue. Khaddam later claimed that the Iraqi regime was unable to provide any concrete evidence of Syrian involvement (Baraka 2011). The Syrians became convinced that Saddam Hussein intentionally destroyed the partnership. The latter would have moved Iraq to the frontline confrontation with Israel; however, Saddam Hussein was unwilling to get involved in this conflict (Khadduri 1988, 74–8). Obviously, the two countries pursued two different aims. While Iraq pushed for the unification of the Ba'ath party and states' apparatuses under its own pre-eminence, Syrian leaders were looking for the regional benefits of unity with Iraq without losing their independence and power in Syria. Henceforth, relations between Damascus and Baghdad degenerated into a cycle of mutual recrimination. By September 1979, Syria accused Saddam Hussein of arming and financing the Muslim Brotherhood[32] to destabilise al-Assad's regime. In less than a year, Syria's strategy of relying on Iraq to balance Israel proved a failure, and Baghdad turned from being an asset into Syria's most dangerous neighbour.

After the partnership between Iraq and Syria formally failed, Saudi Arabia consolidated a new partnership with Iraq and isolated Syria even further. On 17 September 1979, Saudi Minister of the Interior Prince Nayif concluded an agreement with Iraq on security cooperation. Damascus' fears increased when a parallel Jordanian–Iraqi rapprochement emerged. Throughout 1979, these bilateral arrangements

---

[31] Hikmat al-Shihabi (1931–2013) served as the Syrian Army chief of staff from 1974 until 1998.

[32] For details about the relationship between the Muslim Brotherhood and the al-Assad regime, see Rabil (2010) and Talhamy (2009).

developed into a tacit alliance between Iraq, Jordan and Saudi Arabia. This rearrangement of allegiances in the region increased Syria's insecurity, as the Arab focus on regional politics shifted from the Arab–Israeli sphere to the Gulf (Sunayama 2007, 59–60).

This isolation did not only affect the position of Syria at the Arab–Israeli front. The change in the balance of power in Iraq's favour following the Iranian Revolution in itself constituted another source of fear to al-Assad's regime. Iraq's aspiration for regional hegemony was manifested in its military build-up. Following the increase in the oil prices during the 1970s, Iraq's military forces doubled in size, reaching 242,000 men by 1979. Its defence expenditures increased to US$2.67 billion (The International Institute for Strategic Studies 1980, 42). In short, Syria had to deal both with Israel's military supremacy and with Iraq's ascent, which was not only destabilising on the ideological level but was also, more importantly, a military threat (Marschall 1992, 433–5). Both hostile states shared long borders with Syria, and both had considerable projection capabilities. Syrian leaders were aware that any confrontation with its Arab neighbour would mean compromising Syria's military capabilities on the Golan Heights. Khaddam expressed Syria's physical insecurity as follows: '[Syria] cannot fight hundred wars at the same time' (Salloukh 2000, 405).

The overthrow of the Iranian monarchy and the advent of a regime that was not aligned with Israel provided Syria with an opportunity to balance Israel and limit Iraq's regional ambitions. As Hafiz al-Assad stated, 'This revolution introduced important changes in the strategic balance ... [Iran] supports the Arabs, without hesitation, ... for the sake of liberating our lands ... How can we ... lose a country like Iran of the Islamic Revolution...with all its human, military, and economic potential' (quoted in Ehteshami and Hinnebusch 1997, 93). Al-Assad condemned Saddam for 'launching the wrong war against the wrong enemy at the wrong time'. He also argued that 'to fight Iran was folly: it would exhaust the Arabs, fragment their ranks and divert them from "the holy battle in Palestine"' (Seale 1989, 357).

The outbreak of the Iran–Iraq War in September 1980 presented the Syrian regime with an acute challenge. Syria had to now deal with the regional consequences of a potential Iraqi victory in the east, all while continuing to face a militarily superior Israel in the south. For a regime that assumed 'any imbalance [*khalal*] in any part of the region affects all the region', a rapid Iraqi victory would mean the cementing of

Syria's regional isolation. In other words, Syria would find itself encircled between Israel's military supremacy and Iraq's hegemonic aspirations. Khaddam portrayed Syria's fear in this context as follows: 'the Iran–Iraq War was two wars: one against Iran and the second against Syria' (Baraka 2011). In short, Syria sided with Iran to protect its regional position from the unbearable consequences of an Iraqi victory (Chalala 1988, 112–13; Hunter 1993, 198–210; Seale 1989, 353–8). The alliance with Iran was popular neither within Syrian public opinion nor among the cadres of the Ba'ath party, but Syria's physical security dictated the choice of its enemies and friends regardless of any domestic opposition (Batatu 1999, 284–5; Ehteshami and Hinnebusch 1997, 64).

Thus, al-Assad's decision to join Iran to counterbalance Iraq and Israel may said to have been dictated by a *raison d'état* (Ehteshami and Hinnebusch 1997, 102). This fear of Iraq's military ambitions was reinforced by ideological differences between the Ba'ath party in Syria and its counterpart in Iraq. These ideological differences dated back to the 1960s and stemmed from the parties' elites to preserve independence and control over their respective societies. Under the rule of Saddam Hussein, the Ba'ath party in Iraq attempted to weaken its counterpart in Syria. Under processes of state consolidation, many subversive attempts were considered by the al-Assad regime as existential threats to its survival (Hinnebusch 2014b; Kienle 1990; Kienle et al. 1993). As the sources of danger and harm were clear, Syria's identification of enemies and friends came as a response to the regime's physical insecurity. The observed dangers led the regime to reinterpret its identity and its related self–other identification to accommodate physical security needs. This path was conditioned by Syria's limited policy options in navigating the relative power distribution.

The Syrian Regime Identity: A Strategic Adaptation

After accusing Egypt of challenging the very core of Arabism, al-Assad found himself in a similar position a year later. By allying with Iran against Iraq, Syria violated the most conventional pan-Arab norm. Against the fundamental principle of Arabism, according to which Arabs should only unite with Arabs, al-Assad aligned with a major non-Arab state threatening Arab states across the Gulf. In a futile attempt to save Syria's Arab façade, Khaddam stated: 'We told Iran that in the case of any aggression on any Arab state, Syria will follow the Pan-Arab dictates and support the Arab state' (Baraka 2011). However, the statement completely ignored the inconvenient fact that Iraq is an Arab state.

The Islamic Revolution in Iran did not affect the identity security or stability of the Syrian regime, which prior to 1979 had maintained a stable, distinct identity based on Syrian nationalism and Arabism. Syria's strategic isolation imposed high constraints on the regime's physical security at the regional level, which led to the reframing of identity narrative. Such a reframing was possible by the flexible and malleable nature of the Syrian regime identity since the early stages of state formation (Phillips 2012, 42–4). The following discussion highlights the changes in Syria's identity as a result of its alliance with Iran and of its animosity with Iraq and Israel. First, I present the two principles in the regime identity: pan-Arabism and Syrian nationalism. Second, I present the reframing in the content of the regime identity and its move towards a more defined 'Syrian' nationalism under a pan-Arab label in the context of the Iran–Iraq War. Syria's regime identity underwent two developments. First, the definition of the self became distinct from the Arab nation, and especially distinct from Ba'athist Iraq. More precisely, Syrian nationalism supplanted Arab nationalism. Second, the pan-Arab component in Syrian identity was reinterpreted to be a move away from emphasising the unity between different Arab states to focusing on the struggle against Israel. As Hinnebusch (2001, 140) summarises this change, 'the meaning of Arabism [altered] from a cause for which Syria would sacrifice to a means to reach Syrian ends'. In short, the source of distinctiveness became based not on Arabness but on animosity towards Israel. Accordingly, Iran became explicitly integrated within the 'us' category. This section explores the basic tenets of Syria's identity and, then, traces the changes imposed by the physical security needs of the regime.

Throughout the twentieth century, the Syrian regime identity combined elements from two poles: pan-Arabism and Syrian nationalism. Pan-Arabism represents a total commitment to the idea of Arab unity to the extent of denying any separate identity to territorial states. The ideology portrays the Arab world as one Arab nation divided between artificially established Arab states. The ultimate goal of pan-Arabism was (and to a lesser degree remains today) to merge these territorial states into a 'true' Arab nation-state. Until then, the *raison de la nation Arabe* should take precedence over the narrow *raison d'état* (Khalidi 1978, 696). From this perspective, the 'Arab Homeland' (*al-waṭan al-'arabī*) is the primary source of self–other distinction. On the other hand, Syrian nationalism presupposes the existence of a distinct Syrian identity, which corresponds to a greater Syrian state to be established within the natural geographic borders of *Bilad al-Sham* (Zisser 2006). Greater Syria comprises four states in terms of today's political units – Syria, Lebanon, Jordan, Israel and the Palestinian territories including the Gaza Strip and the West Bank (Pipes 1990, 13–14).

Since the early days of state formation, Syrian leaders sought a middle ground that would combine these two poles. They adopted an 'Arab-Syrian' identity. Syria became portrayed in the official discourse as the 'beating heart of Arabism' or 'the cradle of Arabism'. On its independence day, President Shukri al-Quwatli outlined the state identity that guided Syrian foreign policy for decades:

Bilad al-Sham [which] was the cradle of the concept of 'uruba and the home of its first champions and martyrs . . . has been the first Arab country to carry its civilisational mission to parts of the world as far away as . . . the hills of al-Andalus and the wall of China, declares today that it believes in 'uruba . . . we shall not accept that any flag other than that of Arab unity (*wahda*) will fly over this country. (Quoted in Kienle 1995, 58)

The official name of the Republic – 'the Arab Syrian Republic' – expressed the declared priorities of the state identity.[33] Pan-Arab nationalist considerations took precedence over the particular interests of the Syrian state. The Ba'ath party that has dominated Syrian politics from 1963 to the present was established under the same ideology. 'The unity of the Arab nation and its freedom' [*wahdat al-'umma al-'arabiya wa huriyatahā*] was the first principle enshrined in the 1947 party constitution (Kedar 2006: 35).

From independence through the late 1970s, pan-Arabism remained predominant in Syria's identity. Consequently, Arab solidarity and unity occupied a privileged place in the regime's foreign policy discourse.

---

[33] This idea can be compared to the one signalled by Anwar al-Sadat, who changed the official name of Egypt from 'The United Arab Republic' to 'The Egyptian Arab Republic' in 1971. This alteration, placing 'Egypt' in a prior position vis-à-vis Arabism, reflected a change in the order of state's priorities.

Before 1979, Syria initiated nine attempts for Arab unity (Khūrī 1988). Syrian foreign policy was often explained in Arab nationalist terms. Although it was initially imposed by the elites, this meaning of Arabism eventually reached the people who developed a real sense of integration into a larger community and a strong belief in its realisation. Syrian foreign policy always privileged Arabs over non-Arabs. In countless public speeches and interviews, al-Assad emphasized that the cure for all Arab problems lies in the unity of all Arab states. In 1975, al-Assad emphasised: 'the division we are living leads to a growing regional spirit threatening the fate and the future of the Arab nation ... We should resist this division ... it is the greatest threat ... and if we beat this threat then we would beat any other threat all over the Arab world' (al-Assad 1975).

This pan-Arab dimension manifested itself in Syrian foreign policy towards the Arab–Israeli conflict and the Palestinian question in particular. Syrian leaders assumed Syria to be the motherland of the other countries in the Levant – Palestine, Jordan and Lebanon – and considered the struggle with Israel to be a conflict for 'Greater Syria'. Aware of inter-Arab rivalries, the Syrian regime distinguished between long-term Arab nationalist objectives and short-term pragmatic ones. The most important long-term nationalist goal remains the unity of all Arabs under a federative state that would respect the historic idiosyncrasies of each country [quṭr]. As this objective became difficult to attain, Syrian leaders identified short-term objectives: recovering the territories occupied in 1967, retrieving Palestinian rights, and balancing Israel's military power in the region. Despite this pragmatism and flexibility, Syria's definition of the self remained centred around a sense of 'Arabness'. Syrian public speeches and media statements were populated with references to the 'Arab people' and the 'Arab Umma', while references to the Syrian entity were ambiguous and minimal (Kienle 1995, 58–61). Arab nationalism was portrayed in the regime identity as the struggle to unite the Arab lands from Morocco to Iraq under one Arab state where the 'nation' and the 'state' coincide (Dawisha 2003; Valbjørn 2009). On 17 October 1978, Minister of Defence Mustafa Talas declared: 'the Arab–Syrian [region] is the only Arab [region] which has undertaken to hoist above its flag the standard of Arab unity' (quoted in Kedar 2006: 29).

Accordingly, Syrian leaders excoriated the Egyptian exit from the Arab–Israeli conflict and described it as a violation of the basic principle of the Arab nation. Leading the third Steadfastness and Confrontation meeting against Egypt, al-Assad expressed his frustration as follows: 'yesterday, al-Sadat and I planned the October war against Israel and he told us at the time we are the most honourable fighters. Today, he left the most honourable fighters alone in their trenches' (al-Assad 1978). The Syrian media considered the Camp David Accords to be 'a plot', 'a treacherous treaty', and 'a treaty of surrender' (Kedar 2006: 195).

Syria's alliance with Iran and its subsequent identification of Iraq as an enemy created the potential for an inherent instability within the Syrian regime identity. In other words, a contradiction within the identity narrative could emerge, possibly triggering a case of ontological insecurity. A secular pan-Arab regime with a Ba'athist ideology allied with Iran, a non-Arab Islamic regime, against a fellow Arab Ba'athist regime in Iraq. In this sense, the Iranian Revolution did not disrupt the stability of the Syrian regime as the Syrian regime was able to maintain its self–other distinction. Nevertheless, accommodating Syria's physical needs held the potential of creating a contradiction within the identity narrative. Syrian leaders, hence, reframed their identity. This process involved two dimensions: widening the definition of the self and reframing the self–other distinction to conform to Syria's new physical security needs. In doing so, the Syrian regime identified the Iranian other as a friend whereas Iraq was portrayed as a threatening other.

Although the constitutive elements of Syrian nationalism were present since independence, the move towards the consolidation of this 'territorial entity' into a 'nation-state' was slow and ambivalent until 1980 (Pipes 1990, 45–52). The failure of several Arab unity schemes and the different military clashes with neighbouring states – Israel, Lebanon and Jordan – slowly led the Syrians to imagine and construct their own community (Sadowski 2002, 150). In other words, a sense of 'otherness' emerged that differed from the broader pan-Arab vision. Slowly, Syrians came to appreciate that they are not just Arabs or Muslims, but that they belong to a distinct state called 'Syria'. In the 1980s, al-Assad actively intervened in this process and redefined the Syrian self 'from above'. As Sadowski (2002, 151) summarises this development, 'Assad has tended to act as neither a pan-Arabist nor a pan-Syrianist but a Syrian'. Although Arab legitimacy remained the guiding theme of the regime's public statements, the self–other distinction underwent spectacular changes.

The primary change was the emergence of 'Syria' as a relatively autonomous entity whose interests are not necessarily compatible with those advocated by pan-Arabism. 'Syria', instead of the 'Arab Homeland' (*al-watan al-'arabi*) increasingly became an essential point of reference in the legitimation of government decisions. Even though Hafiz al-Assad and other representatives of the regime avoided using an explicit notion to herald this change, they consistently employed implicit references to the Syrian people as a distinct entity. After 1979, al-Assad's speeches pointed to 'the Syrian people' instead of 'the Arab people of Syria' and 'the Syrian citizen' instead of 'the Arab citizen in Syria'. Moreover, the regime's policies were justified as being in 'Syria's *qawmi* and *watani* interest' or at least serving 'Syria' (Kienle 1995, 61). In this regard, al-Assad appealed to the experiences of the Syrian people and highlighted the military institution as a nationally recognisable one (Phillips 2012, 52).

The over-arching regime identity of pan-Arabism was weakened. Still, instead of announcing its decline, the regime maintained the fervour of pan-Arabism, while reinterpreting its meaning in light of the material constraints necessitating the alliance with Iran. Arabism is not defined based on intrinsic characteristics–such as the Arab language or ethnic origins. Rather, it evolved around the struggle against Israel, which defines who the Arabs are and who their allies are. According to this nuanced Arab identity claimed by the Syrian regime, Iran's change of strategy towards Israel and its commitment to the Palestinian cause turned it into a new ally. In other words, Iran was no longer portrayed as a hostile other, but as a friendly one. Accordingly, Syrian media praised Khomeini's opposition to the Israeli–Egyptian peace settlement. As *Al-Thawra's* headline on 27 October 1979 stated, 'Iran: we are in the same trench as the Arabs' (Kedar 2006: 179–80). Syrian Foreign Minister Faruq al-Shar' summarised the change in the Syrian conception of Arabism as follows:

It was not long after the signing of the Camp David Accords in 1979 that the Islamic Republic of Iran was suddenly attacked for no reason. The attack came immediately after the success of its revolution, after it closed the Israeli embassy in Tehran and gave it to Palestine, and after it adopted Arabic as an official language in the country. It was very strange indeed for Muslim Iran to be attacked by an Arab capital that sponsored the Arab National Charter and the Arab summit, which came as a reply to the visit to Jerusalem and the Camp David Accords. (Quoted in Rubin 2000, 22)

In short, pan-Arabism was redefined to suit Syria's military needs vis-à-vis Israel and became a concept devoid of its crucial component: Arabness. Instead of being centred on Arab unity, it became focused on the struggle against Israel.

Conclusion

This chapter examined Syrian and Saudi divergent threat perceptions in the context of the Iran–Iraq War through the prisms of ontological and physical security. In the Saudi case, identity does the causal work in explaining threat perception, as the material power distribution at the time in question was ambiguous and vague. The ontological insecurity that the Saudi regime endured was the primary driver behind its threat perception. To (re)institute its distinctiveness and identity stability, the Saudi regime narrowed down its identity narrative from pan-Islamism to Sunni Islam, a process that involved the redefinition of the Saudi self–other distinction. This distinction not only marked the development of the Kingdom's identity but also guided the choice of allies within an ambiguous relative power distribution. In the Syrian case, however, the material power distribution was clear and determinate. The regime sought an alliance with Iran as a response to physical security needs. Nevertheless, this alliance held the potential for contradictions and instability within the regime identity narrative. Therefore, the regime identity underwent accommodation and adjustment. This reframing was possible due to the flexibility and malleability of the Syrian regime identity.

These empirical cases contribute to the development of this study's theoretical framework in many ways. Looking at the interaction between ideational and material forces is only possible because ontological security is distinct from and not reducible to physical security. This two-layered conception of security paves the way for further interaction and engagement between material forces and questions of identity. The cases of Syria and Saudi Arabia demonstrate that physical concerns have to be combined with a configuration of self–other processes. In some cases, the self–other distinction guides the identification of physical security threats. In other cases, physical security threats emerge as the primary driver behind the self–other reconfiguration. These two mechanisms are conditioned by the multiplicity of policy options and the fluidity of regime identity.

In addition, the divergent cases of Syria and Saudi Arabia help identify the different mechanisms according to which actors (re)institute their ontological and physical security. Actors can restore their ontological security by demonising the other and reinventing their identity distinctiveness. Physical security can be reinstituted through privileging a particular self–other distinction. Beyond this major theoretical proposition, the empirical cases discussed earlier are two examples of how identity narratives provide a bridge between domestic and external spheres. In the process of self–other reconfiguration, Syria and Saudi Arabia reinvented their identity narratives by emphasising certain existing components of their identities. These elements did not exogenously emerge at the relational level but were deep-rooted in the domestic texture of those political entities.

Although Syrian and Saudi threat perceptions during the Iran–Iraq War demonstrate the benefit of analytically dissociating ontological and physical security, they also illustrate the interaction between both spheres. In the Saudi case, ontological insecurity led to a sense of physical insecurity. To consolidate its distinctiveness and ontological security, the Kingdom went further to portray Iran not only as a distinct and different other, but as an eminent enemy. This interaction has implications for the theoretical argument of this study. Although actors can be located in one of the four combinations of ontological and physical security presented in the previous chapter (see Table 2 of Chapter 2), ontological and physical security affect each other. The Saudi Kingdom initially experienced a situation of ontological insecurity and physical security. By identifying Iran as an enemy and supporting Iraq, the Kingdom's subsequent foreign policy led to physical insecurity by supporting the regional ambitions of Iraq, which eventually threatened the Kingdom especially during the Gulf War (1990–91). In short, in the process of restoring its ontological security, the Kingdom moved to a situation of ontological security and physical insecurity.

The Syrian case reflected a different dynamic. The al-Assad regime initially faced a situation of ontological security and physical insecurity. The alliance with Iran was an attempt to increase Syria's physical security vis-à-vis Iraq's regional ambitions and Israel's military supremacy. One of the consequences of this alliance was a challenge to the consistency of al-Assad's regime identity. In other words, the Syrian regime moved to a situation of ontological insecurity and physical security. To avoid exacerbation of this inconsistency, the regime undertook a reframing of its identity.

4 | *The 2006 Lebanon War*

[This war] exposed half-men and people with half-positions, and exposed all [people with] 'delayed' positions, i.e. those who waited to see where the scale of power would settle before aligning their positions.

Bashar al-Assad, August 2006 (al-Assad 2006b)

This chapter examines Saudi and Syrian threat perceptions during the 2006 Lebanon War. Although the war occurred between Israel and Hezbollah in Lebanon, its implication transcended the boundaries of the Lebanese–Israeli conflict and caused regional divisions. The Saudi Kingdom, conventionally portraying itself as the main supporter of the Arab cause against Israel, appeared to side with Israel against a resistance movement. In the meantime, Hezbollah was perceived as a source of threat to the Saudi Kingdom and as a source of instability in the region. A controversial question arises: Why would a non-state actor with limited capabilities – located, moreover, far from Saudi borders – be perceived as a threat? Meanwhile, Syria, a Ba'athist secular regime, oppressing Islamist movements at home, supported Hezbollah and engaged in a pan-Arab discourse. This chapter looks at these two cases of threat perception through the two-layered conception of security: ontological and physical. Whereas Hezbollah constituted a source of identity instability for the Saudi Kingdom and, hence, endangered its ontological security, Israel's military supremacy constituted the primary source of danger to the physical security of the Syrian regime.

The chapter proceeds as follows. I first outline disparate regional reactions to the 2006 Lebanon War. I then examine Saudi enmity towards Hezbollah. By looking at the relative power distribution at the regional level, I demonstrate that the physical security of the Kingdom was not affected by the war. However, Hezbollah's version of Islamic identity and its conception of 'Islamic resistance,' inextricably related to Iran, endangered the ontological security of the Kingdom. The Kingdom's fixed identity around a pan-Islamic narrative made its identity stability and security vulnerable to ideational threats. I then examine Syria's threat perception. I argue that the regional power distribution and the material constraints following the 2003 Iraq war isolated Damascus and endangered its physical security. In this context, Hezbollah's regional role as a strategic asset for the Syrian regime increased significantly. In the meantime, Syria's identity fluidity allowed the accommodation of these material constraints; the Syrian regime identity underwent a reconfiguration of the self–other.

The 2006 Lebanon War and Regional Reactions

Following the Israeli withdrawal from southern Lebanon in 2000, the struggle between Israel and Hezbollah continued on a small scale. Hezbollah maintained the legitimacy of the 'resistance' against Israel by focusing on two issues: the recovery of the Shab'a Farms[1] and the liberation of Lebanese prisoners held in Israel. This state of affair collapsed in the summer of 2006 when Hezbollah kidnapped two Israeli soldiers with the intent of using them in prisoner exchanges. Although this action had a precedent in previous prisoner exchanges, Israel retaliated with a massive attack that lasted from 12 July through 14 August 2006. Throughout the thirty-three days of the war, popular and societal expressions of support for Hezbollah resounded throughout the Arab world ('Aḥmad 2006). Regional opinion polls ranked Hezbollah's leader, Sayyid Hassan Nasrallah, as the most admired Arab leader (Telhami 2007).

Although Arab societies expressed unified support for Hezbollah, the war was a source of contention among Arab regimes. Alongside its violent conflict with Israel, Hezbollah engaged in a bloodless clash with Saudi Arabia, Egypt and Jordan. Saudi officials spoke of Hezbollah's 'reckless adventurism'. Egyptian President Hosni Mubarak and King Abdullah II of Jordan accused Hezbollah of 'dragging the region into adventures' (Rasid Al-Ikhbariyya 2006). Whereas Syria continued its support for Hezbollah due to the fear of Israeli military supremacy in the region, its position constituted a regional exception. Although the Kingdom portrayed itself as a long supporter of the Arab cause against Israel, the Saudis astonishingly condemned Hezbollah.

[1] Shab'a Farms is a small strip of disputed land at the intersection of the Lebanese–Syrian border and the Israeli-occupied Golan Heights.

In addition, it identified this resistance movement as endangering Arab interests and putting the stability of the region at risk.[2]

Two politicised narratives emerged to explain the divergence in Arab positions. The first was articulated by the US Secretary of State Condoleezza Rice who asserted that the region was divided between 'violent radicals' and 'moderate reformists'. The former group was constituted of Hezbollah, Hamas, Syria and Iran.[3] Egypt, Saudi Arabia and Jordan led the other camp, in a way that conformed to the United States' vision for a 'New Middle East'. As Lynch (2010) notes, 'The Bush administration sought to polarise the Middle East into an axis of "moderates" – grouping Saudi Arabia, Egypt, Jordan, and other like-minded Sunni autocrats with Israel – against "radicals" such as Iran, Syria, Hezbollah and Hamas'. Another narrative was sponsored by the so-called moderate camp, which described their clash with Hezbollah using sectarian terms. Talks of a 'Shiite axis' comprising Hezbollah, Syria and Iran became widespread. In December 2004, King Abdullah of Jordan coined the term 'the Shiite crescent' (Cole 2006, 20). Accordingly, the 2006 Lebanon War was portrayed as a proxy war designed by Iran to destabilise the region. In Saudi Arabia, this position was supported by the regime-owned media outlets, such as the newspaper *Al-Sharq al-Awsat* and the satellite channel *al-Arabiya*. Some scholars have also embraced this sectarian narrative (Nakash 2011; Yamani 2008; Zisser 2009a). For example, Susser (2007) argues that 'the fault line between Middle Eastern states is no longer monarchies versus republics or pro-US governments versus pro-Soviet one, but the Sunni-Shi'ite divide'. Similarly, Nasr (2006) predicts that cleavages within Islam would shape future political dynamics in the Middle East. Beyond these politicised narratives, IR scholars have refrained from conducting theoretically informed studies of Arab regimes' behaviour during the 2006 Lebanon War.[4]

This chapter argues that threat perception is more complex than sectarian or moderate-radical narratives. The alliance between Syria and Hezbollah is far from being driven by religious convergence.

---

[2] Some accounts went further to claim that Saudi Arabia implicitly supported Israel (Bilqīz 2006, 70).

[3] Also called *Jabhat al-Muqāwama wa al-Mumāna'a* [Resistance and Defiance Front].

[4] For an exception, cf. Bank and Valbjørn (2010, 2007), Valbjørn and Bank (2012) and Ahmad (2006).

Similarly, Saudi fear from Hezbollah is not related to Shiism *per se*. I argue that a two-layered conception of security – ontological and physical – provides a fruitful third approach for understanding seemingly odd foreign policy choices in the course of the Lebanese–Israeli conflict. For this reason, the aim of this present chapter is to move beyond these politicised and simplistic narratives to offer more rigorous and theoretically grounded explanations for Syrian and Saudi threat perceptions in 2006.

Saudi Arabia: Resisting the Resistance

From a realist perspective, scholars have argued that Saudi animosity towards Hezbollah represented a balancing strategy against an expanding Iranian influence in the region (cf. Gause 2007). Nevertheless, this argument does not explain how a non-state actor fighting Israel on southern Lebanese borders can be considered a threat to the security of the Saudi Kingdom.[5] In the following section, I demonstrate that Hezbollah, despite its alliance with Iran, could not endanger the physical security of the Kingdom. Instead, I argue that Saudi Arabia feared Hezbollah's Islamic conception of resistance, which endangered Saudi conception of the self. In 2006, the Saudi Kingdom's physical security was not endangered. Nevertheless, the fixity and rigidity of its identity narrative made the Kingdom vulnerable to other Islamic models in the region. Furthermore, the Kingdom disposed of limited manoeuvres to reframe its identity narrative. To bolster its ontological security, the Kingdom framed its self–other distinction based on a sectarian narrative, which influenced its perception of the relative power distribution and its choice of allies.

The Relative Power Distribution: Saudi Physical Security

Following the overthrow of Saddam Hussein in 2003 and the destruction of Iraq's military capabilities, Iran gained prominent influence in the Arab world (Rajab 2010, 293–9). Considering Hezbollah's strategic

[5] Rubin (2014) unravels similar paradoxes in his study of Saudi and Egyptian fears of Sudan despite its military weakness. Later, in his book, he also asked similar questions about Saudi threat perception of the rise of the Muslim Brotherhood to power in Egypt in 2012 at a time of Egypt's declining economic and military capabilities.

alliance with Iran and Syria, Saudi opposition to Hezbollah might be read as a *raison d'état* reaction to balance Iran in the Middle East. Nevertheless, this realist-inspired narrative alone is insufficient for explaining Saudi opposition to Hezbollah. First, US military capabilities in the region are more important than Iranian ones. Second, this narrative assumes that regional actors lack agency. Hezbollah is not a mere Iranian offshoot in Lebanon.

The fall of the Ba'ath regime in Iraq following the US-led invasion in 2003 removed a critical set of military threats to the Saudi Kingdom and brought a new power distribution to the region. As its conventional military forces were destroyed, Iraq no longer posed any conventional military threat to the Saudis or to any of its neighbours. Before the invasion of Kuwait, Iraq had over one million men in uniform, 5,500 battle tanks, and one of the largest deployed air defence systems in the world. The Gulf War (1990–91) destroyed around 40 per cent of Iraq's military capabilities. After the Gulf War, Iraq could not repair this damage as it was not allowed to import arms (Cordesman and Obaid 2005, 3). By 2003, Iraq had approximately 400,000 men under arms, and demonstrated little conventional warfighting capabilities (The International Institute for Strategic Studies 2003, 110–11). With the US-led invasion, Iraq's land forces, its naval forces, and its air defence were entirely destroyed within few weeks. In short, any potential Iraqi conventional military threat to Saudi Arabia vanished for decades.

The destruction of Iraq's conventional capabilities led to an unprecedented vacuum in the Persian Gulf. As the Gulf monarchies were unable to fill this void, Iran emerged as the only rising power in the region. Iran's military capabilities seemed predominant compared to those of the six Gulf monarchies. Whereas the Gulf monarchies had approximately 10,391,795 men in uniform in 2003, Iran had 18,319,545 men in 2004 (Langton 2004, 121–40). The conscript in Iran was approximately 540,000 as opposed to 330,800 in the six Gulf monarchies (Cordesman 2004, 2–3). Despite its failure to export the Islamic Revolution to the Arab world throughout the 1980s, Iran deployed successful efforts to expand an indirect influence in Iraq, Lebanon, and among the Palestinians. In Iraq, the Islamic Republic has enjoyed political and military influence, supporting the Shiite governments from 2003 onwards. Iran swiftly recognised the transitional government on 17 November 2003 and restored full diplomatic relations with Iraq on 18 April 2004

(Rajab 2010, 294). In addition, by the time of the Lebanese–Israeli conflict, the Iranian influence had extended to the Israeli–Palestinian struggle. During the Palestinian Intifada of 2000, Supreme Leader Khamenei referred to Palestine as 'a limb of our body' (quoted in Wehrey et al. 2009, 23). Alongside the verbal support, Iran became a major player in Gaza through its financial support for Hamas and the Palestinian Islamic Jihad (PIJ).

Since its establishment in 1982, Hezbollah was identified as an Iranian ally. In the wake of Israel's invasion of Lebanon in 1982, a group of clerics drifted away from Musa al-Sadr[6] movement *Ḥarkat al-Maḥrūmīn* [Movement of the Dispossessed] (1974) and established a militia to resist the Israeli invasion (Fuller 2007, 141–2). This militia constituted the basis for Hezbollah, whose organisation was officially announced in 1985 with an 'open letter' to the 'Downtrodden in Lebanon and the World' (translated in Norton 1987, 167–87). This document clearly reflects an ideological inspiration from Khomeini's interpretation of *vilayat-e faqīh* [The Rule of Jurisprudence]. The founders of the group expressed their loyalty to the Islamic Revolution and pronounced themselves as '[abiding] by the orders of a single, wise and just command represented by the guardianship of the jurisprudent, currently embodied in the Supreme Ayatollah Ruhollah al-Musawi al-Khomeini ... who has detonated the Muslims' revolution, and who is bringing about the glorious Islamic renaissance'.

The document framed its worldview around struggle of the oppressors versus oppressed. Whereas the oppressors identified by Khomeini in the context of the Islamic Revolution were the Shah's regime and Western powers (particularly the United States). Hezbollah's oppressors were the invading Israelis and supporters, the United States including. The document explicitly states that 'Imam Khomeini has stressed time and again that America is behind all our catastrophes, and it is the mother of all vice ... The US, its NATO[7] allies, and the Zionist entity in the holy land of Palestine [Israel] attacked us and continues to do so without respite' (Alagha 2011, 40–1). Moreover, Hezbollah leaders have often expressed their loyalty to Ayatollah Khomeini and his successors (Hamzeh 2004, 38–48).

---

[6] Al-Sadr was an Iranian cleric who came to Lebanon in the late 1950s and assumed a prominent role in mobilising the Shia community on the social and political levels. For more details, cf. Norton (2007).

[7] North Atlantic Treaty Organisation.

Beyond this ideological subscription to the Islamic Revolution, Hezbollah has been a prominent recipient of financial support from Iran, which has been reflected in the group's social and philanthropic programs.[8] In addition, Iranian funding has extended to military assistance (El Husseini 2010, 809; Levitt 2007, 137). According to reasonable estimates, this support has been of approximately US$25–50 million per year (Cordesman 2006a, 3). Beyond financial and military aid, Iran provided Hezbollah with logistical support. In the early days of Hezbollah, the Iranian Revolutionary Guard Corps (IRGC) trained the party of God's members in Iran or in al-Beqaa Valley in Lebanon (Fuller 2007, 142; Mus'ad 2006, 301–2; Qassem 2005, 240). Even after their official withdrawal from Lebanon in the early 1990s, Iran's Islamic Revolutionary Guards continued to train Hezbollah's members (Hamzeh 2004, 71).

In this context, Saudi discourse was able to portray Hezbollah as an offshoot of the Islamic Republic in Lebanon. On 29 July 2006, Saudi-owned daily newspaper *Al-Sharq Al-Awsat* published a detailed article on the assistance that Iran's Revolutionary Guard extended to Hezbollah. The article went as far as claiming that officers from the Revolutionary Guards were fighting along with Hezbollah (Zādah 2006). Saudi Columnist Mshari al-Dyadhi expressed the fear of an expanding Iranian influence as follows: 'examine all the big Arab portfolios – Lebanon, Palestine, and Iraq. They are being stolen from Arab hands . . . and turned over to Iranian hands gradually' (quoted in Wehrey 2011, 22). Other Arab regimes – mainly Egypt and Jordan – seconded this Saudi position during the meeting of Arab foreign ministers on 16 July 2006, as they announced their 'complete refusal to all projects that aim to turn Lebanon into a theatre for open confrontations to achieve regional and international goals at the expense of the national interest of the Lebanese people and their security and stability' (Al Riyadh 2006; Ḥasīb 2006, 44–5).

Considering the Hezbollah–Iran connection, the Saudi perception of Hezbollah as a threat can be seen through the lens of physical security needs, according to which Riyadh needed to balance Teheran's infiltration in the region, especially in the context of Iran's re-emerging nuclear programme. I argue that this realist-inspired narrative misses

---

[8] This assistance did not officially come from governmental channels. Instead, it came from charitable foundations affiliated with the Supreme Leader.

the bigger picture. Despite its connection with Iran, Hezbollah could not and did not pose a threat to the physical security of the Kingdom.

First, even though Iran could be considered to pose a conventional military threat to Saudi Arabia at this juncture, this does not mean that the Iranian power was left unbalanced. Ever since its involvement in Iraq in 2003, the United States has been willing to increase its military presence in case its geostrategic interests were threatened, such as the flow of oil from the Gulf. Moreover, the United States maintained military bases in various Gulf states (Figure 1). They also deployed large military forces in countries neighbouring Iran from the east

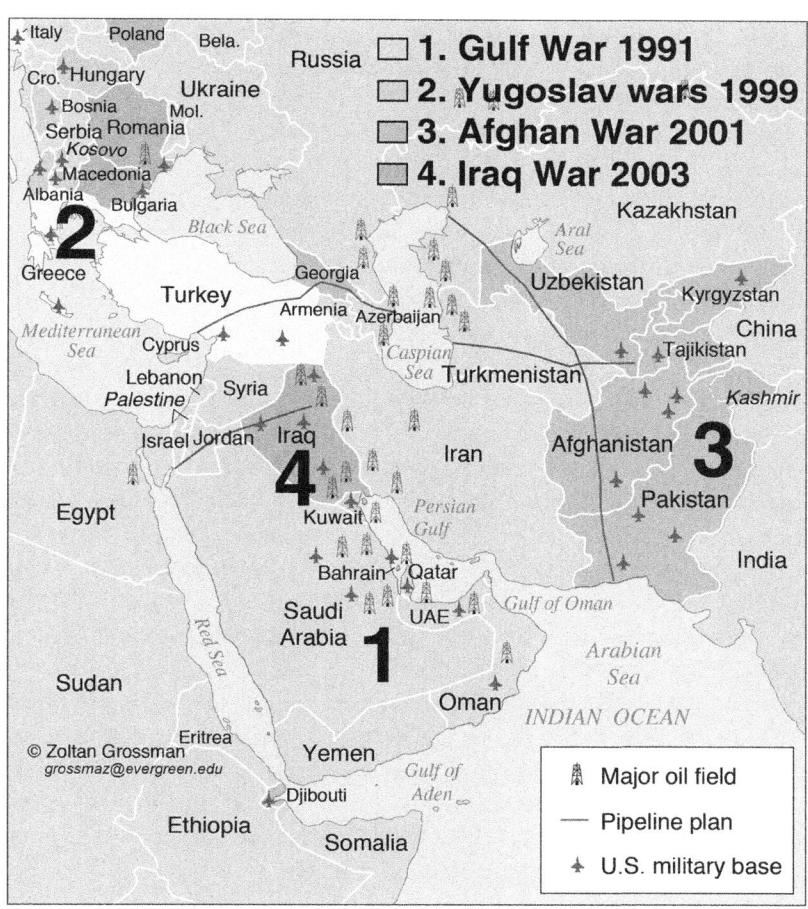

Figure 1 US Military Bases in Central Asia and the Middle East.

(Afghanistan) and the west (Iraq) (Kam 2004, 18–20). Accordingly, the military presence of the superpower in the region constituted a considerable source of pressure on Iran. As shown in Figure 1, after 2003 Iran became surrounded virtually on all sides by countries associated with the United States and hosting US military bases, with considerable projection capabilities (Piven 2012). In this context, Iranians became aware of their limited capabilities. As Iranian Minister of Foreign Affairs Javad Zarif explained, 'Do you think the United States, which can destroy all our military systems with one bomb, is scared of our military system?' (quoted in Chubin 2014, 66). Alongside the superpower's presence in the region, the collapse of Iraq's military power provided Israel with a set of opportunities to entrench its military supremacy, which in itself would also impede any Iranian expansion in the region.

Second, Iran's infiltration in the region might be considered a sign of weakness rather than power. As Wehrey et al. (2009, 22) argue, 'Iran's hyperactivism on pan-Arab issues is not necessarily proof of its influence, but rather just the opposite – an effort to overcompensate for its fundamental isolation from the rest of region'. In other words, appealing to 'Arab' issues reveals Iran's failure to export its revolution and to mobilise any mass-based opposition to existing regimes in the Arab world. Even though some scholars characterised Iran's ability to exert such influence as a sign of 'soft power',[9] which also points to its inability of using hard power in exerting influence. Moreover, Iran is separated from Saudi Arabia by an oceanic moat (the Gulf) and lacks meaningful technological capabilities to project its military power across the Gulf or even to the Arab–Israeli sphere (Chubin 2014). In addition, Iran's infiltration in the region does not mean that it will become a dominant power. As Gause (2011, 182) eloquently notes, 'If the United States, with all its power, could not dominate the region post-2003, it is hard to imagine that Iran could'.

Moreover, Iran's conventional military power is far less modern than it was during the time of the Shah, or during the Iran–Iraq War. Most of its military equipment is aging, and arm imports have considerably decreased since the eight-year conflict. According to US estimates, Iran imported US$8.8 billion worth of arms between 1988 and 1991, but only US$2 billion between 1996 and 1999, and

---

[9] See, for example, Mabon (2013).

US$600 million between 2000 and 2003 (Cordesman and Obaid 2005, 16). Its overall military expenditures were comparatively limited in the last two decades. The International Institute for Strategic Studies (IISS) estimates the Iranian military expenditure of US$3.051 billion in 2003 and US$5.2 billion in 2005. In contrast, according to the IISS, Saudi Arabia spent US$18.747 billion in 2003 and US$18.4 billion in 2005 (The International Institute for Strategic Studies 2003, 2006). If Iran's military expenditures can be compared to that of the Gulf monarchies, it is hard to argue that it aspires to military hegemony (Cordesman 2014). As Chubin (2014, 65) succinctly states, 'by orthodox standards Iran is militarily weak, and cautious, defensive and prudent in resorting to force'.

Third, the role of Iran's nuclear programme in triggering Saudi threat perception has been often advanced by media commentators as the main source of concern with regard to the Hezbollah connection to Iran as it might embolden Iranian proxies. It is obviously impossible to know for certain how much fear of hard power can be factored in the calculations of leaders, especially as ideational and material sources of threat can emerge at the same time. Saudi leaders consider Iranian acquisition of nuclear capabilities to be a serious threat to regional stability and have constantly threatened to develop their own nuclear programme, with some speculations that Saudi leaders have been already in the process of considering acquiring nuclear capabilities (Cigar 2016). While it is difficult to isolate Saudi responses to particular sources of threats, but it is clear that fear of Iran and Hezbollah is more ideational than military. Quantitatively, there has been an imbalance between military expenditure between Saudi Arabia and Iran. According to Stockholm International Peace Research Institute (SIPRI) database, Saudi Arabia's military expenditures in the past two decades consistently doubled or tripled the amounts of Iran's military expenditures. In particular, Saudi military spending has skyrocketed since 2005 (SIPRI 2016). That being said, these military acquisitions are hardly ways to balance against a nuclear threat. At the same time, these arms purchases could also be a way of acquiring status and prestige (Darwich 2018).

A direct nuclear attack is not the primary concern for the Saudi Kingdom among other Gulf countries. Instead, the direct threat stems from the implications that a nuclear Iran might have on regional dynamics (Kaye and Wehrey 2007). For example, a nuclear Iran would lead to a nuclear race in the region where other regional powers, such as Egypt, will attempt to achieve the nuclear bomb. Furthermore, Saudi leaders mostly fear the loss of control and leadership in the Gulf area. Should Iran possess a nuclear bomb, its leverage and power over small states in the Gulf would increase drastically, which will lead to eclipse of Saudi ambitions of regional leadership in the Arab world. A nuclear Iranian power will further raise questions about the extent to which the United States intends to provide security shields for the Saudi Kingdom. Even before the 2011 uprisings, Saudi leaders feared a potential nuclear agreement between the United States and Iran, and a subsequent rapprochement (Wehrey 2012, 3). That being said, the circumstances encircling the nuclear programme in Iran and the relationship with Hezbollah suggested an ideational balancing rather than material one during the 2006 Lebanon War (Rubin 2014, 113–15). The development of nuclear capabilities in Iran does not necessarily translate into more increased Iranian influence in Iraq, Lebanon and the Palestinian–Israeli conflict, etc. In other words, the Iranian nuclear programme might have intensified Saudi perception of Hezbollah as an ideational threat in 2006, but it was not the main driver.

Fourth, and most importantly, the Hezbollah–Iran connection cannot be seen as a mechanical transfer of Iranian power to Lebanon. Iran was accused of using Hezbollah as a card in its negotiations with the United States, especially with regard to the nuclear programme. For example, Makovsky (2006) mentioned that on the eve of the kidnapping of the two soldiers, Ali Larijani, Iran's head of the Supreme National Security Council, threatened that the West 'will suffer if the Iranian nuclear issue was taken back to the United Nations Security Council'. Despite these claims, there is no evidence of any Iranian control over Hezbollah. The Hezbollah–Iran connection can be rather considered a conventional form of alliance. In responding to the claims that Iran directed Hezbollah, Hassan Nasrallah declared, 'This is a great lie. We are an independent Lebanese organisation. We do not take orders from anyone. However, this does not mean that we are not going to form alliances' (*CounterPunch News Service* 2006). Most analysts have argued that despite the financial and ideological linkage with Iran, Hezbollah is an independent local organisation. Based on interviews with Israeli decision-makers conducted in August 2006, Cordesman (2006b) stresses that no Israeli officer thought that Hezbollah was acting under Iranian command. According to Hezbollah Deputy Secretary General Sheikh Na'im Qassem (2005, 56–7),

There is no connection between the internal administration of the Iranian state and Hezbollah's administration. These are two separate issues, each having its own particularities and bodies of administration, despite the commitment of both to the commands and directions of the Jurist-Theologian.

Furthermore, Hezbollah's relations with Iran have wavered over time. The death of Ayatollah Khomeini as well as the end of the Cold War led to significant changes in Iranian foreign policy towards Lebanon, and towards Hezbollah in particular (El Husseini 2010, 807; Norton 1999, 18). As a result, Hezbollah's leaders turned to the domestic sphere and made a considerable effort to transform the militia into a Lebanese political party. Since the 1991 elections, Hezbollah has participated in all Lebanese parliamentary and municipal elections. This process is often termed as the 'Lebanonisation' of Hezbollah.[10] The 2009 New Hezbollah Manifesto unmistakably reflected this process. The document defers the ideologically inspired goal of establishing an Islamic state in Lebanon. Moreover, it places Hezbollah's relationship with Iran squarely in the context of its relations with other Islamic countries. The New Manifesto explicitly states:

In this context, Hezbollah considers Islamic Iran to be a focal nation in the Islamic world. For Iran was the country that thwarted the Zionist-U.S. scheme through its national revolution, supported resistance movements in our region, and stood with courage and determination alongside Arab and Islamic causes, at the forefront of which is the Palestinian cause. (Alagha 2011, 131)

Signs of this wavering relationship between Iran and Hezbollah were manifested even during the 2006 war. Beyond verbal support, Iranian officials denied any military intervention to support Hezbollah. In his meeting with Lebanese Foreign Minister Fawzi Salloukh, Iranian Ambassador Muhammad Rida stated that 'There is no military defence treaty between Iran and Lebanon, similar to the one we have with Syria. Regardless of this matter, historical records clearly show that Iran has been, still is, standing behind Lebanon' (*Al-Hayat* 2006a). In response to allegations that the Revolutionary Guards were assisting

---

[10] For further details on this process, cf. Hamzeh (1993) and Norton (1999).

Hezbollah, Hamid Rida Asifi, the spokesman of Iran's foreign minister, denied the existence of any Iranian soldiers in Lebanon and stressed that Iranian support for Hezbollah is limited to 'political, diplomatic, and humanitarian support' and if 'there was any military support, Israel would be defeated long before' (Al-Hayat 2006b).

From this perspective, Hezbollah did not, in the run up to the 2006 war, pose a physical security danger to Saudi Arabia. The organisation's linkage with Iran or Syria did not even imply any Iranian influence in the region that could threaten the physical security of the Kingdom. Israel's supremacy in the Arab–Israeli sphere would not allow Hezbollah to play a military role beyond Lebanon's borders. Why then was a Lebanese local organisation identified as a threat to the Kingdom? The following section argues that Hezbollah's Islamic identity threatened the identity stability of the Kingdom. The process of ontological security restoration involved reframing the self–other narrative based on sectarian terms. This self–other distinction predominated the Saudi threat perception and choice of allies during the 2006 war.

Regime Identity and the Ontological Security of Sectarianism

Since 1967, Saudi Arabia has played a prominent role in the Arab struggle against Israel through financial and diplomatic means. Despite this traditional position against Israel, the Saudis astonishingly condemned Hezbollah in July 2006. For the first time in the history of the Arab–Israeli conflict, an Arab state claiming the leadership of the Muslim world condemned a resistance movement and inadvertently backed Israel (Yamani 2008, 153). This section argues that Hezbollah's Islamic identity narrative challenged the stability and the distinctiveness of the Saudi regime. The vulnerability of the Saudi Kingdom is related to the rigidity and fixity of its identity narrative. Relying on Islam as a main pillar in its identity narrative has limited the Saudi elites' ability to reinvent their self when faced with a similar other. As a response, the Kingdom framed a self–other distinction based on sectarianism (Sunni versus Shiite). This newly framed 'other' was furthermore identified as an enemy.

The Saudi involvement in the Arab–Israeli conflict manifested itself in two aspects. First, the Kingdom financially supported the frontline states – Egypt, Jordan, Syrian, and the PLO – in their struggles against

Israel, especially after 1967. Second, the Kingdom emerged as the primary regional mediator in the conflict (Al-Dakhīl 2007; Kamrava 2013; Kostiner 2009). The Kingdom put forward a progressive agenda that portrayed the Arab interest as pacifying the Arab–Israeli conflict through the peace process. Furthermore, this role became embedded in the Saudi Islamic narrative.

The first Saudi mediation was in the early 1980s with the Fahd peace plan (1981),[11] which illustrated the Saudi vision supporting a peaceful settlement of the Arab–Israeli conflict. In contrast to the Egyptian initiative in Camp David, which was based on bilateral negotiations with Israel, Saudi Arabia promoted a comprehensive peace plan including all Arab states in order to avoid any rift within the Arab camp. Among the eight points proposed by the Fahd plan, the seventh point stipulated that all Middle East states have the right to live in peace. In other words, if Israel withdraws from the territories occupied in 1967, it will be given the right to live in peace with the other states in the region (Kostiner 2009, 419). The peace initiative was a Saudi attempt to bring the whole region to order, while positioning the Kingdom as the maestro of this concert.

This Fahd plan constituted a compromise that enabled Riyadh to capitalise on its relationship with Washington, while maintaining a consistent Islamic identity narrative (Sela 1998, 274). During the 1970s, the Egyptian–Israeli peace treaty created a rift in the Saudi–US partnership, as the Kingdom found itself forced to participate in the Arab Steadfastness and Confrontation Front boycotting and punishing Egypt (Kostiner 2009, 418; Sunayama 2007, 54–5). While promoting its pan-Islamic narrative in the region by demonstrating solidarity against Israel, Saudi Arabia employed the peace plan to portray itself in the West as a promoter of peace. Nevertheless, the initiative was not successful. The Fahd plan encountered Syria's opposition and was foiled by the absence of the Syrian delegation from the Arab summit in Fez, Morocco, (session one) in 1981. Following this Arab objection, the Saudi initiative was reintroduced with changes at the Fez Summit in September 1982 (session two). The seventh point stressing that all states in the region have the right to exist in peace was eliminated (Kostiner 2009, 419–20).

---

[11] For more details on the Fahd Peace Plan, see Long (1986).

In 2002, Saudi Arabia recultivated the same strategy through the Abdullah peace initiative – also known as the 'Arab Peace Initiative'. Instead of offering Israel mere 'recognition', this new plan offered full 'normalisation' with Israel in return for the complete withdrawal to the pre-1967 borders. This new Saudi initiative reflected Arab states' weakness; Egypt under the leadership of Mubarak was unwilling to play a regional role, and Iraq was extremely weakened and isolated ever since the invasion of Kuwait. All Arab states unanimously accepted this initiative during a summit in Beirut in March 2002 (Bahgat 2009a).

In the meantime, the peace-making strategy became embedded in the Kingdom's identity narrative. In other words, the Saudi role in the Arab–Israeli conflict became inextricably related to the Kingdom's position as the guardian of Islam's holiest sites. Religious *ulama* close to the royal family claimed that from a religious perspective seeking peace is more favourable than taking risks and going to war. As Abdel Muhsen al-Ubayykan[12] (2006) stated,

[A] condition of Jihad is the possession of sufficient power to defeat the enemy, repulse its evil, and ensure the safety of the Muslim people's lives, property, and honour and safeguard them from assault and loss, namely, the squandering of resources, violation of honour, and loss of lives. ... If we consider [the prophet's example] and compare the two situations, *we will find that at this time we are required to make a truce with the Jews or seek peaceful political solutions* on the grounds that the Muslims lack the requirement of sufficient military strength. This can continue until the time when the Muslims are prepared to regain their rights because they have sufficient power. In this way we will be obeying the Prophet's example in word and deed. (Emphasis added)

By linking its role in the peace process to an Islamic narrative, the Kingdom tied the legitimacy of its foreign policy to the stability of its identity narrative. Accordingly, Hezbollah's conception of 'Islamic resistance' not only challenged the Saudi role in the conflict but also endangered the stability of its identity narrative, which was heavily reliant on this Islamic component.

---

[12] Al-'Ubayykan is a senior ultraconservative Wahhabi cleric. He was a member of the Shura Council and a consultant for the Ministry of Judiciary. Moreover, he was an adviser to the Royal cabinet until he was dismissed in May 2012.

Whereas Saudi Arabia claimed that the Arab Peace Initiative was the only solution capable of preserving the 'Arab interest' (Teitelbaum 2009, 19), Hezbollah presented a competing vision based on armed resistance (*muqāwama*). Since the party's foundation in the early 1980s, Hezbollah's *raison d'être* has been intimately tied to resistance against the Israeli occupation of South Lebanon. Hezbollah has defined itself as a '*jihadi* movement', whose ultimate priority has been the liberation of the Lebanese territory from Israeli occupation as well as the Liberation of Palestine. Accordingly, for Hezbollah, resisting the occupation took precedence over the goal of establishing an Islamic state. In addition, this declared objective could only be achieved through armed resistance (Saad-Gorayeb 2002, 112–17). Because it considers Israel an oppressive occupying force, Hezbollah defines '*Jihad*'[13] as a 'defensive' duty (Mahmoud 2010, 42–4). Consequently, by capturing the two Israeli soldiers on the morning of 12 July 2006, Hezbollah considered itself to be taking a legitimate action to restore its rights, which included liberating the Shab'a farms, exchanging the soldiers for Lebanese and Palestinian war prisoners, and deterring Israel from any expansion in Lebanon (Ḥasīb 2006, 26–8). As Sheikh Qassem (2007) declared, 'The confrontation with Israel is not an elementary choice for the resistance, but it is a current and future defensive choice'.

Behind the logic of armed resistance lies a strong belief in the unviability of the 'land-for-peace' based negotiations with Israel. First, this position stemmed from Hezbollah's non-recognition of Israel, which the party considers to be an unjust oppressor state.[14] Second, the negotiations have so far proven fruitless. As Abbas al-Musawi, Hezbollah's former secretary-general, has expressed it, 'Any rational person who thinks objectively will reach one conclusion: that force is the only option when political activity and negotiations are of no avail. We announce that resistance is our only choice and that our talk is based on logic' (quoted in Saad-Gorayeb 2002, 120). According to Hezbollah, Israel cannot be trusted, and the conflict will continue until all Muslim territories are liberated (Bilqīz 2006, 48–50). According to Sheikh Qassem (2007), 'Confrontation with Israel is inevitable. If we refuse the occupation of our lands, we should expect violent

---

[13] '*Jihad*' is derived from the Arabic word '*Juhd*' [effort]. Jihad means the exertion of any effort in God's cause.

[14] For further details on Hezbollah's view of injustice, refer to the first Manifesto in Alagha (2011, 39–55).

confrontation because Israel is aggressive, expansionist, and self-oriented'. Hezbollah believes that even if Israel was granted recognition by the entire Arab region, it would not withdraw from the occupied territories (Mahmoud 2010, 43). This belief was based on Hezbollah's experience; Israel withdrew to the security zone in 1985 and from the south of Lebanon in 2000 only because of the armed resistance.

Nevertheless, Hezbollah's armed approach to the conflict per se did not challenge the Kingdom. Instead, it was the Islamic colour of the resistance that disrupted the stability of the Kingdom's identity. Although Hezbollah's pan-Islamic ideology and its related goal of establishing an Islamic state in Lebanon has wavered and become increasingly replaced by political pragmatism, the party is still fighting Israel under a banner of 'Islamic resistance' (Bassedas 2009, 18–28; Norton 2007, 83). This Islamic dimension has been based on the concept of Jihad. Although Hezbollah's concept of Jihad borrowed heavily from Khomeini's doctrine, its ideological flexibility and its exclusive focus on fighting Israel made it appealing to Arab public opinion. In addition, Hezbollah's path of *Jihad* against Israel and its commitment to the Palestinian cause has served a role model for other groups, such as the Palestinian Islamic Jihad and Hamas (Hamzeh 2004; Khashan and Mousawi 2007). In short, Hezbollah's logic of resistance has undermined the Saudi identity narrative favouring peace negotiations. Furthermore, it has impeded the Kingdom from speaking in the name of Islam.

The Saudi official position towards Hezbollah reflected the regime's anxiety. Following the outbreak of the Lebanese conflict, a Saudi formal statement on 13 July 2006 accused Hezbollah of 'not serving the Arab interest', which can be implicitly understood as the stability of the region based on the peace process promoted by the Kingdom. Resenting Hezbollah's logic of armed resistance, the statement distinguished between 'legitimate resistance' and 'miscalculated adventures'. Saudi Arabia accused Hezbollah of 'adventurism' as its actions were carried 'without consultation or coordination with Arab countries'. The Saudi statement further described Hezbollah as threatening the Arab interest by 'creating a gravely dangerous situation exposing all Arab countries and its achievements to destruction with those countries having no say'.[15] On 14 July 2006, the same statement was issued

---

[15] The full text of the Saudi statement can be found on www.spa.gov.sa/English/details.php?id=375383

again with the same text with the following added concluding paragraph: 'The Kingdom will continually seek for security and stability in the region, exerting everything that it can do to protect the Arab nation from an Israeli oppression and transgression'.[16] This Saudi leading role in defining the Arab–Israeli agenda was seconded on 14 July 2006 by the joint statement of King Abdullah of Jordan and President Mubarak of Egypt, who condemned Hezbollah's actions and assigned the responsibility for the suffering of the Lebanese people to the party.[17] From this perspective, Hezbollah's actions against Israel emerged as threatening to the status of Saudi Arabia as a normative leader in the Arab–Israeli sphere.

In the process of restoring its ontological security, the Kingdom attempted to demonise Hezbollah's Islamic identity by claiming that Hezbollah was serving Iranian interests. Moreover, the Saudi regime promoted a sectarian discourse to distinguish its own identity from that of Hezbollah's. Whereas Nasrallah framed the struggle against Israel in religious terms: 'A defeat for us is a defeat for the whole Muslim nation', Saudi Arabia portrayed Hezbollah's 'irresponsible acts' as providing Iran with an opportunity to extend its influence in the region (Amba 2006).

In addition, the Kingdom found in sectarianism a mechanism to reinforce its distinctiveness and the security of its identity narrative vis-à-vis other Islamic movements in the region, including Hezbollah.[18] The Kingdom reinforced a sectarian self–other definition, which identified Hezbollah as a threatening 'other' because of its Shiite roots. On 18 July 2006, shortly after the Saudi official statement condemning Hezbollah, the Saudi Press Agency republished an old fatwa of Sheikh Abdullah bin Jibrin[19] and circulated it through state-influenced media outlets. Originally published in 2002, this fatwa states:

---

[16] For the full text of the second statement, cf. www.spa.gov.sa/English/details.php?id=375423

[17] For the full text of this statement, cf. www.ahram.org.eg/Archive/2006/7/15/ARAB6.HTM

[18] Scholars have often pointed to the use of sectarianism by the Saudi Kingdom as a tool for survival (Al-Rasheed 2011) and ontological security (Darwich 2016).

[19] Ibn Jibrin was the second top leading scholar in the Wahhabi movement. He was also a member of the Permanent Committee for Islamic Research and Fatwa in Saudi Arabia.

It is forbidden to support this *rafiddi*[20] party, joining it or even praying for it to achieve victory, I advise all Sunnis to deny this party and those who join it and to explain its hostility to Islam and Muslims, specially that such rejecting parties have always been hostile to Sunnis and tended to expose their shortcomings. (*Rasid Al-Ikhbariyya* 2006)

Religious *ulama* closely related to the royal family have expressed hostility towards Hezbollah based on religious considerations. Sheikh Nasir al-'Umar described Hezbollah as 'the party of the devil'. In addition, he claimed that 'Hezbollah does not represent Sunni Muslims' resistance in Palestine or any other place, but it serves the Iranian Revolutionary Guards' (Fattah 2006). Similarly, Safr al-Hawali issued a fatwa according to which 'it is forbidden to pray for Hezbollah or to provide any support for its war against Israel' (Al-Rashid 2013). From this perspective, the Sunni–Shiite discourse served as a mechanism to re-establish Saudi ontological security.

This framing of a sectarian distinction between Hezbollah and Saudi Arabia allowed the regime to preserve some identity stability and ontological security. That being said, such reframing has its limits. Following these reactions, the Arab public opinion reacted to the condemning positions of Arab regimes in Egypt, Saudi Arabia and Jordan through protests and marches supporting Hezbollah as a 'resistance movement' and rejected the sectarian characterisation of the conflict. Therefore, Valbjørn and Bank (2012) described this dynamic as the rise of a cultural Arabism across the region that unravelled a struggle between regimes and societies in the Arab world. Other scholars mentioned the rise of 'Arab' public sphere that transcends national and sectarian divisions (Lynch 2006; Phillips 2012; Rinnawi 2006). Instead, Sheikh Hassan Nasrallah became an Arab hero whose photos were posted across Arab streets, which led Saudi Arabia and other Arab regimes to downgrade their framing of the group as an existential threat (MacFarquhar 2006). To appease the public opinion, the Kingdom started distancing itself rhetorically from US and Israeli condemnations of Hezbollah. Furthermore, they announced several humanitarian aids for the Lebanese people and promised to revive the Arab Peace Initiative. Such limited backtracking from the Saudi Kingdom following the rejection of this narrative by the Arab public opinion shows the limit in pursuing ontological security

---

[20] A word used by Wahhabi clerics to refer to Shiites.

through reframing self–other distinction, as such reframing requires internalisation and acceptance by the domestic audience, which can be a long-term process. Following the 2006 Lebanon War, the Saudi regime maintained the sectarian characterisation of Hezbollah as a threatening other, and this narrative was diffused by its media outlets and religious scholars, and eventually this sectarian narrative became gradually embraced at the societal level and culminated in persuading the Arab League and Gulf states years later to label the group as a 'terrorist organisation' (CNN 2017; Reuters 2016).

Syria: The Quest for Physical Security

Whereas several Arab regimes condemned Hezbollah and blamed it for the devastating effects of the war, the Syrian regime's alliance with Hezbollah against Israel since the 1980s culminated and reached a high point in 2006. When asked about the possibility of a regional war, Syrian Foreign Minister Walid al-Mu'allim replied as follows: 'Welcome to the regional war; we are ready for it and we do not hide our preparations'. He then added: 'I am ready to be a soldier under the leadership of Hassan Nasrallah' (quoted in Ziadeh 2011, 117).

This section argues that Syria's increasing support for Hezbollah during the 2006 Lebanon War was driven by Syria's physical security needs, whose survival became increasingly dependent on the axis of refusal. Indeed, Syria played a direct role in the establishment of Hezbollah.[21] Throughout the 1980s, the Syrian regime had allowed Iranian units to enter Lebanon to provide logistical and operational support for the party. Given this historical context and this long-standing alliance, two erroneous assumptions predominated accounts of the 2006 Lebanon War. The first assumption claims that Hezbollah is only a 'proxy' or a 'pawn' implementing Syria's and Iran's will in Lebanon. Following the abduction of the two Israeli soldiers by Hezbollah on 12 July, Western governments accused Syria and Iran of being accomplices.[22] As the US National Security Council spokesperson Frederick Jones stated, 'We charge Syria and Iran who support Hezbollah with the responsibility for the attack and the violence which followed it' (quoted in Ziadeh 2011, 115). The second assumption

---

[21] Cf. Zerden (2000).
[22] Cf. White House statement on the kidnapping of two Israeli soldiers (2006).

considers the alliance between Syria and Hezbollah to be driven by sectarian affinities between Hezbollah, described as a Shiite group, and Syria's Alawite ruling elite (Amidror 2007). Yet these assumptions do not reflect the complex nature of this alliance.

Thinking of Hezbollah as Syria's proxy is inaccurate. Prior to 2005, while Syria had 20,000 troops stationed in Lebanon, the chiefs of Syrian *istikhbarat* (military intelligence) exerted considerable influence over Hezbollah's operational planning (Perthes 2006, 36). Following Syria's military withdrawal from Lebanon in 2005, the Syrian regime could no longer control Hezbollah's strategic actions. The group asserted itself as an independent actor with operational autonomy and a distinct decision-making process (El-Hokayem 2007). During the 2006 war, the two actors asserted dissimilar policy imperatives. For this reason, Syria's alliance with Hezbollah should be understood as a strategic decision made by the regime. With Syria's regional isolation, this alliance became strategically more vital to Syria than to Hezbollah.

Ideological convergence is hardly a driver behind this 'marriage of convenience'. Despite the seemingly sectarian affinity, the alliance between the Alawite ruling elite in Syria and Hezbollah is driven by strategic factors more than by ideational affinities. The Islamic nature of Hezbollah's identity narrative has been the source of discomfort to a Ba'athist pan-Arab secular regime oppressing its own Islamic movements (El-Hokayem 2007, 36). However, the repeated convergence of interests has enabled the protracted cooperation between both actors (El Husseini 2010). As Norton (1999, 11) puts it, 'Syria has no eternal allies and no perpetual enemy in Lebanon' and Hezbollah is a 'wary ally of Damascus'.

This section explores Syria's threat perception in 2006. I argue that Syria's physical insecurity was endangered by Israel's military supremacy following the US-led war in Iraq (2003). Those fears were substantiated with the failure of Syrian–Israeli peace negotiations, Syria's military withdrawal from Lebanon, and its regional and international isolation. Furthermore, despite the improvement in the relationship between Ankara and Damascus after the rise of the AKP to power, Turkey's strategic alliance with Israel remained resilient at that time. The alliance with Hezbollah provided the Syrian regime with leverage in its struggle against Israel's military threat and international isolation led by the United States and the only viable policy option to ensure physical security.

Although the Syria–Hezbollah axis has evolved over the years since the 1980s, the 2006 war constituted an important episode in this alliance; Hezbollah is a crucial ally in implementing Syria's regional strategy and not just an ally in Lebanon. Particularly after the Syrian withdrawal from Lebanon, the strategic importance of Hezbollah to Syria shifted from the status of a 'resistance card' to an indispensable strategic ally. As El-Hokayem (2007, 36) notes, 'Syria [became] more pro-Hezbollah than Hezbollah is pro-Syria'. With the rise of Hezbollah as a regional resistance movement that gained appeal and support from Arab public opinion across the region, the Syrian regime became more dependent on Hezbollah, and the refusal axis in general, to gain regional legitimacy and leverage in its negotiations with the international community. In other words, Hezbollah became a crucial asset for Syria to break its isolation at both regional and international levels.

Despite the secular pan-Arab nature of the Syrian regime, the success of Hezbollah in the 2006 war in gathering regional support across the masses along with the gradual Islamisation of Syrian society compelled the regime to adapt its own identity narratives to align more closely to the Islamic identity of Hezbollah. Bashar al-Assad's domestic ideational power and, hence, regime survival became increasingly reliant on the 'resistance' credential of Syria's external ally, Hezbollah (Sottimano 2016; Stein 2017, 678). In 2006, the Syrian regime underwent an important development in the sources of regime identity to capitalise on its alliance with Hezbollah for its physical survival, that is an alteration in the official identity narrative to include an Islamic aspect alongside nationalist and pan-Arab elements. In what follows, I first examine the relative power distribution that led to Syria's physical insecurity and viable policy options to escape isolation. I then examine how the regime in Damascus adapted its identity to capitalise on the success of Hezbollah as it became more dependent on the axis of resistance for physical survival.

The Relative Power Distribution: Surviving Isolation

Following the US-led invasion of Iraq in 2003, Syria suddenly faced a new geopolitical situation that fostered its regional isolation and made its position in the Arab–Israeli balance more fragile than it had been. These regional developments made the alliance with Hezbollah more vital for Syria's interests than ever before and the only policy option in the face of physical insecurity.

The conflict with Israel maintained its centrality in Syria's security priorities. Although the Syrian–Israeli front had been relatively quiet since 1967, the outbreak of war always remained in the background. Syria's ruling elite was aware of the country's military incapability of defending itself in the case of an open military confrontation with Israel. On the one hand, absolute numbers reflected a military imbalance in Syria's favour. In 2003, Syria's armed forces counted approximately 319,000 active soldiers, 548 combat aircraft, and 4,500 main battle tanks. Israel could field approximately a total of 167,000 active soldiers, 438 combat aircraft, and 3,950 main battle tanks (The International Institute for Strategic Studies 2003, 111–12, 122–3).[23] On the other hand, Syria's military hardware has not been modernised since the collapse of the Soviet Union; it has been poorly maintained, and its technical standards have lagged far behind those of Israel. For instance, more than half of the Syrian tanks are T-55 or T-62s – models from the 1950s and 1970s. In the case of war, Israel's air force would predominate, and its troops would be in Damascus before any Syrian troops could enter Israel's territory. Syria's military capabilities were limited in launching a surprise attack on Israeli instalments in the Golan Heights or to shoot Scud missiles at Israeli cities. Despite Syria's effort since the 1970s to contain Israel within its 1967 borders by bringing its military capabilities to par with Israel – what has been known as the strategic parity policy – Syria was not able to alter or control the balance of power. In the late 1990s, Syria had to abandon its strategic parity with Israel. Russia, the successor of the Soviet Union, had no interest in funding the Syrian army. Therefore, since the demise of the Soviet Union, the asymmetry between Syria and Israel kept steadily widening (Drysdale and Hinnebusch 1991, 165).

Under these circumstances, the strategic value of Weapons of Mass Destruction (WMD), from a Syrian perspective, multiplied to deter and contain Israel. By almost every report, Syria was known to possess a chemical weapon programme that was developed as a deterrent strategy against Israel's nuclear arsenal (Shoham 2002). Furthermore, US efforts to persuade Syria to renounce its WMD programme have been a failure despite the harsh economic sanctions (Jouejati

---

[23] For similar figures, cf. Feldman and Shapir (2001) and Kam (2004).

2005; Zisser 2004). Furthermore, the Syrian regime attempted to build a nuclear reactor that Israel destroyed in 2007 (Agence France-Presse 2018; Harel and Benn 2018). Yet, these WMDs were often perceived as a defensive strategy. In short, Syria could not effectively balance Israel, and Syria's deterrent capabilities against an Israeli attack were limited.

In addition to the Israeli threat, Syria felt vulnerable to a US-dominated regional environment. A quick look at the map supports this argument. Syria shares around 900-miles of border with Turkey – a NATO ally of the United States. Although Syrian–Turkish relations improved under Bashar al-Assad, the underlying issues that are sources of tensions between these two states were not resolved. Also, Turkey maintained its strategic alliance with Israel until the end of 2008. To Syria's east lies Iraq, where the United States has deployed over 14,000 soldiers since 2003. To the south, Syria maintains an uneasy relationship with Jordan – also known to be a strong US ally. Finally, on Syria's west coastline, the US sixth fleet is stationed in the Mediterranean.

At the outbreak of the 2006 war and under the conditions of military imbalance in favour of Israel and the US-dominant security environment, the Syrian regime had two policy options. First, Syria could move away from the Iran–Hezbollah axis and closer to the so-called moderate camp. In this case, Bashar al-Assad would mend the fences with the United States, seek peace with Israel, and further enhance the relationship with Turkey. This option would allow the Syrian regime to escape its regional isolation and re-establish itself as an active regional player through mediating between the Iran–Hezbollah axis and other Arab regimes. For domestic reasons, Bashar could endorse this policy only in return for the Golan Heights, Arab financial support to the Syrian economy, and strategic influence in Lebanon. In short, if it took this option, Syria would bandwagon with the United States in the region and give up any balancing behaviour against Israel. Initially, the Syrian regime expressed willingness to consider this policy option through engaging in peace negotiations with Israel in the early 2000s. This first option was, however, unlikely to materialise as both the United States and Israel rejected the idea of integrating the Syrian regime into the peace process. Moreover, Israel rejected the notion of returning the Golan Heights. Bandwagoning would, therefore, threaten rather than protect the regime (Salloukh 2009, 165).

The second policy option was bolstering the Syria–Iran–Hezbollah alliance, or the refusal axis, to counterbalance the Arab 'moderate' camp, Israel, and the United States. This option meant participating in anti-US and anti-Israeli operations. It provided Damascus with strategic depth vis-à-vis Israel. In other words, Syria could – and did – take advantage of its alliance with Hezbollah in Lebanon to advance its political and military interests, for example, by using any Hezbollah attack against Israeli forces in South Lebanon as a leverage for Israeli concessions in the Golan (Rubin 2000, 18). Regional observers called this strategy 'the resistance card' (Perthes 2001, 41). In addition, observing US failures in Iraq and Israel's poor performance against Hezbollah, Syrian leaders could reassert their regional role without making any concessions to the United States or other Arab regimes.

Syria initially attempted to go with the first option and to end its isolation by engaging in peace negotiations with Israel. Nevertheless, the failure of the peace negotiations, the withdrawal of Syria from Lebanon in 2005, the resilience of the Israeli–Turkish alliance, and Syria's isolation from the other Arab countries made Syria increasingly dependent on the alliance with Hezbollah and Iran as the only option for preserving Syria's physical security.

Since the 1990s, aware of Syria's inability to either balance or deter Israel and wanting to escape from international isolation, Hafiz al-Assad sought a peaceful settlement for the conflict with Israel. Between 1991 and 2000, Damascus participated in the US-brokered peace talks with Tel-Aviv in a bid to regain the Golan Heights in exchange for peace and recognition of Israel (Goodarzi 2013, 46–7). Syria's approach to the negotiations was best characterised as a zero-sum game, according to which Israeli gains were considered Arab losses. After numerous US-sponsored meetings between Syrian and Israeli representatives, the failure of the peace talks became evident in 2000.[24] In November 2000, Syria turned back to its old enemy – Iraq – for support. Despite the fact that Syria supported Iran in its war against Iraq (1980–88) and provided troops in the coalition effort to liberate Kuwait in 1991, Iraq – which was desperate for any regional ally – gave Damascus the opportunity to break its regional isolation.

---

[24] For further details on the Syrian–Israeli peace talks, cf. Ma'oz (2007a), Miller (2000), and Ziadeh (Forthcoming).

In this context, the fall of Saddam Hussein was a substantial setback for Damascus, as it became deprived of its regional ally. Bashar al-Assad provided Saddam Hussein with military supplies, hosted Iraqi refugees, and allowed Islamist jihadist to cross the borders to Iraq to support the resistance against the United States. The Iraqi developments heightened Syria's exposure to the US foreign policy in the region. The swift US victory in Iraq raised fears among Syrian ruling elites that Syria could be the next target in the Bush administration's 'war on terror' (Goodarzi 2013, 47). In the post-9/11 environment, the Bush administration categorised states as being 'for' or 'against' terrorism. In this context, the term 'rogue states' resonated with neoconservative proposal to extend the war on terror beyond al-Qaeda to states that sponsor terrorism. From Washington's viewpoint, Syria supported terrorist groups (Hamas, Hezbollah and the Palestinian Islamic Jihad) and possessed WMDs. Syria was on the top of 'rogue states' list (Lesch 2005). Following the fall of Baghdad, prominent figures in the Bush administration voiced their desire to see 'a regime change' in Damascus. As Deputy Secretary of Defence Paul Wolfowitz declared, 'there will have to be a change in Syria' (quoted in Salloukh 2009, 164).[25]

The Syrian elite's fear gained saliency when the US army cut the Iraqi oil pipeline to Syria shortly following the invasion of Iraq. On 12 December 2003, the US Congress signed a bill titled 'Syria Accountability and Lebanese Sovereign Act'. According to this bill, the US required Syria to stay away from Iraq and to close down the offices of Palestinian organisations in Damascus. Moreover, Syria should not interfere with the 'road map' of the Israel–Palestinian talks. The United States indirectly pressed Syria to restrain Hezbollah and withdraw its troops from Lebanon. If Syria failed to comply with these requirements, military measures would be used (Lesch 2005, 99; Perthes 2004, 50–1). Although Syria opposed the US invasion of Iraq, the Syrian elite responded to the Act by backing away from any overt support for Iraqi resistance. In addition, Syria extended an offer to reach an understanding with Washington. Syrian leaders offered to provide intelligence against al-Qaeda and to help stabilise Iraq through tightening the control over the borders (Hinnebusch 2009, 19–20; Ziadeh 2011, 88–90).

---

[25] Cf. Seale (2003).

At the same time, al-Assad was reluctant to comply with all US requirements in the Accountability Act, as it would lead to Syria's weakness and dependence on the United States for security. Accordingly, these negotiations revealed Syria's strategic isolation in this new geopolitical situation. Syria became locked between Israel on the south and a US-dominated Iraq on the east. This line of thinking was best described in General Bahjat Sulayman's article in the Lebanese newspaper *al-Safir*. Sulayman, former head of Syrian intelligence, suggested that Syria would help control Hezbollah and Palestinian Jihad and would contribute to the stability of Iraq in exchange for US guarantees regarding the survival of the regime and Syria's reintegration into the peace process (*al-Safir*, 15 March 2003). Nevertheless, Washington was not willing to bargain or negotiate with Damascus; it expected full compliance with its demands and insisted on isolating Syria (Salloukh 2009, 164–5).

This new geopolitical situation aggravated Syria's regional predicament and its physical security, especially vis-à-vis Israel. In a final attempt to enhance its position, Syria renewed the peace talks with Israel. In December 2003, Bashar al-Assad implored Israel's Prime Minister Ariel Sharon to return to the negotiating table. In the history of peace talks, this was the first time that Syria independently proposed talks with Israel over the Golan (Simon and Stevenson 2004). This Syrian initiative reflected the increased pressure over Damascus and its attempt to survive under these unfavourable conditions. Nevertheless, Bashar's offer for peace negotiations was rejected by the Bush administration as well as Israel.

Instead of surrendering to the United States' requirements, the Syrian regime undertook a number of actions aimed at counterbalancing the United States and Israel. Damascus continued to provide discreet support to the Iraqi resistance. In addition, Syria bolstered its alliance with Iran, especially in terms of the latter's activities in Iraq. In an attempt to prevent the United States from using Iraq as a base to launch attacks on Damascus or Teheran, both regimes fuelled the insurgency in hopes that it would pin down US forces. On the one hand, Teheran maintained close relations with all groups in Iraq in order to ensure that the new government in Iraq would not take any hostile positions towards it. On the other hand, Damascus aided the passage of Arab and Sunni foreign fighters from Syrian territory to Iraq (Goodarzi 2013; Ma'oz 2007a).

These counterbalancing measures aggravated Syria's isolation at the regional level. Arab regimes – Egypt and Saudi Arabia in particular – traditionally gave the Syrian regime strategic depth in its conflict with Israel. They supported the al-Assad regime in the peace process and approved of Syria's position in Lebanon. In addition, Syria was one of the principal recipients of Saudi aid. In return, Syria accepted a Saudi influence in Lebanese affairs. But these relationships were deeply affected by the disagreement over Iraq. Following the invasion of Iraq, al-Assad furiously attacked pro-US Arab regimes for siding with the US strategy towards Iraq. Moreover, Bashar al-Assad regularly denounced Arab regimes for not cutting relations with Israel. This Arab populist rhetoric – which was directed towards Egypt, Jordan and Saudi Arabia – led to the animosity of Arab regimes (Perthes 2004, 47–8). Syria's active diplomacy in the Arab world declined, especially in regards to the Israeli–Palestinian conflict. In July 2003, an Arab summit was organised in Sharm al-Sheikh to give an impetus to the 'road-map', which is a plan to solve the Palestinian–Israeli conflict suggested by the United States, Russia, the European Union and the United Nations. Only the so-called moderate Arab states – Egypt, Jordan, Saudi Arabia, Bahrain and the Palestinian Prime Minister Mahmoud Abbas – were allowed to attend. Although Syria had played a crucial role in the region for decades, it became completely isolated (Ziadeh 2011, 94–5).

Syria's regional predicament reached its peak following the assassination of Lebanese Prime Minister Rafik al-Hariri, as Syria had to withdraw its forces from Lebanon in 2005. Lebanon has always been a sphere of influence, granting the Syrian regime a strategic depth vis-à-vis Israel. Losing such depth, especially considering the above regional developments, only increased Syria's physical insecurity vis-à-vis Israel. Therefore, holding on to its strategic relationship with Hezbollah became a necessity. Remaining in the Syria–Iran–Hezbollah axis became Damascus' only option. In other words, Syria had no choice but to 'defy the hegemon' (Hinnebusch 2005a).

In an attempt to break Syria's international isolation and deprive Israel from its regional ally, Bashar al-Assad took a pragmatic step to establish a close alignment with Turkey, especially after the rise to power of the Justice and Development Party (AKP). Since the formation of both modern states of Turkey and Syria, territorial, political, economic and ideological grievances have contributed to a long uneasy relationship between these two antagonistic neighbours. Turkey has long considered Syria an unsettling enemy that supported Ankara's enemy, the Kurdish Worker's Party (commonly known by its Kurdish acronym PKK), by providing them training camps in Lebanon and then in Syria to execute attacks against Turkey (Larrabee and Lesser 2003, 145–7; Phillips 2011, 35). In 1995, some reports further suggested that there was a tacit pact between Syria and Greece to encircle Turkey (Mufti 1998, 35). Consequently, deterring Syria became a mutual interest for both Turkey and Israel. In 1996, both countries signed the most comprehensive strategic agreement, that is, the Military Cooperation and Training agreement. The agreement covered intelligence sharing, surveillance, joint training, naval strategies, and weapon sales. This agreement was later expanded to include a Free Trade Pact, which led to the increase of bilateral trades between partners from US$54 million in 1987 to US$1 billion in 1999 (Stern and Ross 2013, 117). Throughout the 1990s, the Turkish–Israeli alliance has grown out of similar concerns regarding Syria and the aim was to restrain Syria from taking hostile actions against both allies. The hostility between Syria and Turkey led to an open crisis in 1998. Turkish officials openly declared that Syria was waging an 'undeclared war' against Turkey and, hence, Turkish officials threatened a strike in Syria, and Turkish military reinforcements were deployed on the borders with Syria. The crisis ended in October 1998 with the Adana agreement, according to which Syria was forced to end its support for the PKK and expel the PKK leader Abdullah Ocalan from Damascus (Larrabee and Lesser 2003, 145). Although this agreement did not lead to cooperation between Turkey and Syria, it put certain conditions and prevented the escalation of the conflict.

At the beginning of the twenty-first century, Turkish–Syrian relations have witnessed a turn with domestic changes in both countries. In Turkey, the rise of the Justice and Development Party (AKP) led by Recep Tayyib Erdogan's rise to power in 2002 had direct ramifications for Turkey's foreign relations. The AKP government formulated a regional policy based on 'zero problems with neighbours'.[26] According to this policy, Turkey would replace defensive policies with cooperation and economic engagement with neighbours. Consequently,

---

[26] For an overview of this policy, see Aras (2008).

Turkey's perception of Syria changed from an enemy to a business partner.[27] This development in Turkey coincided with Bashar al-Assad's rise to power in Syria and his attempt to break Syria's regional and international isolation. In 2004, Bashar al-Assad visited Ankara on the first presidential trip to Turkey since Syria's independence in 1946 (Stern and Ross 2013, 118). Bashar al-Assad stated in 2005 that 'Turkey became one of the friendliest countries toward Syria in the region, one which pursues not only good relations at a bilateral level but also cooperates with Syria on a number of regional issues' (Aras 2008, 4). Furthermore, al-Assad appeared to be willing to make substantial sacrifices to cultivate a new friendship with Turkey, such as dropping long-standing Syrian claims to the Turkish province of Hatay and accepting Turkish sovereignty in 2004 (Perthes 2004, 47; Phillips 2011, 36).

Despite this shift in Turkish–Syrian relations, this rapprochement did not alleviate Syria's international and regional isolation. First, the military cooperation between Syria and Turkey remained symbolic at best as many scholars concluded. Turkey seemed reluctant to risk its relationship with the United States by forging a strong military cooperation with al-Assad (Phillips 2011, 38). Second, the rapprochement did not mean that Turkish leaders stopped considering Syria a dangerous neighbour. Turkish leaders remained wary of Syria's secret military programmes focusing on chemical and missiles development (Larrabee and Lesser 2003, 146). Henceforth, the AKP was not considering untying the strategic cooperation with Israel. Under the AKP government, Turkey signed several trade agreements with Israel. In 2004, bilateral trade hit a record of US$2 billion compared to US$200 million in 1993 (Inbar 2005, 591). Military cooperation also flourished between Israel and Turkey, through the transfer of military technology, the sale of Israeli surveillance equipment to Turkey, and the conduct of joint military exercises (Inbar 2005, 592; Stern and Ross 2013, 119). In 2005, Prime Minister Recep Tayyib Erdogan visited Israel (Myre 2005), and Israeli Prime Minister Ehud Olmert reciprocated the visit in 2007 and again in 2008 (Uzer 2013, 100). The relationship between Turkey and Israel remained resilient until

---

[27] For an elaborate account of the shift in Turkish foreign policy towards Syria and Iran, see Aras and Polat (2008).

the Israeli offensive on Hamas during the Operation Cast Lead on the Gaza Strip in 2009. The relationship deteriorated significantly only in 2010 (Uzer 2013).

In this context, the alliance with Hezbollah became indispensable for the Syrian regime. On the one hand, Hezbollah and the Syrian regime converged in their struggle against Israel. On the other hand, reinvigorating the alliance enabled Damascus to escape its regional isolation. According to a high-ranking member of the Ba'ath Party, 'after Syria left Lebanon, the West thought the regime was dead, and so Damascus used its support to Hamas and Hezbollah to prove that it was alive' (quoted in Perthes 2006, 39). Therefore, Damascus understood any attempt to defeat Hezbollah militarily or politically to be an effort to emasculate and isolate Syria. During the 2006 war, Damascus considered Riyadh's animosity towards Hezbollah and its refusal to offer overflight rights to Iranian supply planes as part of a strategy of encircling the Syrian regime (Salloukh 2009, 171).

The Regime Identity: Widening Pan-Arabism

Although the physical insecurity of the Syrian regime shaped the regime's threat perception and its choice of allies, this choice did not affect the stability of its identity or, in other words, its ontological security. Syria's support for Hezbollah during the 2006 war conformed to its previous self–other distinction. Yet, the 2006 Lebanon War showed that the Syrian regime became more and more dependent on Hezbollah and the axis of refusal for survival. Henceforth, such security dynamics reflected on the identity narrative as Syrian leaders expanded the pan-Arab dimension in the regime identity narrative to accommodate Islamic aspects to the narrative, which enabled the regime to capitalise on Hezbollah's gains to enhance its legitimacy at domestic and regional levels in the contexts of increasingly Islamised Arab societies. Whereas the Syrian regime faced limited policy options in achieving physical security, fluidity and flexibility in Syria's regime identity narrative led to its reframing and accommodation to Syria's physical needs. Syria's regime identity developed by mixing pan-Arab, Syrian nationalist and Islamic elements.

The alliance between Syria and Hezbollah has often been attributed to the Shiite nature of the Alawite ruling elite in Syria (cf. Talhamy 2009). Describing the Syrian regime as a minority-based regime by referring to the Alawi minority is simplistic.[28] As stated by Ismail (2009, 14–15), the case of the Syrian regime is described as 'the sectarianism of the authority' rather than 'the authority of the sect'. In other words, the Alawi elite does not rule, but the authority consecrates the Alawi sect and relies on alliances with other sects when their interests coincide. Instead, the regime identity narrative is based on a nuanced pan-Arabism, where the struggle against Israel constitutes the source of distinctiveness. This pan-Arab narrative coincided with Hezbollah's struggle against Israel. Despite this apparent convergence in their ideas,[29] Hezbollah's identification as an ally has presented a potential for inconsistency within the Syrian identity narrative. The Syrian regime has been claiming a secular identity oppressing Islamist movements at home, while Hezbollah is an Islamist movement with an active pan-Islamic call. Syria's strategic need for this partnership led Damascus to reframe its identity by embracing Islamic and anti-imperialist dimensions from Hezbollah's worldview. Syria's regime identity illustrated exceptional flexibility in allowing a mix of various elements from pan-Arabism, Syrian nationalism and Islamism. Such flexibility allowed the Syrian regime to focus on its physical survival, while accommodating its identity narrative accordingly through mixing elements of pan-Arabism, Syrian nationalism and Islamism.

The Iran–Iraq War, the Egyptian–Israeli peace treaty, and the rise of the 'me-first'[30] policies across Arab states led to the growth of a reconsidered 'Syrian identity'. Instead of rejecting pan-Arabism, the regime maintained its commitment to this ideology but reframed its meaning to suit Syria's physical security needs. Since then, Syria's definition of Arabism has been based not on the 'Arab' component but one that developed around a 'resistance identity' that is focused on the struggle against with Israel. A slow emergence of Syrian nationalism was consolidated throughout the 1990s. Driven by a strategic and economic quest for regional reintegration, the Syrian regime decided to

---

[28] This argument is strongly present in Pipes (1990), Van Dam (1996) and Ma'oz (1988).

[29] Some scholars argue that 'ideology' might be a better lens than 'identity' to explain the convergence among Hezbollah, Syria and Iran (Haas 2012; Haugbolle 2016; Rubin 2014; Stein 2017).

[30] These policies reflected the endeavour of Arab states to consolidate their national identities and to drift away from pan-identities. For instance, Egyptian leaders point to an 'Egypt-first' policy, according to which the interests of the state should come first, then those of the Arab nation.

join the US-coalition to liberate Kuwait in 1991. This decision further solidified a renovated Syrian nationalism. During the Syrian–Israeli negotiations throughout the 1990s, Hafiz al-Assad often explained his participation in the peace process as based on Syria's interests (Hinnebusch 1996; Seale 1992). On 16 January 1994, Hafiz al-Assad declared:

Syria seeks a just and comprehensive peace with Israel as a strategic choice that secures Arabs right; ends the Israeli occupation; and enables the people of the region to live in peace, security, and dignity. In honour we fought; in honour we negotiate; and in honour we shall make peace ... we want the peace of the brave, a genuine peace which can survive and last, a peace which secures the interests of each side. (Rabil 2006, 105)

When he commenced his rule in 2000, Bashar intended to follow his father's legacy in mixing elements of pan-Arabism and Syrian nationalism. Bashar initially pursued pragmatic regional policies towards Arab states, Turkey and the United States. More importantly, Bashar expressed his adherence to pan-Arabism defined in Syrian terms (Ma'oz 2007a, 11). Throughout the 1980s and 1990s, Syria's physical security needs led Hafiz al-Assad to pursue the course of peace and redefined the notion of pan-Arabism. During the 2006 war, this identity narrative fit well with Syria's physical security needs and its alliance with Hezbollah in balancing Israel.

Under these circumstances, the regime identity narrative appealed to a pan-Arab identity, according to which the main line of self–other distinctiveness evolved around the struggle against Israel. Bashar appealed to audiences beyond Syria and expressed his loyalty to the Arab nation and the resistance. His speeches, especially to regional audiences, depicted Syria as a stronghold of Arabism or as 'the beating heart of Arabism'.[31] On 21 January 2006, in an interview with *al-Hayat*, Bashar publicly declared that he considers 'Syria the heart of the Arab world', and that his main goal was to 'reinvigorate Arab unity' (quoted in Kandil 2008, 430). He also stated the following:

Many have tried in the past to destroy the Arab national perception by attempting to position it in confrontation with feelings of 'local patriotism', which ostensibly are contaminated by separatism. Some tried to position

[31] Cf. Bashar al-Assad's Speech at the Arab Parties General Conference (al-Assad 2006c).

Arabism in confrontation with Islam ... Others even tried to turn Arabism into the equivalent of backwardness and isolationism ... But none of this, of course, is correct. (Quoted in Zisser 2006)

Bashar went further to widen the definition of pan-Arabism beyond Syria's interests. Whereas Hafiz al-Assad limited the idea of 'a comprehensive peace' to Syrian interests, which ruled out the Lebanese and the Palestinians, Bashar declared that any agreement would not constitute a comprehensive peace plan without 'a balanced Lebanese, Palestinian, and Syrian axis'. He noted that 'signing an accord with Syria would not be enough to solve the problem and attain the purpose of coordinating other policies' (quoted in Ziadeh 2011, 85). From this perspective, Bashar highlighted not only the importance of achieving a comprehensive peace but also the necessity of establishing an agreement with all Arab states to resist the 'Zionist project'. He harshly criticised the so-called moderate Arab regimes – Egypt, Jordan and Saudi Arabia – for backing the Saudi-sponsored Arab peace initiative (2002). He claimed that Arabs should reconsider their policy of 'peace as a strategic option' vis-à-vis Israel and cut their diplomatic relations with Israel (Ma'oz 2007a, 12).

In this context, the Syrian regime's identity converged with the discourse of resistance promoted by Hezbollah. On 15 August 2006, Bashar gave a significant speech to the Syrian Journalists Union, where he declared that Hezbollah's resistance to Israel followed the tenets of Arabism. He claimed that 'resistance and peace' are not contradictory or mutually exclusive and 'constitute one pillar rather than two pillars, and who supports part of it has to support the other part'. The innovation in Bashar's pan-Arab rhetoric lay in condemning the past failure of Arabism. He argued that Arab weakness and failure is the main reason for Israeli supremacy: 'The only thing Israel possesses is the destructive force at the military level and some other factors at the international level, but at the same time it possesses a very big force; namely the weakness of the Arabs, both morally and physically' (al-Assad 2006b). He also conceded that Arabs talked much and hardly achieved anything in their history. For that matter, al-Assad considered Hezbollah to be a model of a regional Arab resistance against Israel (Wikas 2006).

This pan-Arab narrative, however, belied an inherent contradiction with Hezbollah's identity. This contradiction could potentially endanger the stability of the regime identity narrative and the regime's legitimacy at the domestic level. Syria's pan-Arabism was secular in nature. In addition, the regime oppressed Islamist movements domestically and criticised their identity. With the rise of Hezbollah's importance in Syria's physical survival, Bashar al-Assad included an Islamic aspect in the regime identity narrative. Bashar further widened Syria's identity narrative by mixing pan-Arabism with elements of Syrian nationalism and Islamism.

First, Syrian nationalism became more pronounced alongside pan-Arabism in Bashar's speeches. On several occasions, he speaks of 'We in Syria'. In his inaugural addresses in 2000, Bashar mentions 'Arab' seventeen times and 'Syria' ten times. In 2007, he mentions 'Arab' twenty times and 'Syria' forty-nine times. Looking at the following excerpt from Bashar al-Assad's speech given at the Fourth General Conference on the Journalists Union in Damascus on 15 August 2006, pan-Arab and Syrian elements are balanced.

I would like to say to the Syrian Arab people that the word 'proud' is not enough at all to express what a human being feels towards the greatness of your support to our Lebanese brothers ... But, the great people of Syria always surprise the adversary by what is not expected ... you were the beating heart of Arabism in every sense of the word regarding the heat that will rise and the meaning which will be more powerful when we liberate the Golan by our hands, will and determination. The destiny of Syria is to be proud of Arabism and to defend and maintain it because it is the only base for a bright and honourable future we build for our children. We have to implant in our hearts and minds that there is no place in this world but for the strong. Strength starts by the power of mind, will and faith and this is the base of resistance and the only way to achieve victory. (al-Assad 2006b)

Bashar's discourse is both pan-Arab and Syrian nationalist. He emphasised the Arab element in Syria's identity by describing Syrians as 'the beating heart of Arabism' and as 'the Syrian Arab people'. Meanwhile, he speaks of 'the destiny of Syria' and 'the future we build for our children' (Phillips 2012, 60–1).

Second, the regime identity started adding an Islamic element alongside pan-Arab and Syrian nationalist discourses. The regime started adding Islamic trimmings to its discourse. In 2003, the Syrian government allowed soldiers to pray on military bases and let women wear headscarves in school, which had been forbidden before. The regime started promoting a melange of pan-Arabism and pan-Islamism (Rubin 2007, 237–9). In 2005, especially after the withdrawal of Syria from Lebanon under international pressure, Bashar al-Assad started including some Islamic rhetoric in his speeches. He started using slogans like 'God protects Syria', which was particularly unusual for a very secular regime (Phillips 2012, 59). Billboards displaying the picture of Bashar al-Assad and a map of Syria with the colours of the national flag and the slogan 'God protects you, oh Syria' [*Allah yahmiki ya Suriya*] were spread across the country (Pinto 2011, 191). The creation of this language showed a fusion of Islamic reference with Arab and Syrian nationalism that was embraced by the society and was shared by different groups as a discursive framework for the Ba'ath regime as it faced regional and international isolation after the 2003 Iraq War. Furthermore, Bashar al-Assad was portrayed in the media, the billboards and posters as a pious Muslim (Pinto 2011, 192).

Such inclusion of Islamic reference in the Syrian identity discourse was often received as a superficial sign and that the regime in Syria remained secular throughout (Phillips 2012, 59). Despite the minimal presence of some Islamic symbols emerging under Hafiz al-Assad, the use of religious symbols and vocabulary by the Syrian state took another dimension under Bashar. This change shows the strength of Islam as a cultural idiom and its utility in encouraging nationalistic support, especially when Syria's physical survival is at stake at the regional or international level. In other words, Bashar al-Assad deferred to the cultural power of Islam to project the identity of resistance and gather domestic and regional support around the policies that guarantee Syria's physical survival. As Syria became increasingly dependent on the axis of refusal to guarantee its physical security, the regime included Islamic references in its identity narrative.

This strategy of mixing Islamic and Arab references in a nationalist identity became more pronounced during the 2006 Lebanon War. During the 2006 Lebanon War, Bashar embraced Nasrallah's worldview in his opposition against the United States, describing it as a struggle against the 'oppressor' (El-Hokayem 2007, 43). An example can be found in the speech delivered to the conference of Arab lawyers in Damascus on 21 January 2006.

[the US policy] is meant to target Syria and Lebanon as part of an integrated project to undermine the region's identity and reshape it under different names that finally meet Israel's ambitions to dominate the region and its resources ... But what is targeted are [not only Syria and Lebanon, but all] *the Arabs and even the Islamic nation* ... What is happening now [with Syria and Lebanon] is part of a big conspiracy. (al-Assad 2006a)

During the 2006 Lebanon War, Bashar adopted the same rhetoric. He described the Israeli aggression as 'Israeli in tools, but ... American in decision shared by certain Western countries' (Al-Assad 2006b). In short, Syria's pan-Arab narrative was broadened to include non-Arabs and Islamists dimensions alongside Syrian nationalist references to accommodate Syria's physical security needs, which became increasingly dependent on the axis of refusal.

Conclusion

This chapter examined Saudi and Syrian threat perceptions during the 2006 Lebanon War and their divergent reactions towards Hezbollah's fierce confrontation with Israel. The Saudi case reflected a situation of ontological insecurity and physical security. Despite Iranian and Syrian support, Hezbollah – a non-state actor that does not share any borders with the Kingdom and is militarily focused on its war against Israel – cannot pose a danger to the Kingdom's physical security. Instead, it was Hezbollah's Islamic narrative that constituted a serious challenge to the regime identity narrative in Saudi Arabia. In order to restore this identity stability, the Kingdom demonised the Islamic credibility of Hezbollah, while reinforcing Saudi self–other distinction based on a sectarian narrative (i.e. Sunni versus Shiite). This self–other distinction was framed in negative terms.

Compared to its Saudi counterpart, the al-Assad regime was in a situation of ontological security and physical insecurity. Whereas Hezbollah and Israel did not endanger Syria's identity stability, its physical security was endangered, especially during the years preceding the 2006 Lebanon War. This chapter explored the geopolitical imperatives that impelled al-Assad regime to support Hezbollah unconditionally. Alongside an increasing military imbalance in favour of Israel, Syria suffered severe regional and international isolation, which was aggravated by US policies towards Syria following the 2003 invasion of Iraq. Despite the rapprochement between Turkey and Syria in 2004, the Turkish–Israeli strategic alliance remained robust. In a regional environment dominated by the United States and its allies encircling

Syria, al-Assad's regime perceived significant threats to its physical survival.

Under these circumstances, and despite the longevity of the Syria–Hezbollah axis since the 1980s, Hezbollah became indispensable to Syria's survival. The exigencies of physical survival led to some changes in the identity narrative of the regime. Although the Ba'ath regime is a secular pan-Arab regime oppressing Islamist movements at home, which were always portrayed as 'others', Syria's self–other distinction underwent an accommodation to integrate Hezbollah's narrative and capitalise on its victory in the region. Even though the alliance between Hezbollah and the Ba'ath regime lasted for decades, it has gained a new dimension in 2006 as Hezbollah emerged as a regional champion in the Arab world. To capitalise on Hezbollah's regional gains, al-Assad regime reframed the regime identity narrative from Syrian pan-Arabism to a wider pan-Arabism that includes any actor involved in confrontation with Israel, whether it be Islamist or secular. Furthermore, al-Assad regime started including elements of pan-Islamism in a Syrian nationalist identity framework. These changes were also congruent with the Islamic revival and the increase in piety at the domestic level in Syria.

The divergence in both cases is conditioned by the nature of Saudi and Syrian identities as well as the policy options offered by the relative power distribution. Once again, Hezbollah has exposed the inability of Saudi elites to reinvent their identity narrative beyond the Islamic component. This lack of fluidity in their identity narrative was coupled with a less acute structure of the relative power distribution. On the other end of the spectrum, Syrian identity was fluid, which enabled the elite to reinvent their pan-Arabism to be inclusive of an Islamic dimension. Nevertheless, the relative power distribution offered the Syrian regime very limited options in ensuring its physical survival.

One of the most important implications of the cases examined earlier for the theoretical framework of this study is that identity framing and reframing are important mechanisms to restore ontological security in both the Syrian and Saudi cases. Saudi Arabia had a stake in maintaining a sectarian discourse to differentiate itself from Hezbollah and its ally, Iran. Syria, on the other hand, broadened its pan-Arab framing to include Islamist movements to avoid inconsistencies.

5 | The 2009 Gaza War

Hamas, Hezbollah, the Muslim Brotherhood, and Tehran have decided to put the Palestinian cause and its martyrs into Iran's hands. However, everyone is forgetting one important point – namely, that we will not hand over our people's capabilities to lunatics who hide out in Syria and who fire not a single bullet at Israel ... there is a plan to set the entire region ablaze, and to kill as many Palestinian and Lebanese martyrs as possible, in order to expose the helplessness of Egypt, Saudi Arabia, and the [entire] moderate Arab axis.

Mohamed Ali Ibrahim, *Al-Gumhouriyya* (Egypt), 29 December 2009

This chapter examines the divergent Saudi and Syria threat perceptions during the 2009 Gaza War. On 27 December 2008, Israel launched a military operation called the 'Cast Lead' in Gaza against the Palestinian militant group, Hamas – also known as the Islamic Resistance Movement (*Harakat al-Muqāwmah al-Islāmiyya*). Although the Palestinian–Israeli conflict has its own internal dynamic, Arab reactions reflected other dynamics that yield empirical and theoretical insights. Saudi Arabia, traditionally a supporter of the Palestinian cause and the main funder of Hamas since 1987 until 2007,[1] surprisingly condemned the resistance and blamed it for the suffering of the Palestinian people. While Syria supported Hamas – that is, a Sunni Islamist movement with Muslim Brotherhood origins – the al-Assad regime simultaneously continued oppressing a group with a similar ideology at home. This chapter examines the puzzle of why Saudi Arabia perceived Hamas as threatening, while Syria considered it to be an asset in its struggle against Israel's military supremacy in the region.

This chapter addresses these questions by looking at the interplay between the physical and ontological security spheres, which led to two

---

[1] For details on the development between the relations between Saudi Arabia and Hamas, see Al-Jazeerah (2015) and Stratfor (2015).

outcomes. Whereas Saudi Arabia demonstrates a case of ontological insecurity and physical security, Syria is a case of ontological security and physical insecurity. Hamas challenged the Saudi regime's Islamic identity. At the same time, while struggling for survival in a hostile regional and international environment, Syria found in Hamas an opportunity to advance its regional leverage. Although Syria's alliance with Hamas could have created an internal contradiction in the regime's identity, the al-Assad regime pre-empted this problem by widening its pan-Arab discourse to include some Islamic elements in such a way that Syria's secular pan-Arabism does not contradict the Islamic ideology of Hamas.

As the previous two empirical case studies showed, identity and material power intersected in the process of threat perception. Saudi and Syrian threat perceptions during the Gaza War are a least-likely case study, or a crucial case, that presents a harder test for the theoretical argument. The previous two cases have established that sectarian identities *per se* were not the driving force behind threat perception. Instead sectarian identities served as a mechanism to reinforce ontological security and distinctiveness, especially in the case of Saudi Arabia. The previous chapters also showed that the widely spread narratives about the Shiite nature of the Syria–Iran–Hezbollah axis are mistaken. An examination of threat perception towards Hamas provides further evidence confirming the previous findings. The Hamas case in the context of the 2009 Gaza War presents a least-likely case study for the theoretical argument of this book.

As opposed to the Islamic Republic in Iran and Hezbollah, Hamas is a political Islam movement that finds its origins in the Muslim Brotherhood, which belongs to a Sunni school of thought. Despite the identity convergence between Hamas and Saudi Arabia, the Kingdom perceived Hamas as a threat. Also, the Ba'ath regime, which is often depicted as Alawite in nature and oppressing the Brotherhood at the domestic level, has perceived Hamas as an ally. The Gaza War provides an uncontroversial evidence that threat perception is not driven by sectarian identities *per se*, and, thus argues that ontological security approach provides a fresh view of the sectarianism in international relations of the Middle East, according to which leaders in the Middle East have a stake in maintaining and promoting sectarian narratives. Furthermore, the case challenges regime security approaches in the study of international relations. Hamas emerged as a strategic ally to the al-Assad regime despite oppressing an offshoot of the same group at the domestic level. From a regime security approach, al-Assad regime should have feared the rise of Hamas to power in Gaza as it can be a source of inspiration and empowerment to the opposition movement in Syria. From a similar perspective, the Saudi regime would have been expected to support Hamas considering the centrality of the Palestinian question in its identity narrative and domestic legitimacy. Yet, both Saudi Arabia and Syria deviated from the expectations made by regime security approaches and essentialist approaches to sectarianism in the international relations. Instead, an approach that takes into account the interplay between ideational and material forces in threat perception allows a comprehensive explanation of this crucial case study.

Along these lines, this chapter aims to contribute to the wider literature on the study of sectarianism as a significant texture undergirding Middle East international relations. Sectarian identities at the regional level have gradually spurred growing scholarly interest, especially since the outbreak of the Islamic Revolution in Iran. Broadly, threat perception and alliance decisions have been situated within the debates between primordialists (essentialists) and rationalists. The primordialist approach belongs to this major trend in IR Theory that puts emphasis on culture and identity as determinants of conflict and cooperation among actors. Primordialists have analysed 'Sunni' and 'Shiite' identities as the core conflict in the region since the seventh century, and these continue to shape its political dynamics (Abdo 2013; Nasr 2006). Based on Huntington's (1993) famous argument about the 'clash of civilisations', according to which conflicts would erupt around cultural divides, some scholars argued that the 'clash' is within Islam (Sadiki 2014). This approach clearly fails to explain threat perceptions during the Gaza War.

Rationalists have, however, adopted an instrumentalist top-down approach, which derives from neorealism. As the structure is constituted of relative power distribution, identities and norms are instruments manipulated to legitimise actors' material interests (Kedourie 1992; Walt 1987). From this perspective, the Sunni–Shiite divide in the region emerged as a prop of power and material interests in the region (Berti and Paris 2014; Gause 2007, 2014b; Lynch 2013; Wehrey 2013; Wehrey et al. 2009; Zubaida 2014). Instrumentalist approaches clearly answer more questions than primordial ones do. Nevertheless, this top-down approach leaves many questions unanswered: If leaders are motivated by material interest, how and under which conditions they can manipulate identities as they wish. Moreover, by reducing identities to superstructures, rationalists cannot unravel why Saudi Arabia feared a non-state actor that is situated far from its borders and with limited military capabilities.

In this context, this chapter provides an understanding of sectarianism that goes beyond primordial and instrumental approaches to identities. It argues that ontological security provides a third way to examine the role of sectarian identities in the processes of threat perception. This chapter argues that states have a stake in maintaining and reinforcing sectarian differences in order to achieve distinctiveness and uniqueness in their identity narrative.

The chapter proceeds as follows. I, first, present the context in which the 2009 Gaza War occurred and the subsequent regional reactions. I then explore Saudi enmity towards Hamas. The relative power distribution demonstrates that the war did not endanger the physical security of the Saudi Kingdom. Instead, Hamas' Islamic Sunni identity put the ontological security of the Kingdom at risk, as it endangered the distinctiveness and consistency of the Saudi identity narrative. Throughout the 1980s and 1990s, the Saudi regime has preserved its distinctiveness by maintaining a sectarian narrative based on Sunni–Shiite divisions. The emergence of a Sunni Islamist movement challenged the distinctiveness of this narrative. By presenting a resistance strategy based on an alternative Sunni Islamic narrative in the region, Hamas challenged the Saudi regional role and the Kingdom's related Sunni Islamic identity. Third, I explore Syria's threat perception. I argue that the relative power distribution and the unfavourable regional and international environment endangered the physical security of the Ba'ath regime. In this context, Hamas emerged as a strategic ally of Syria in its struggle against Israel. I then examine how the Syrian regime revived a pan-Arab narrative inclusive of Islamic elements to accommodate its alliance with a Sunni Islamist movement and avoid a situation of ontological dissonance.

The 2009 Gaza War and Regional Reactions

On 27 December 2008, Israel began a series of air attacks on Gaza, which was later expanded into a ground offence. This war underscored the regional divisions that crystallised during the 2006 Lebanon War between two camps: the so-called moderate regimes – Egypt, Saudi Arabia and Jordan – and the resistance – Iran, Syria, Hezbollah and Hamas. Syrian and Saudi perceptions towards Hezbollah in 2006 were replicated in regards to Hamas in 2009.

During the extraordinary Arab summit in Doha on 16 January 2009, Bashar al-Assad declared: 'we should show our clear support for the Palestinian resistance. I suggest that this summit official calls the Zionist entity a terrorist entity' (BBC 2009). As opposed to this clear and explicit support for the resistance movement, the Saudi Kingdom criticised Hamas for abandoning the cease-fire with Israel and blamed it for the war casualties in Gaza. As Prince Saud bin Faisal, Saudi Arabia's foreign minister, declared: 'This terrible massacre [from the Gaza war] would not have happened if the Palestinian people were united behind one leadership, speaking in once voice' (Black 2009a). Hosni Mubarak, the Egyptian president, echoed the same sentiment: 'You all know that efforts Egypt had undertaken to extend the cease-fire and our warnings that a refusal by factions to extend it was an open invitation to Israeli aggression' (Reuters 2009).

Saudi newspaper *al-Sharq al-Awsat* compared Hamas' reckless instigation to Hezbollah's move that had led to the 2006 Lebanon War. Similarly, Egypt explicitly blamed Hamas for abandoning the cease-fire with Israel. As Foreign Minister Ahmed Abulgheit stated, 'Hamas served Israel the opportunity on a golden platter to hit Gaza' (Erlanger 2009b). Egypt and Saudi Arabia portrayed Hamas as a mere pawn of non-Arab Iran and, hence, accused it of serving Iranian instead of Arab interests. Consequently, critics of Saudi and Egyptian foreign policies accused the so-called moderate regimes of collusion with Israel, the Arab and Islamic world's bitter enemy.

Although Arab reactions to the 2009 Gaza War underscored the intra-Arab divisions that emerged during the 2006 Lebanon War, these events pose further questions. In contrast to the Shiite religious identity of Hezbollah, Hamas is a Sunni movement recognised as an offshoot of the Muslim Brotherhood ideology, combining a traditional pan-Islamist ideology with Palestinian nationalism. Situated at the heart of the Arab–Israeli conflict and with a Sunni background, Hamas should have attracted the support of the Saudi Kingdom, a monarchy with a Sunni pan-Islamic ideology. Paradoxically, the Al Saud, a ruling elite claiming the leadership of the Islamic world and of the support for the Palestinian cause, condemned the resistance. The Syrian regime – a secular regime oppressing the Muslim Brotherhood at home – explicitly sided with Hamas and supported it verbally and financially.

Saudi Arabia and the Struggle for Consistency

The Palestinian question has traditionally been the subject of ideational and religious sensitivities in Saudi foreign policy. Saudi Arabia, as the custodian of the two most important holy cities of Islam, Mecca and Medina, sees itself as having a divine mission to protect the holy sites of Islam. From this perspective, Palestine, especially Jerusalem, is particularly important to Saudi Arabia's self-conception, historically pledging to defend and support the Palestinian cause. The following extract is a speech addressed to those making *Hajj* (pilgrimage) to Mecca in 1997, by King Fahd bin Abdul Aziz and Crown Prince Abdullah bin Abdul Aziz:

The Kingdom of Saudi Arabia has continued to hold the same position of giving support to a just and comprehensive peace which will bring an end to oppression and which will return occupied Arab lands to their own people in Palestine, Syria and Lebanon. In relation to Jerusalem and the construction of Israeli settlements there, the stand of the Kingdom of Saudi Arabia is one which is completely clear and to which it has given expression many times. The Kingdom deplores and condemns all actions in Jerusalem, which are in conflict with the nature of the city and with the legitimate rights of its Arab population therein. (Quoted in Khan 2004, 176)

Although the Kingdom has never been a frontline state in the Arab–Israeli conflict and has never had any troops involved in military operations against Israel, the Palestinian cause has remained at the centre of Saudi international and regional diplomacy.

Following the defeat of the Arab forces in the 1967 Six-Day War, the Al Saud became actively involved in continuing the struggle against Israel, henceforth serving as the primary financial supporter of the frontline states. From that moment, the Saudis financially and diplomatically supported the Palestinians, particularly their primary organisation, the Palestinian Liberation Organisation (PLO), and later Hamas during the 1990s. During the 1970s, the Kingdom provided the PLO with hundreds of millions of dollars, and an estimated US$1 billion in the 1980s (Bowen 2008, 124–5). With the Egyptian withdrawal from the conflict (1979) and the Jordanian–Israeli peace treaty (1994), Saudi Arabia opted for a regional role, through leading and facilitating mediation in Lebanon and the Palestinian–Israeli peace process. From the early 1990s onwards, the Kingdom provided financial support to the Palestinians to attend peace talks and participated actively in some regional talks that led to Madrid Peace Conference 1991 and Oslo Accords 1993 (Wilson and Graham 1994, 125). Throughout, the Saudis consistently portrayed themselves as supporters of the Palestinian resistance, an image they bolstered by funding secular leftist Palestinian groups as well as Islamist groups such as Hamas and the Islamic Jihad.

Saudi Arabia and Hamas have a long history of interaction. Since the first Intifada in 1987, the Saudi Kingdom has been one of Hamas' chief patrons. According to some estimates, the Kingdom provided 50 per cent of Hamas budget (Stratfor 2015). The Saudi regime has provided Hamas with financial support officially twice in 1988 and again in 1998. This support has intensified especially after the PLO's support to Saddam Hussein during the 1991 Iraqi invasion of Kuwait and allowed Hamas to open an office in Jeddah. In addition, the Kingdom allowed Hamas the opportunity to collect charitable funds from the region without restrictions (Al-Jazeerah 2015). In 2007, Riyadh played a role in negotiating a compromise and a coalition government between Fatah and Hamas. Until then, Saudi Arabia maintained financial support to Hamas. Following the collapse of the negotiations and Hamas took over the Gaza strip in June 2007, the relationship between the Saudi Kingdom and Hamas deteriorated, and the Saudi Kingdom started cutting funds. At the same time, Iran started increasing its support to Hamas through military assistance and helped Hamas in meeting its monthly budget requirements. In 2009, the Saudi Kingdom perceived Hamas as an eminent threat. Such perception constitutes a paradox considering pervious cooperative relations and convergence in Saudi and Hamas identities based on Sunni Islam.

To explain this paradox, I argue that Hamas, despite its alliance with Iran, did not pose any threat to the Kingdom's physical security. Instead, Hamas' Islamic ideology endangered the Kingdom's ontological security, as it questioned the Saudi claim of Sunni leadership and its associated position as a sponsor of the peace negotiations in the Arab–Israeli conflict. Following the Islamic Revolution, the Saudi Kingdom promoted a sectarian narrative to distinguish its identity from the revolutionary claim of pan-Islamism in Iran. Instead, the

Kingdom reduced its identity as the leader of Sunni Islam. Therefore, the rise of Hamas and its resistance identity based on Sunni Islam constituted a far greater threat to the ontological security of the Saudi Kingdom. This threat was even greater considering the fixity and the limited flexibility of the identity narrative in the Saudi regime. In what follows, I first examine the relative power distribution before and at the outbreak of the 2009 war. I argue that Iran's support for Hamas did not at the time make it a source of physical insecurity to the Kingdom. I, then, examine the ideational challenge Hamas posed to the Saudi regime's identity narrative.

Saudi Physical Security: Is Hamas a Threat?

Saudi perception of Hamas as a threat in 2009 has been often read as a realist strategy, in accordance with which the Kingdom was balancing Iran's expanding influence in the region. Considering Iran's support for Hamas and other Palestinian groups, this realist logic seems accurate at first glance. Upon further examination, however, the story appears to be more complex. Iran's support for Hamas did not necessarily mean any Iranian military presence and, hence, did not endanger the physical security of Arab states, the Kingdom including. Furthermore, this argument erroneously assumes that Hamas is not an independent actor. This section argues that Hamas' drift towards Iran did not contribute to any military imbalance in the region. Instead, the balance of power in the region remained in Israel's favour, and Iran's support of Hamas could not threaten the physical security of the Kingdom. Hamas' behaviour in the following year challenged the assumption that Hamas is a mere proxy. In the context of the Syria crisis in 2013, Hamas shifted its alliance and distanced itself from the al-Assad regime and Iran (Milton-Edwards 2013; Napolitano 2013).

The 2009 Gaza War broke out under conditions similar to those of the 2006 Lebanon War. The regional configuration that emerged following the 2003 US invasion Iraq was manifested in 2006 and again in 2009. The fall of Saddam Hussein's regime and the destruction of Iraq's military capabilities changed the regional power distribution. Israel's military supremacy became evident in the Arab–Israeli sphere, especially with the tenacity of the Egyptian–Israeli peace treaty since 1979 and the conclusion of the Jordanian–Israeli peace treaty in 1994. Moreover, by 'shattering' the Iraqi state, the United States eliminated

Iraq's power as a regional buffer vis-à-vis Iran, which in turn attempted to fill the vacuum and expand its own influence (Roy 2007). This meant that the traditional stable triangle of Iran, Iraq, and Saudi Arabia – in which the three powers balanced one another – collapsed and left room for a Saudi–Iranian confrontation (Fürtig 2007). Arab states became fragmented around two camps. On the one hand, the US-backed coalition consisting of Saudi Arabia, Egypt and Jordan supported the peaceful settlement of the Arab–Israeli conflict. Moreover, this camp identified Iran as the most substantial threat to the stability of the region. The second coalition included Iran, Syria, Hezbollah and Hamas. This camp, often called the 'resistance axis', considered the United States and Israel to be the ultimate sources of threat in the region. The fragmentation of the region around these two camps has often been termed as the 'New Arab Cold War'.

From this perspective, Hamas' threat to the so-called moderate axis was often exacerbated by Iran's support for the organisation. Hamas was accused of serving Iranian interests rather than Arab or Palestinian ones. It was also portrayed as a threat because it allowed Iran to expand its influence over the Palestinian question, thereby acting counter to the so-called Arab interest. The portrayal of Hamas as an Iranian pawn was abundant in the Arab media coverage, especially in Saudi media outlets. Hamas was accused of assisting Iran in taking over the Middle East (Carmon 2009). For example, Tarik al-Humayd, a journalist in the Saudi newspaper *al-Sharq al-Awsat*, questioned whether Iran's support for Hamas and Hezbollah and their designation as 'freedom fighters' or 'liberation movements' amounted to the 'hijacking [of] Arab causes to serve Iran's interests' (Chubin 2009, 170). In the Saudi daily *Al-Riyadh*, Saudi Columnist Ali Al-Mahmoud warned about Iran's 'octopus-like expansion'. In his view, 'Iran wants to control the region, not by spreading its ideology ... but by maintaining armed organisations [in Arab countries] it violates their loyalty to their homelands, replacing it with loyalty to Iran' (*Al-Riyadh*, 29 May 2008). In the Saudi daily *Al-Watan*, Saudi columnist Ali Sa'd Al-Moussa wrote that Arab countries were being subjected to 'Persian colonialism'. He added:

Iran has become a major and central player in Arab politics . . .. Today we are seeing new signs of Persian colonialism. This is a [new] more advanced colonial model: We are no longer talking of troops occupying [certain] regions or of flags [flying] over public buildings. The colonialism of the modern era is manifested by the submission of [various regional forces to Iran] ... Iran chose [regions] on the Arab map and attacked them without [even] pulling the trigger. Arabs are implementing its entire plan. (*Al-Watan*, 29 May 2008)

In light of this, it is not surprising that Saudi state-influenced newspapers presented the Israeli attack on Gaza as an attack on Iranian influence in the region.[2] Leading Saudi columnist Khalaf al-Harbi accused the Saudi state-led propaganda of marketing the idea that 'any support for the [Hamas] resistance is an incitement to terrorism' (Al-Harbi 2009).

Existing explanations of Saudi fear from Hamas, I argue, have conflated physical and ontological security spheres. Iran's support for Hamas did not in fact mean a change in the balance of power and did not transform Hamas into a material threat to the physical security of the so-called Arab moderate countries, Saudi Arabia included. By the time of the 2009 war, Iran's support for Hamas did not mean any military presence in Gaza. Instead, Iran's support for Hamas remained mostly ideological.

Since the Islamic Revolution, Iran has considered Israel to be its ultimate enemy in the region and – for religious reasons – the Palestinian issue has featured as a core component of Iranian foreign policy. The Iran–Hamas relationship developed during the 1990s and matured in the wake of Hamas' international isolation after 2006. The relationship started in 1992 when Israel expelled hundreds of Hamas' leaders to Lebanon, where they met with representatives of the Iranian Revolutionary Guard. Since this meeting, Iran has been funding and training Hamas. The relationship was consolidated during the Oslo Accords in 1993 and the following Israeli–Palestinian peace negotiations in 1996. Following its isolation in 2006, Hamas relied more extensively on the so-called axis of resistance for funding. In addition, the organisation was inspired by the successful model of Hezbollah in its war against Israel in 2006 (Frankel 2012).

Iran became Hamas' biggest donor. Estimates of Iranian financial assistance to the organisation have varied significantly between US\$30 and US\$250 million per year (Al-Mughrabi 2013; Haaertz 2006; Levitt 2008, 172–4). Nevertheless, this Iranian support for Hamas

---

[2] This was the case of Egyptian and Jordanian newspapers as well.

did not mean any Iranian military presence in Gaza that could threaten neighbouring Arab states. On the geopolitical level, whereas Iran was able to support Hezbollah logistically through sending military hardware via Syria, the same was not possible in the case of Hamas. As Head of Iran's Revolutionary Guards, General Mohamed Ali Jafari declared,

Gaza is under siege, so we cannot help them. The Fajr-5 missiles have not been shipped from Iran. Its technology has been transferred and (the missiles are) being produced quickly. (CBS News 2012)

In other words, military assistance consisted of the transfer of technical know-how necessary for manufacturing weapons (rockets and anti-tank missiles). This knowledge transfer also included military training for Hamas members (Szorm 2009). Throughout, even though Iran might have possessed the potential military capabilities to balance Arab states, it was unable to project these capabilities far beyond its borders, because Iran's economic capacity was not sufficient to support such expansionism (Chubin 2009).

More importantly, Hamas cannot be considered as a mere Iranian proxy devoid of agency. Although Iran was its primary funder of Hamas since 2006, Tehran did not have any control over the Palestinian group. As Sadjadpour (2009) puts it, 'Iran supports Hamas, but Hamas is no Iranian puppet'. Hamas' agency became evident after the 2009 war when the organisation broke its alliance with Iran and turned to Egypt during the short-lived rule of the Muslim Brotherhood under President Mohamed Morsi (2012–13). In other words, the alliance between Iran and Hamas around the time of the 2009 Gaza conflict was built upon shared interests. On the Palestinian side, Hamas was encircled and isolated after winning the elections in 2006, as Arab states followed the United States in isolating Hamas and cutting funds. From this perspective, Iran filled a vacuum. On the Iranian side, the support for the Palestinian cause served the interests of Iranian foreign policy, as it enabled Iran to overcome its regional isolation and to enhance its leverage in the negotiations over its nuclear program (Chubin 2009).

Hamas' sense of agency was evident, as Hamas had the choice between the support of Sunni Arab states and Iran's support. According to Ahmed Yusuf, the adviser to Hamas Leader Ismail Haniyah, 'our relations with Iran have angered Saudi Arabia but sometimes we have no choice. We would prefer to have closer relations with Saudi Arabia and maybe that will come' (Urquhart 2007).[3] Hamas' leaders had two options: moderating their core principles in order to ensure the support of Arab states, or accepting Iranian support while maintaining a bellicose stance against Israel. As Egypt and Saudi Arabia followed the US boycott of Hamas, the organisation's leaders opted for the latter option. They took into consideration Iran's uncompromising position on Israel and turned to the Islamic Republic for financial support. In short, Hamas took advantage of the region's rivalries to enhance its own position (Kostiner and Mueller 2010). In other words, the relationship between Hamas and Iran is merely strategic, and the former will not act on behalf of the latter. Salah Bardawil, a member of Hamas' political bureau in Gaza, insisted that in case of war between Israel and Iran, 'Hamas will not be part of such war' (quoted in Sherwood 2012). The same position was seconded by Gaza leader Ismail Haniyeh: 'Hamas is a Palestinian movement that acts within the Palestinian arena and it carries out its political and field actions in a way that suits the interests of the Palestinian people' (Nakhoul and Stott 2012).

The subsequent Gaza wars of 2012 and 2014 decisively demonstrated Hamas' independence from Iran and Syria. Following the breakout of the Syria crisis, Hamas refused to follow Iran in supporting the al-Assad regime against the rebels. Iran considered Hamas' position to be a betrayal to the axis of resistance and fiercely scaled back its support and cut financial aid to the Palestinian group (Al-Mughrabi 2011). Under these circumstances, and with the rise of the Muslim Brotherhood to power in Egypt in 2012, Hamas shifted its alliance back to Egypt (Qassir 2014). Hamas leaders also sought a rapprochement with Turkey and Qatar (Abu Amer 2013).[4] Still, despite Iran's waning support for Hamas in 2014, Saudi perception of Hamas as a threat persisted (Riedel 2014). Whereas the Kingdom refrained from condemning Israel's assault on Gaza that year, it openly blamed Hamas for the suffering of the Palestinian people; the Saudi royal elite was thereafter accused of colluding with Israel in destroying Hamas (Kirkpatrick 2014).

[3] See also the interview with Khalid Meshaal on ABC Channel (Willacy 2006).
[4] Nevertheless, this alliance shift was intermittent. With the fall of the Muslim Brotherhood in Egypt, Hamas sought to re-activate its relationship with Iran (Al-Mughrabi 2013).

The Kingdom has often justified its fear of Hezbollah by referring to a sectarian narrative, i.e., Sunni versus Shiite. Hamas is, however, a Sunni Islamist movement. Despite the seemingly sectarian convergence, the Kingdom has portrayed Hamas as a threat. The following section examines this paradox. I argue that Hamas' Islamic nature endangered the stability of the Kingdom's identity narrative and, hence, its ontological security.

Saudi Regime Identity: 'Othering' Hamas

The Palestinian question has been central to the Kingdom since the early stages of its formation (Kazziha 1985; Piscatori 1983). As King Fahd bin Abdul Aziz stated:

The cause of Palestine which the Kingdom of Saudi Arabia has always placed at the top of its priorities will always have that position for us because this issue is linked to positions of principle and to an encompassing vision which embraces the higher Arab interest and necessities of comprehensive Arab security.[5]

As already discussed in the previous chapters, the Palestinian question and Jerusalem are constitutive of the Islamic dimension in the Saudi identity narrative. According to Esposito (1998, 114), 'The liberation of Jerusalem and the creation of a Palestinian state became a major component of Saudi foreign policy and an Islamic issue to which [King] Faisal rallied worldwide Muslim support'. In other words, the Palestinian question has constituted a core element in Saudi self-conception at the regional and domestic levels (Khan 2004, 175–8).

As already discussed in the previous chapter, since the 1980s, the Saudi Kingdom has developed a vision for the conflict based on a comprehensive peace. The Custodian of the Two Holy Mosques King Fahd launched the first peace initiative in 1982, while he was still crown prince. In February 2002, following the Palestinian Intifada in the West Bank and Gaza (2000), Crown Prince Abdullah presented a second peace initiative, which was later endorsed by the Arab League and became known as the 'Arab Peace Initiative'.[6] The proposal was an explicit expression of the Saudi stance on the conflict and offered

---

[5] www.saudinf.com/main/x003.htm.
[6] For further details on this initiative, cf. Kostiner (2005).

Israel full normalisation of relations with its neighbours in return for full withdrawal to the 1967 borders; it did not, however, lead to real negotiations. In 2007, King Abdullah attempted to revive the 'Arab Peace Initiative' during the Riyadh Summit in order to boost a new round of negotiations between the Palestinians and Israel.

At the same time, the Saudi Islamic narrative enabled the Kingdom to play a crucial role in the inter-Palestinian mediation between Fatah and Hamas. As a result of the 2006 elections, Hamas won the majority of seats in the Palestinian National Council, with its leader Ismail Haniyah becoming the Palestinian prime minister. Hamas' growing power in relation to Fatah, together with the struggle over the new government, created acute tensions. In February 2007, King Abdullah invited both factions to Mecca to negotiate the terms of a 'unity government'. The Saudi King also promised US$750 million in aid to the unity government (Kostiner 2009). The mediation was a failure, as following the Mecca agreement, tensions between the two factions crystallised and led to a split in the government: Fatah ruled over the West Bank and Hamas ruled Gaza.

The Saudi vision favouring negotiations was a strategy developed to combine the Kingdom's physical security needs related to its partnership with the United States and its identity narrative inextricably related to the support of the Palestinian cause. By mediating between Palestinians and Israel, the Kingdom was able to actively portray itself as the guardian of the Palestinian cause. In the meantime, it conformed to the US narrative by playing the role of the maestro of a 'moderate' Arab coalition aiming to counterbalance 'radicalism' in the region. Moreover, by engaging in negotiating intra-Palestinian conflicts, the Saudis aimed to lure Hamas back into the Arab fold in order to deprive Iran of its influence in the Palestinian question. This strategy constituted a compromise for the Al Saud, balancing their interest in bringing Hamas back to the Arab camp and limiting the Iranian influence in Palestinian issues without controverting the Western boycott of Hamas. More importantly, this strategy allowed the Kingdom to maintain a consistent identity narrative.

As the Palestinian question is at the heart of Saudi identity, the Al Saud had to link their strategy with their identity narrative. The late senior Saudi Mufti Ibn Baz issued a *fatwa* stating that peace between Jews and Muslims was compatible with *shari'a*, citing the Prophet's example. Ibn Baz even issued another *fatwa* permitting Muslims to visit Al-Aqsa mosque as a way to facilitate peace with Israel (Chubin and Tripp 1996, 59). By tying its strategy in the Arab–Israeli conflict to its Islamic identity narrative, the Kingdom risked a loss of credibility in the face of alternative strategies. All the while relying on a Sunni Islamic identity narrative similar to that of the Saudis, Hamas presented an alternative vision of the conflict based on the concept of 'resistance'. Henceforth, Hamas vision endangered the stability of the Saudi regime identity, as inconsistencies between its claim of support for the Palestinian question and its opposition to Hamas' rejection of the peace process emerged.

From this perspective, Hamas presented a two-fold challenge to the Saudi regime identity. The Saudi elite already condemned Hezbollah's mode of struggle against Israel by relying on a sectarian discourse based on the Sunni–Shiite divide. Following this Saudi self–other distinction, one would expect the Kingdom to support Hamas. However, by presenting an alternative approach to the conflict based on armed resistance linked to a Sunni Islamic narrative, Hamas questioned the Saudi dedication to the Palestinian cause and, hence, to its related identity narrative. In short, Hamas' Islamic identity associated with the resistance endangered the Saudi exclusive identity narrative portraying the Kingdom as the champion leader of the Sunni world.

Hamas' regional policies and narratives came in stark contrast to the Saudi plea for a peaceful settlement. The Palestinian group has embraced as a fundamental tenet the belief that independence and freedom will be achieved only through armed struggle. According to Hamas, this is the only logic that Israel understands. From this point of view, peace with Israel is not an option for Hamas. As Hamas leader Khalid Meshaal stated, 'Our enemy only comes under pressure when they are under fire and as our rockets hit them they were forced to hold talks with us' (Bakr 2014). Although Hamas has consistently opposed peace negotiations with Israel, it has considered the *hudna* (cease-fire) to be a strategic option. Sheikh Ahmed Yassin launched this idea in the early 1990s. In his view, 'Islam permits a temporary truce for a limited period with the Jewish enemy if necessary' (quoted in Jensen 2008, 34). Despite Hamas' moderation throughout the 1990s and after it won the elections, the armed struggle against Israel was and remains at the heart of its ideology and raison d'être.

Hamas' ideology exposed the inconsistencies in the Saudi Kingdom and, hence, raised questions about the credentials of its Islamic identity narrative. In other words, the stability of the Saudi regime identity and its ontological security were shaken. This challenge did not only affect the external dimension of the Kingdom's identity narrative, it exposed this identity inconsistency to Saudi public opinion, garnering Hamas admiration among domestic Islamic groups within Saudi Arabia. As a consequence, the Arab public, including the Saudi one, came to resent the positions of the so-called moderate Arab regimes and to largely sympathise with the resistance. Massive demonstrations took place in Jordan, Egypt, Lebanon, as well as in the Gulf, showing support for Hamas and virulently criticising the positions of Arab regimes (Pollock 2009). In order to escape these inconsistencies in its identity narrative, the regime attempted to restore its ontological security through various mechanisms aiming at demonising and othering Hamas.

First, the Saudis blamed Hamas for calling the 2009 war upon itself by refusing the negotiations with Israel. Indeed, the Gaza War broke out, at the end of a six-months cease-fire (June 2008 through December 2008) between Hamas and Israel, as on-going negotiations between Israeli and Palestinians failed. In other words, the Saudis blamed Hamas for being the cause of the Palestinian suffering in Gaza that could have been avoided if the organisation had complied with the Saudi vision of conflict resolution. This Saudi narrative became even more explicit during the second and third Gaza Wars (2012 and 2014), where the Saudi King explicitly blamed Hamas. In 2014, in a stunning statement, King Abdullah called the Hamas–Israel war a 'collective massacre' caused by Hamas (Batrawy and Al-Shihri 2014).

Just as the Saudi mediation on the Palestinian–Israeli level failed to temper Hamas' stance towards Israel, the Kingdom's interference in the intra-Palestinian split also failed. A few months following the 2007 Mecca agreement, the situation evolved into a civil war that ended in Hamas' control of the Gaza strip with Fatah remaining in control of the West Bank. Accordingly, the Saudi Kingdom considered the Israeli war on Gaza in 2009 to be a direct result of Hamas' failure to unite with Fatah. As Saudi Foreign Minister Prince Saud bin Faisal declared, 'This terrible massacre [from the Gaza war] would not have happened if the Palestinian people were united behind one leadership, speaking in one voice' (Erlanger 2009a).

Moreover, to fend off domestic discontent, the Kingdom attempted to portray Hamas as other by questioning the organisation's religious credibility. For example, the Kingdom did not recognise Palestinian causalities as martyrs (*shahīd*), a position clearly reflected in the Saudi media, such as the TV channel *al-Arabiya* (Rubin 2014, 110). Second, Hamas was portrayed as an Iranian agent undermining the so-called Arab interest, defined in Saudi terms as the peace process with Israel. Finally, the regime relied on the 'ulama's religious discourse to delegitimise the protests supporting Hamas. Abdul Aziz Al Sheikh,[7] the grand mufti in the Kingdom, issued a *fatwa* forbidding protests in support of Gaza and describing these acts as *ghawghā'iyya* [demagogic]. Instead, the grand mufti stated that the best way of helping the Palestinians is to send aid and financial support (Al-Ifrig 2009). In addition, the Kingdom aimed at improving its regional credibility by offering financial support to the Palestinians. At the end of the war, the Al Saud offered to donate US$1 billion for rebuilding Gaza (Al-Faisal 2009). In short, despite their shared Sunni ideology, the Kingdom demonised Hamas and portrayed it as other. This similarity exposed Saudi identity inconsistencies and threatened the stability of its regime identity narrative. Moreover, the sectarian (Sunni–Shiite) discourse employed by the Kingdom to distinguish and distance itself from the 'axis of resistance' seemed losing credibility.

Syria: Reinforcing Pan-Arabism

Whereas the Saudi regime perceived Hamas as a threat despite their shared Sunni background, Syrian policies operated based on an entirely different logic. Under the secular Ba'ath regime, Syria fostered a strategy that combines the oppression of the Syrian Muslim Brotherhood at home and support for Hamas, a Palestinian offshoot of the Muslim Brotherhood in the Gaza strip. In an interview on Al-Jazeerah, senior Hamas Leader Mahmoud al-Zahar highlighted this paradox: 'Syria has very good relations with Hamas, but terrible relations with the Muslim Brotherhood group. More than 24,000 people [members of the Muslim Brotherhood] were killed in 1982 in Hama by the Syrian regime' (Al-Zahar 2009).

Although the Syrian regime perceives Islamist movements as its bitter enemy at home, this did not impede al-Assad allying with

---

[7] He is the grand mufti and head of the Permanent Committee for Islamic Research and Issuing Fatwas.

Hamas, while maintaining a broad pan-Arab identity in response to physical security needs in the run up to the 2009 war. Due to Israel's perpetual military supremacy, the Syrian regime perceived Hamas as an asset in its quest to counterbalance the southern neighbour. The regime further understood that an alliance with Hamas would allow Syria a strategic depth in its struggle against Israel and enhance its leverage in pushing Israel back to the negotiation table. Accordingly, Syria's support for Hamas included providing refuge in Damascus to senior Hamas figure Khalid Meshaal. In addition, the Syrian regime provided the Palestinian ally with arms and military training (Ghadry 2009; Karmon 2008, 33–4). In 2009, Syria's threat perception represented a case of ontological security and physical insecurity.

I argue that Syria's physical insecurity and its regional isolation dominated the regime's threat perception. This perception led the secular Ba'ath regime to support Hamas' Islamic narrative, a group that it heavily oppressed at the domestic level. Although Hamas' identity narrative *per se* did not challenge the Syrian regime identity, alliance with the group held the potential of unravelling the contradictions within Syria's identity narrative. To avoid imminent ontological insecurity, the regime maintained an extensive pan-Arab discourse that includes support for any other group engaged in a struggle against Israel, regardless of its secular or Islamic nature. In other words, the al-Assad regime maintained the same discourse that emerged during the 2006 Lebanon War. The following first section outlines the regional environment affecting Syrian foreign policy in the aftermath of the 2006 Lebanon War up until the 2009 Gaza War. The second section examines how Hamas' Islamist narrative converged with Syria's broad pan-Arab vocation.

The Relative Power Distribution: Escaping Isolation

In the early years of Bashar al-Assad's presidency, the regional system established by Hafez al-Assad collapsed, and Syria became internationally isolated and regionally estranged. The Ba'ath regime in Syria became a target of the US war on terror under the George Bush administration following a series of events that led to a serious fracture in Syria–US relations: the outbreak of al-Aqsa Intifada (2000), the 9/11 attack on the United States, and the 2003 Iraq War. In addition, Syria became isolated at the regional level following its rapprochement with

Iran and Hezbollah, which created a rift in Syria's relationship with the so-called moderate camp. This regional fragmentation culminated during the 2006 Lebanese War, when Bashar al-Assad called the leaders of Saudi Arabia and Egypt 'half-men' (al-Assad 2006b). Following Hezbollah's performance in 2006, the isolation of the Syrian regime became partially alleviated, as international and regional actors understood the al-Assad regime's value in managing Middle East conflicts. This section argues that despite these improvements in Syria's position, it remained under a condition of severe physical insecurity. Alongside the constant risk of an Israeli attack, the Syrian regime feared a return to its isolation.

Following the 2006 Lebanon War, Syria's influence in the Iraqi and Lebanese spheres of conflict made the Ba'ath regime a 'sought-after player' (Zisser 2009b). As Martin Indyk, a former American Ambassador to Israel, stated at the time, 'Syria is a strategic linchpin for dealing with Iran and the Palestinian issue' (quoted in El-Khawas 2011). This influence constituted Syria's card in the negotiations with Israel over the Golan Heights. At the same time, despite a long history of enmity, Syria moved into a close alliance with Turkey. The empowerment of Kurds in Iraq following the 2003 Iraq War gradually brought Syria and Turkey together (Hinnebusch 2014a, 229). Despite an Iranian objection, Turkey even sponsored the renewal of peace talks between Syria and Israel in May 2008 (Bronner 2008).

During the same year, Syria's participation in the 2008 Doha agreement – which eased the tensions in Lebanon – made Syria indispensable for European and US efforts to stabilise the region. As French President Nicolas Sarkozy broke with the US policy of isolating Syria, Bashar al-Assad was invited to the Paris launch of the European-Mediterranean Union, with Syria's accession to this partnership on the agenda. The overall improvement in relations was made possible by leadership change, as Nicolas Sarkozy replaced Jacques Chirac in France and Barack Obama replaced George W. Bush in the United States. The Obama administration adopted a more conciliatory approach to the Ba'ath regime and opened a cautious dialogue to explore the possibility of improving relations with Syria (Hinnebusch 2010a). At the regional level, tensions between Syria and Saudi Arabia appeared to ease in 2007, especially during the Arab summit in Riyadh, when King Abdullah expressed his wishes to restore Syrian–Saudi détente (Kabalan 2010, 39–42).

Although the severe isolation and the regional estrangement of Syria seemed alleviated in 2008, its physical insecurity persisted due to its protracted geopolitical predicament vis-à-vis Israel. Syria was unable to sustain a conventional military balance with Israel as a growing technological and airpower gap opened between the two countries. Such an imbalance in Israel's favour is quantitatively evident. Israel was predominant in several aspects, including land weapons, air forces, artilleries, arm deliveries, mobilised army manpower, and military expenditures. Worse, from Syria's point of view, this Israeli predominance was not only quantitative. After the 2006 Lebanon War, Israel sought to make considerable progress in developing the quality of its reserve manpower and making technological advances in conventional military hardware (Cordesman and Burke 2008). In the face of this situation, Syria sought to consolidate its alliance with Iran, Hezbollah and Hamas (Goodarzi 2013). Moreover, it turned to Russia for arms purchases. From 2007 to 2010, the value of Russian arms deals with Syria more than doubled – from US$2.1 billion in 2003 to US$4.7 billion in 2006 (Herszenhorn 2012). The continuation of Israel's occupation of the Golan Heights remained a constant pressure on the Syrian leadership. Unable to recuperate the occupied lands by military means, the regime was aware of its inability to compel Israel to withdraw to the 1967 borders. The only alternative means to achieving this goal was through negotiations.

The possibility of a war with Israel was always in the background. In March 2018, the Israeli newspaper *Haaretz* published a long investigative report on how Israel destroyed a nearly completely nuclear reactor in Syria in 2007 (Harel and Benn 2018). The reactor was funded by Iran and built by North Korea (Serr 2018). The incident shows that during this period, Israel was considering several strategies from a limited attack on the reactor to an open war with Syria, with possible support from the United States.

When the Gaza War broke out in December 2008, the Ba'ath regime saw an opportunity to enhance its position in the negotiations with Israel as well as in its relationship with the United States. In other words, Syria sought to replicate the 2006 Lebanon War scenario, which led to Syria's reintegration at the regional and international levels. By hosting Hamas' leadership and allowing them to maintain permanent offices in Damascus, the Syrian regime demonstrated a strong support for the Palestinian resistance during the Gaza conflict.

On the ground, Syria backed Hamas' military efforts by relaying information on Israeli air sorties that were detected by Syrian radar installations. Domestically, the Syrian regime facilitated a donation campaign for the Palestinians in Gaza (ACRPS 2014). Moreover, Syria, together with Qatar, spearheaded an effort to convene an extraordinary Arab summit aimed at supporting the resistance and bringing the Israeli aggression to an end. During the extraordinary Arab summit in Doha in mid-January 2009,[8] Bashar al-Assad expressed his full support for Hamas and stated that Israel only understands 'the language of blood'. In addition, he called on the Arab world to boycott Israel, to close any Israeli embassies in the region, and to sever all 'direct and indirect ties with Israel'. Furthermore, he announced the suspension of peace talks between Israel and Syria ('Bashar al-Assad Speech in the Doha Summit' 2009).

The Syrian support for Hamas cannot be understood without a detailed examination of the relative power distribution and Syria's physical insecurity in its geopolitical environment. Developments immediately post 2006 encouraged Syria to play a more confident role. Its alliance with Iran and Hezbollah made it a regional asset indispensable in solving Middle East conflicts. As Jimmy Carter summarised it: 'Syria is a key factor in an overall regional peace' (Carter 2009, 174). The Syrian leadership employed its support for non-state actors in the Middle East as a strategy to manage its regional isolation and acquire leverage during the negotiations with Israel to recuperate the Golan Heights. As this strategy led to a partial alleviation of Syria's regional isolation, the Syrian regime finally managed to obtain a foothold in-between two networks in the region. On the one hand, it was a constituting part of the Iran-led 'resistance axis', pursuing a policy of defying the West made sustainable by economic relations with Asia and renewed economic and military relations with Russia. On the other hand, Syria's relationship with the West was revived, which manifested itself in the détente in the relationship with France, the Turkish-sponsored peace talks with Israel, the cautious dialogue with

---

[8] The divisions among Arab states over Gaza manifested during the preparation for Arab summits. Whereas Syria and Qatar pushed for an extraordinary Arab summit in Doha aiming to put an end to the Israeli aggression, Egypt, Saudi Arabia, and other Arab states boycotted the Doha summit and discussed the Gaza issue one week later in Kuwait during the Arab Economic summit (Black 2009b).

the United States, and the détente with Saudi Arabia. The Syrian regime aimed at maintaining such a balance with the ability to tilt towards one camp or the other with the view of obtaining benefits from both sides.

Yet, Syria still found itself in an unfavourable physical security environment that made it, at the end of the day, inclined to support Hamas in 2009. Despite the Obama administration's willingness to open the dialogue with the Ba'ath regime, it maintained continuity with Bush's policy by setting preconditions and making demands on Syria. The United States offered to play a role in Israeli–Syrian negotiations, remove Syria from the list of states sponsoring terrorism, and lift the economic sanctions, if Syria severed its relations with Iran, Hezbollah and Hamas. In other words, improving the relationship with the United States and the 'moderate' axis in the region could only come at the expense of depriving Damascus of all its 'cards', especially in the negotiations with Israel (Hinnebusch 2010a). The Syrian regime remained suspicious of US motives and refused to sever its relationship with the 'axis of resistance'. As Bouthaina Sha'ban, al-Assad's political and media advisor, stated, 'improved relations with US would not come at the expense of Syria's relationship with Iran' (*Al-Quds Al-Arabi*, 19 March 2009).

Consequently, in 2009, the Syrian regime believed that its ability to maintain a dialogue with the United States and leverage over Israel during the negotiations stemmed from its ability to influence the political and military outcome in Gaza, especially given that the military balance heavily tilted in Israel's favour. Therefore, Bashar al-Assad steadfastly backed Hamas, even though this led to the suspension of the Turkish-sponsored negotiations with Israel. As former Syrian Information Minister Mahdi Dahlallah explained,

The most important factor that brought about the change [in U.S. policy] is the Arab resistance camp, [comprising] Syria, the Lebanese and Palestinian resistance, and the Iraqi people, who refused [to accept] the occupation. Additional [factors] are the Iranian position, which refuses to accept the [American] hegemony, as well as the new Russian policy ... Had Bush been able [to implement] his policy without meeting opposition from anyone, the new administration would have continued the same policy ... The change introduced by Obama ... does not stem from an [American] reassessment of its ideology ... but from [Bush's] failure to achieve the goals that the U.S. was – and still is – pursuing ... [This administration simply] realised that it cannot promote the totality of its interests in the region without a relation-ship with the Syrians. (Quoted in Hinnebusch 2010a, 26)

By backing Hamas during the Gaza War, al-Assad aimed to advance his position against Israel over the Golan Heights and to prevent the United States from weakening his regime. At the regional level, Syria attempted to persuade the United States to abandon the strategy of aligning with the so-called moderate Arab Sunni states as a coordin-ated front against 'Shiite' Iran, Hezbollah and Hamas. In short, the Syrian support for Hamas during the Gaza War seemed tied to Syria's overall regional security strategy of resisting Israel's regional predom-inance and US intervention, both of which threatened the physical security of the Ba'ath regime. According to Patrick Seale (2009), the aforementioned strategy was efficient in guarding the vital interests of the Syrian regime, as it protected Syria's sphere of influence in Lebanon and prevented foreign penetration. In addition, this strategy countered Israeli hegemony in the region by strengthening the Teheran–Damas-cus–Hezbollah–Hamas axis, which continued to steadfastly back the Palestinians. More importantly, the Syrian policy blocked strategy of reshaping the Middle East, or at least that component of it which aimed at bringing down al-Assad's regime.

In 2009, Syria's support of Hamas seemed to result in a slight change in US foreign policy towards Syria. Shortly after the cease-fire in Gaza, the Obama administration opened a dialogue with Bashar al-Assad, as the regional weight of Syria in Middle East issues became evident. In February 2009, four US officials visited Damascus to negotiate Syria–US relations (Islammemo 2009). The negotiations were over the following issues: the stability of Iraq and Lebanon, a comprehen-sive peace process for the Arab–Israeli conflict, and the Iranian–Syrian alliance. In July 2009, US envoy George Mitchell visited Damascus as a prelude to starting the Syrian–Israeli peace negotiations (BBC Arabic 2009). Despite Syrian and US optimism, the negotiations ultimately did not produce the intended détente. By the end of 2009, no agreement was reached, and the United States renewed the sanctions on the Syrian regime. Furthermore, the al-Assad regime was further accused of bombings in Iraq in August 2009 as well of fostering the instability in Lebanon.

The failure to reach an agreement reinforced Syria's fear of a return to isolation and explains the regime's insistence on maintaining its alliance with Iran and its refusal to disassociate itself from Hamas or Hezbollah. In other words, it was this physical insecurity that led the regime to capitalise on its alliance with Hamas. The next section explores how the Syrian regime's pan-Arab narrative converged with its foreign policy choices.

The Regime Identity Narrative and the Resistance Discourse

After 1979, the Syrian regime identity had been narrowed from pan-Arabism to a 'Syrio-centric Arabism', which is a confluence of pan-Arabism and Syrian nationalism. Yet, Syria's physical security needs following the 2003 Iraq War led to the reassertion of an inclusive pan-Arab narrative. This return to pan-Arabism converged with Syria's new regional struggle against the United States and Israel as well as its alliances within the axis of resistance (*muqawma*) or the steadfastness (*muman'a*) front. Despite this apparent convergence between Syria's pan-Arab narrative and Hamas' struggle against Israel during the 2009 Gaza War, this alliance posed a potential source of instability for Syria's regime identity and its ontological security. The secular Ba'ath regime, which oppressed the Muslim Brotherhood at home, found itself allying with Hamas, which was itself an offshoot of the Muslim Brotherhood in Gaza. The Syrian regime avoided this contradiction by maintaining an overarching inclusive pan-Arabism in the context of the resistance against Israel and the United States, similar to the one that developed during the 2006 Lebanon War. This section examines the self–other framing Syria's regime identity narrative in the context of the 2009 Gaza War.

The pan-Arab discourse was discernible in Bashar al-Assad's speech during the extraordinary summit in Doha. He repeatedly referred to the Arab people as 'the Arab nation', a term that targeted Arab public opinion. He described the struggle between the Palestinians and Israel as a struggle between '*Arab* resistance' and 'Israeli terrorism'. The following statement summarised this pan-Arab dimension: 'the destiny of Gaza is not that of Gaza Citizens alone; it is our shared destiny. The battle of Gaza is the battle of every Arab citizen'. From this perspective, Syria's pan-Arabism was inclusive.

In other words, the limited options to ensure Syria's physical security predominated the regime's threat perception and guided the self–other framing in its identity narrative. From this perspective, the definition of the pan-Arab self reasserted an inclusive dimension gathering those secular and Islamic groups who fight against Israel. Al-Assad framed this Arab dimension in the context of the struggle against Israel: 'Israel wants through its aggression on Gaza to change the new realities created by the resistance, especially after the resistance has been victorious in Lebanon, stronger in Palestine, and been spread to the consciousness of the Arab Citizen' ('Bashar al-Assad Speech in the Doha Summit' 2009). On a front-page article in the government Syrian daily *Teshreen*, pro-Syrian former Lebanese MP Nasser Qandil stated that the Doha summit was a turning point in the position of the Arabs, who began to adopt the Syrian discourse:

President Assad's speech at the summit was a prime example of the new [Arab] discourse – a discourse that Syria had used [even] in the midst of the crises and wars, and whose [main principles] are adherence to the resistance and a quest for partners and sources of power within the shifting world [order]. This [will be achieved] by formulating a new Arab conception capable of generating alliances with rising regional powers that are interested in partnership – especially Turkey and Iran – while suspending the [Arab] peace initiative, which has been killed by Israel more than once. (*Teshreen*, 5 April 2009)

Whereas the Syrian regime depicted its struggle with Israel as primarily related to the territory, Hamas portrayed the conflict as one about faith and belief. In this regard, Hamas was known for 'Islamising' the Palestinian–Israeli conflict. In Litvak's words (1998, 149), 'at the heart of Hamas' ideology is the emphasis on "the Islamic essence" of the Palestinian cause'. Interestingly, Bashar al-Assad maintained a broad pan-Arab discourse that embraced and reconciled with the Islamic nature of Hamas' ideology. Hamas was even referred to in his speeches as the 'Arab resistance' ('Bashar Al-Assad Speech in the Doha Summit' 2009). The same struggle against Israel, the United States, and the so-called moderate Arab regimes was pan-Arab for Syria and Islamic for Hamas. Nevertheless, the Syrian regime framed an inclusive pan-Arabism wherein Islamism fit into the discourse. Such identity fluidity enabled the Syrian regime to accommodate its physical security needs.

Leaders cannot, however, manipulate identity narratives whenever and however they need to. Leaders can only activate or deactivate identity elements already present at the domestic level that provides leaders with the 'menu of choices'. In Syria's case, adopting this inclusive pan-Arabism was possible as the domestic audience supported the struggle against Israel. Subsequently, the Syrian official discourse that followed during the 2012 and 2014 Gaza Wars merits further attention because of the way it shifted with the changing political landscape in the Middle East. The Syrian regime's position towards Hamas in the 2012 and 2014 Gaza Wars only confirmed that the resistance axis, including the Syrian–Hamas alliance, was based on strategic interests. It also suggests that leaders cannot easily manipulate regime identity. At the outbreak of the Syrian uprisings on 15 March 2011, Hamas played an ambiguous role and attempted to conciliate the two opposing sides. Once the conflict between the protesters and the regime transformed into an armed struggle, the Ba'ath regime requested Hamas' unconditional support in its struggle against the revolutionary movements. The Iranian regime even echoed this request. When Hamas refused to assist Damascus, the Syrian regime demanded the departure of Hamas' leaders from the Syrian capital and the shutdown of their permanent offices in November 2012 (ACRPS 2014).

Despite Hamas' refusal to support the Syrian regime, al-Assad could not follow the 'moderate' Arab regime in renouncing or condemning the resistance. In his inauguration speech on 17 July 2014, the Syrian president insisted that his government would remain committed to the Palestinian cause. He did, however, make a distinction between the Palestinian resistance and Hamas, which he deemed to be a 'fraudulent' resistance movement. As the following statement summarises,

[We are required] to distinguish carefully between the Palestinian people who resist, whom we must support, and some ingrates among them ... between real resistance fighters, whom we must back, and those amateurs who wear the garb of resistance according to their interests and to improve their image and bolster their power. If we do not do this, then, consciously or unwittingly, we will be serving Israeli goals. (Quoted in ACRPS 2014, 3)

In line with this position, the Syrian official media referred to various Palestinian factions as the 'resistance' and avoided mentioning Hamas. Instead, the media stressed that the faction that allied with the Syrian regime represents the 'genuine resistance', such as the Jihad Jibreel Brigades. Yet, the Syrian regime could not go further in condemning Hamas, which reflects the significance of the Palestinian question in the domestic struggle for legitimacy in Syria. Following a

decade of reviving pan-Arabism in the Syrian regime identity discourse, the Syrian uprisings reversed this process. As a consequence,
in its on-going struggle for survival, the Syrian regime has downgraded
pan-Arabism in favour of a strong Syrian nationalism (Rifai 2014).
On the one hand, the Gaza War, therefore, showed that the fluidity of
Syria's regime identity lessened identity risks and allowed the regime
to accommodate identity narratives to the exigencies of material structures. In other words, ontological and physical security were reconciled through a manipulation in the perception of the alliance with
Hamas as a strategic choice. On the other hand, the Gaza Wars of
2012 and 2014 demonstrated that there are limits to the fluidity of
identity, and that elites do not create identities. The Syrian regime
adopted pan-Arab discourses that embraced the resistance movement
for decades. Yet, when Hamas shifted its alliance and condemned the
Syrian regime, al-Assad could not suddenly go against its earlier
narratives supporting Hamas.

Conclusion

This chapter provided further evidence for the utility of a two-layered
conception of security in explaining divergent Syrian and Saudi threat
perceptions. In 2009, Saudi Arabia, traditionally portraying itself as a
supporter of the Palestinian cause, condemned the resistance movement, Hamas. It is hard to imagine that a non-state actor enclaved in
the Gaza strip could be a material source of threat to the Kingdom,
even though it received financial support from Iran. The analysis
showed that the Kingdom's physical security was not endangered.
The 2009 Gaza War is a crucial case study that provided further
evidence to the analysis that the Saudi Kingdom feared similarity due
to the rigidity in its identity narrative, and confirmed that sectarianism
can be a source of security rather than a source of threat.

With the rise of Hamas to power in Gaza and the challenge to the
Saudi role in mediating the Arab–Israeli conflict presented an insur-
mountable challenge to the stability and distinctiveness of the King-
dom's identity. In the aftermath of the Islamic Revolution in Iran, the
Saudi Kingdom narrowed its identity from pan-Islamism to Sunni
Islam. Since then, the Kingdom has portrayed itself as the leader of
Sunni Islam in the region against a Shiite other. Hamas, a Sunni Islamic
movement presenting an alternative vision of the Arab–Israeli conflict

to that of the Kingdom, was a source of anxiety and ontological insecurity for the Saudi regime. In response, the Kingdom criticised Hamas not only for its war against Israel but for its Islamic identity that was very similar to the Kingdom's. In other words, the Saudi Kingdom redefined its identity and presented a new source of distinctiveness (Muslim Brotherhood versus Salafi), according to which Hamas is considered to be the 'other'.

In contrast to its Saudi counterpart, the al-Assad regime supported Hamas against Israel, which was perceived as a source of danger to Syria's physical security. In this chapter, I examined the geopolitical situation surrounding the Syrian regime. Fearing a return to its regional and international isolation following the failure of the peace talks with Israel, the al-Assad regime identified Hamas as a 'friend' whereas Israel and the United States were identified as the 'enemy'. Based on this physical insecurity, the regime identity adopted a broad pan-Arab discourse according to which the 'us' includes any actor identifying Israel as an enemy, justifying the alliance with Hamas.

This empirical chapter contributes to the development of this book's theoretical framework in several ways. First, the analysis of Saudi threat perception towards Hamas showed that identity convergence and similarity can be a source of threat and conflict. Whereas Saudi Arabia was able to reframe its identity narrative and distinguish it from the Islamic Revolution in Iran and Hezbollah using a Sunni–Shiite discourse, the same narrative was not possible in the case of Hamas. Instead, Saudi Arabia further narrowed down its identity by stressing the Salafi-Wahhabi element and demonising the Muslim Brotherhood ideology. This has also demonstrated the rigidity of Saudi regime identity and the inability of Saudi elites to reinvent their identity away from the Islamic dimension. In other words, this chapter has showed that ontological security provides a theoretical lens through which sectarianism can be seen as a source of security and distinctiveness for the Saudi Kingdom. This empirical chapter provides some insights to examine Saudi behaviour during the 2011 Arab uprisings, especially towards the rise of the Muslim Brotherhood to power in Egypt.

Second, Syrian threat perception towards Israel and its alliance with Hamas showed how states can hold diverging identities and interests. Whereas the Syrian regime oppressed the Muslim Brotherhood at home, they supported an offshoot of the same group at the regional level. This case shows the benefit of examining identities and interests as separate spheres of analysis. A constructivist approach assuming that identities and interests are co-constituted masks these dynamics. In these cases, where identities and interests dictate contradictory behaviour, the chapter demonstrated how the Syrian regime reframed and accommodated its identity narrative to conform to its physical security. The case also showed that holding contradictory identity and interests create a potential for a situation of ontological insecurity. States, therefore, struggle to reconcile actions with the narrative states use to present their self-identity and justify actions at both domestic and international levels. As the Syrian regimes supported Islamist movements beyond its borders – namely Hamas – while oppressing groups with similar ideology at home could be an insurmountable source of inconsistency and, hence, identity risk. To avoid cases of ontological insecurity, the regime had to accommodate its regime identity narrative in a way that conforms to its material interests.

Finally, this chapter contributes to the debate on the role of sectarianism in Middle Eastern international relations. It provides empirical evidence that sectarianism is a complex process that transcends primordial and instrumentalist approaches. On the one hand, Saudi animosity with Hamas – a Sunni movement – seemed like a replica of Saudi behaviour towards Hezbollah – a Shiite movement. On the other hand, al-Assad's regime, often depicted as Alawi, allied with a Sunni movement. Both cases have showed that threat perception is hardly driven by the content of these sectarian identities. This challenges primordialists view of the rise of sectarianism in the Middle East (Nasr 2006). Instead, an ontological security approach shows that actors have a stake in maintaining those sectarian differences, which provide actors with a sense of self and distinctiveness in their environment. Although instrumental and discursive approaches to sectarianism share some elements with this argument, namely that elites play an important role in manipulating narratives. Wehrey (2013) and Rubin (2014, 108) argue that elites use sectarianism to prevent the emergence of broad-based opposition movements and to mobilise the masses around a narrative of a sectarian other. The ontological security lens adds depth to this argument in many ways. Through the lens of ontological security, this chapter provides a third way to examine sectarianism as serving actors' need of distinctiveness and their security-as-being. From this perspective, ontological security is not synonymous to discourses as instruments to serve legitimacy and domestic survival. Instead, ontological security is the 'presence of a stable self-understanding, which can include positive, neutral, and negative components' and a consistent identity and narrative (Mitzen and Larson 2017). Another contribution of ontological security to the debate on sectarianism is related to the level of consciousness in adopting sectarian narratives. Whereas the instrumentalist approach assumes full consciousness and intentionality in promoting particular narratives, ontological security argues that elites maybe conscious in promoting certain narratives, but they do not understand entirely their discomfort or why they choose particular narratives over other to restore the stability of their identity.

6 | *Conclusion*

The exception is more interesting than the rule. The rule proves nothing; the exception proves everything. In the exception the power of real life breaks through the crust of a mechanism that has become torpid by repetition.

Carl Schmitt, *Political Theology: Four Chapters on the Concept of Sovereignty* (1922, 15)

How and why states perceive others as threats and what factors drive the process of threat perception remain core issues for scholars of international relations. To answer these questions, theories have been designed, refined and applied to a broad range of cases. These intellectual efforts have occupied a central place in IR theory as they explain state behaviour and unravel the dynamics of cooperation and conflict. This book shows how threat perception and alliance choices in the Middle East contribute to this theoretical endeavour.

The claim that Middle Eastern international relations, enmity and conflict have been driven by ideational factors is indisputable. Pan-Arabism, pan-Islamism and national and sectarian identities have shaped regional security dynamics. In this regional context, realist lenses treating identity as secondary have proved limited when faced with controversial empirical cases. Similarly, empirical analyses provide compelling evidence that focusing on identity while considering material forces secondary can be equally misguiding. In a region known to be the most militarised in the world, inter-state conflicts and war are still pervasive. According to the Global Militarisation Index (GMI), six of the top ten countries with the highest degree of militarisation are in the Middle East. Nearly all other Middle Eastern states can be found among the first forty positions (Grebe 2014, 6–7). As Gause (2003, 274) puts it, 'if there is one area of the world where fears that a neighbour's military power could be turned against a state should be high, it is the Middle East'. From this perspective, the

Middle East, a region where ideational and material forces are constantly in play, provides an optimal pool for examining anomalies and puzzles that could advance the research programme on threat perception.

The existing literature on threat perception is divided between those who prioritise identity over material power and those who reduce identity to an epiphenomenon or a mere instrument of material power considerations. The endeavour in this book has been to move beyond the 'either ... or' dichotomy to explore how these two phenomena coexist and interplay in the process of threat perception. In particular, the book has explored the conditions under which ideational or material forces become predominant in leaders' threat perception. This concluding chapter briefly summarises the findings. I highlight the implications of the argument for the study of Middle East politics and IR theory in general. I also discuss some of the limitations and anomalies that this book could not address, some of which provide avenues for future research.

Summary of the Findings

This book has offered a different way of thinking about threat perception, by presenting a two-layered conception of security: ontological and physical. Whereas physical security is associated with military threats that endanger the survival of the state, ontological security is associated with those dynamics and processes that centre around the reproduction of identity narratives and the maintenance of a system of certitude. This book advances the debate around the ideational-material nexus in threat perception by examining how these two distinct layers of security interact and, thereby, leading to divergent threat perceptions. Furthermore, it outlines the conditions under which ideational factors override material factors in leaders' perceptions or vice versa.

The book has examined how ideational and material forces interact. Although the two layers of security – physical and ontological – are distinct and have different logics and dynamics, they are systematically intertwined and in constant interaction, which is an aspect that is often overlooked in the study of international relations, and of Middle East politics in particular. The book has shown that leaders fearing for their regime's physical security usually reframe regime's identity narrative to adapt to the constraining relative power distribution. Also, leaders facing instability with regard to their ontological security can mobilise military and material resources to bolster their ideational defensive mechanisms. Furthermore, this book has examined the conditions under which one factor becomes predominant in states' threat perception. These conditions are the multiplicity of policy options in the context of the relative power distribution and the fluidity of the regime identity.

This argument was illustrated through the empirical examination of Saudi and Syrian threat perceptions during three major regional wars in the Middle East: the Iran–Iraq War (1980–88), the 2006 Lebanon War, and the 2009 Gaza War. The findings from the cases suggest that states, or more specifically leaders, perceive their ontological security to be threatened when the other's identity disrupts the continuity or the distinctiveness of their identity narrative. This logic becomes even more apparent if states' physical security is not threatened. In this situation of ontological insecurity and physical security, states tend to restore their identity security through various mechanisms, namely, demonising the other and reinventing their identity narrative. Leaders' strategic options in navigating the relative power distribution becomes driven and constrained by the need to restore their ontological security. The case of Saudi Arabia's situation during the three wars discussed in this book exemplifies this dynamic. Iran, Hezbollah and Hamas were all consecutively identified as Saudi Arabia's enemies. Saudi Arabia, the leader of pan-Islam, perceived other Islamists movements as a source of disruption for its identity distinctiveness. By relying on new sources of distinctiveness, such as Sunni–Shiite sectarian narratives, the Kingdom restored the stability of its identity and, hence, its ontological security. Due to the fixity of the regime identity relying on a version of pan-Islamism linked to a Wahhabi doctrine to tie the different tribes and regions, leaders have limited abilities to manipulate the societal foundation of ontological security. In pursuing physical security, elites choose policy options that are consistent with the perceived ontological security.

In contrast, the case of Syria shows that states could experience a different situation, that of physical insecurity and limited options to ensure survival. Some of the policy options to ensure physical survival could have compromised the Syrian regime's ontological security; a secular Ba'athist regime allying with a non-Arab Iran against an Arab Ba'athist fellow regime in Iraq, or allying with Islamist movements abroad, while oppressing similar groups at home. Regimes then attempt to reconcile ontological and physical security. Otherwise, regimes can potentially suffer from ontological dissonance that might evolve out of contradictions in the identity narrative. In 1979, when the physical insecurity of the regime required an alliance with Iran in order to fend off Saddam Hussein's military ambitions, Syria's main identity narrative was based on Arabism. From this perspective, identifying Iraq as an enemy based on material considerations was a clear violation of the regime identity. To resolve this contradiction, the Syrian regime reframed the regime identity and changed the meaning of Arabism. According to the new narrative, Arabism is no longer based on the ethnic component of 'Arabness' but on animosity towards Israel. Thus, because Iran identified Israel as the major enemy, it fell into the Syrian 'us' category. Likewise, Iraq fell into the Syrian 'them' category as it did not identify Israel as its most important enemy. The same adaptation took place in the cases of the Syrian alliance with Hezbollah and Hamas. Considering their Islamist background, the Syrian regime had to adapt and reframe the secular component in its identity narrative to make it more inclusive. In short, the choice of allies was based on Syria's physical security needs, and Syrian elites reframed their identity narrative to conform to this choice. Without this identity reframing, Syria could encounter future problems of inconsistencies in their identity narratives, ending up in a situation of ontological dissonance. Due to the multi-layered, flexible nature of the Syrian regime identity narrative, the elites were able to shape identity narratives to make preferred policies acceptable.

From this perspective, this book showed that while physical security is obviously important, ontological security is just as important, because its fulfilment affirms state's self-identity and determines how a state sees and defines itself vis-à-vis others. Accordingly, states seek to contributing to restoring its physical security, the Syrian regime's actions were incongruent with its identity narrative. To avoid this incongruence, leaders reframed their identity narrative so that actions and self-identity narratives become consistent.

These arguments and findings come together to form the basis of the theoretical framework that guided the empirical analysis. Saudi threat perception revealed the Kingdom's steady quest for a distinct, consistent narrative of self-identity vis-à-vis other Islamic models emerging in the region. The Islamic character of the Islamic Revolution in Iran (1979), the emergence of Hezbollah as an important regional actor during the 2006 Lebanon War, and the Sunni model of resistance portrayed by Hamas all constituted sources of anxiety to the Saudis, as they threatened the stability of the regime's self-conception as the leader of the Muslim world. In these three cases, it is safe to say that the physical security of the Kingdom was intact. For decades, the Islamic Republic of Iran was weakened and had no interest in launching a war with any of its neighbours. In the cases of Hezbollah and Hamas, the military balance was clearly in favour of Israel. Instead, the Saudi Kingdom saw the tenets of its identity narrative challenged by these three alternative Islamic models, and attempted to demonise them as a defence mechanism. Moreover, the ruling elite tried to draw a clear distinction between their identity own narrative and these models by reframing the Saudi identity narrative, arriving at a new self–other distinction. In relation to the Islamic Republic and Hezbollah, the Kingdom promoted a sectarian distinction based on the Sunni–Shiite divide. Henceforth, the Saudi Kingdom portrayed itself as the leader of Sunni Islam. Therefore, Hamas, a movement with a Sunni background, presented an even more challenging case to the Saudis. To surmount this challenge, the regime aimed to demonise Hamas' Muslim Brotherhood background. Saudi threat

Moreover, Syria was regionally and internationally isolated and deprived of any Arab support. In these three cases, the physical insecurity of the regime guided Syria's alliance choices. Syria allied with Iran, Hezbollah and Hamas to balance the source of military imbalance, i.e., Israel, and also to escape its regional and international isolation. Nevertheless, these alliances created various contradictions in the regime's identity narrative. The Ba'athist secular pan-Arab identity of the regime suffered a potential contradiction in the face of the alliance with a non-Arab Islamic regime in 1979. To a lesser degree, al-Assad supported two Islamist movements (Hezbollah and Hamas) while oppressing their Islamic counterparts at the domestic level. Despite their importance to Syria's physical insecurity, these alliances constituted the potential for future ontological dissonance, due to inconsistency and incongruity between identity narrative and behaviour. To avoid this situation, the regime reframed its identity at each stage. In 1979, the regime changed the meaning of pan-Arabism, from an identity based on an ethnic origin to one defined by the struggle against Israel. In other words, Arabism in the Syrian context does not necessarily lead to alliances with Arabs but with anyone who supports the struggle against Israel. The alliance with Hezbollah and Hamas also resulted in the reframing of Syria's identity narrative, as al-Assad revived a pan-Arab discourse to include Islamist movements in the struggle against Israel. In a word, Syria's pan-Arab identity narrative widened and became more inclusive. Ultimately, the Syrian case demonstrates that states care about ontological security even under severe cases of physical insecurity.

The two cases presented in this study constituted extreme cases: Syria suffered from physical insecurity whereas Saudi Arabia was in a perennial quest for ontological security. The book argued that these situations are often driven by the options of the relative power distribution and the flexibility of regime identity narratives. This leads to an important question: Are some states more prone to suffer from ontological insecurity whereas others are doomed to be victims of physical insecurity? On the one hand, the lack of flexibility in Saudi identity has contributed to its ontological vulnerability. The lack of a distinctive Saudi identity differentiated from Islam has contributed to the Kingdom's anxiety towards other Islamic models. Nevertheless, the study has shown that Saudi identity has narrowed over time from pan-Islamism to Sunni Islam. In other words, regime identities are in constant mutation. One can expect that the Kingdom will develop a more state-focused identity over time, which might lessen the effects of its ontological vulnerability. In the Syrian case, the country has suffered from physical insecurity imposed by the geopolitical situation. Nevertheless, this physical insecurity is unlikely to last. The ever-shifting regional alliances might eventually evolve towards changing Syria's geopolitical position in the relative power distribution. Moreover, the domestic and regional struggle in Syria can pose novel challenges to the consistency and continuity of the regime's identity narrative. Therefore, its situation of relative ontological security might change into one of anxiety and ontological insecurity. In short, although these cases constituted extreme situations of insecurity, this does not mean that states are enclaved in perennial states of physical or ontological insecurity. On the contrary, the second part of the argument shows how the interaction between these two layers of security keeps states' vulnerabilities in constant mutation. States can alternate between possible combinations of ontological and physical security.

Moreover, the cases presented here have shown that ontological and physical security can affect each other through interaction. Ontological insecurity can create or reinforce physical insecurity. In the Saudi case, in responding to ontological security needs the Kingdom pursued a foreign policy behaviour that endangered its physical security. In 1979, to restore its distinctiveness and identity difference in the face of the ontological challenge from Iran, the Kingdom allied with Saddam Hussein in his war against the Islamic Republic; concurrently, the Kingdom discursively framed the Islamic Revolution not only as a threatening other but as one that was physically threatening and endangering the Kingdom's interests in the region. The Kingdom, in other words, pursued a foreign policy based on a particular perception of the relative power distribution, which was necessary to affirm its ontological security. As a result, conflictual relations with Iran preserved the Kingdom's ontological security, but endangered its physical security. As Mitzen (2006) argues, states may remain in conflict and can sacrifice their physical security if it preserves their ontological security. Physical insecurity may also lead to ontological insecurity. In the Syrian case, restoring physical security led to situations of ontological dissonance, as the regime pursued a foreign policy that partially contradicted its identity narrative. In order to avoid possible situations of inconsistencies, the regime adapted and reframed its identity narrative.

Lessons for IR Theory and Middle East International Relations

This book's central argument makes significant empirical and theoretical contributions to the study of Middle East international relations and broader IR theory. Its major contribution is in showing that the treatment of ideational factors as a function of material forces or vice versa has obscured the myriad ways in which both aspects are in constant interaction. Moreover, relying on the ideational versus material argument obscures the dynamics of threat perception and hinders explanations as to why states diverge in this regard. This study has put forward a theoretical framework based on a two-layered conception of security. A major contention of this book has been that the relevant literature on threat perception in both realist and constructivist theoretical frameworks has overlooked the co-existence and the interplay of ideational and material forces in real-world events. Rather than being confined by the '-isms', this research has aimed to advance the debates around substantive mid-range theories by adopting an eclectic approach driven by empirical puzzles.

This study contributes to the broader IR literature by providing an integrative conceptual framework that bridges and links together the specialist literature on ontological security, self–other relations, and neorealism. My analysis both complements and challenges in important ways major international relations theories, including balance-of-threat theory, regime security approaches and constructivism.

First, the analysis adds specificity to Walt's balance-of-threat theory. Although Walt (1987) claims that states balance against the greatest threat, his theory did not specify how threats are perceived or how ideational and material power considerations play out simultaneously in this process. My analysis addresses this issue by showing how ideational and material spheres co-exist in each case of threat perception. Moreover, by focusing on threat perception as a dependent variable, the analysis has considered other relevant foreign policy behaviours beyond alliance formation, such as identity reframing and the consolidation of existing alliances.

My argument has important similarities with and differences from regime security approaches (cf. Gause 2003). Scholars writing in this vein suggest that leaders will resist both external and internal threats to the survival of their regime. My argument obviously shares this focus on the dual levels of threat perception. Regime security approaches focus on transnational ideologies and their diffusion as the ultimate source of ideational threat, proposing that leaders often fear that these ideologies will transcend borders and lead to domestic unrest and instability. I do, however, demonstrate that threats to identity can operate in many other ways. The analysis here shows that the other's identity can also be threatening as it drives actors to question their own identity. Moreover, identity similarity with the other may threaten actors' identity distinctiveness and consistency. These threats are external, but they also relate to domestic vulnerabilities. From this perspective, identity threats emerging from the interaction with the external other can lead to domestic rifts and struggle, as the identity narrative that holds the political community together is threatened. From this perspective, looking at the separate dynamics of ontological and physical security has allowed the analysis to delve further into this concept of 'regime security', which has many meanings and dynamics beyond the ones already identified in the literature.

Barnett's constructivist account offers the most direct challenge to my understanding of the ideational sources of leaders' threat perception. Consequently, his account of Arab politics constitutes the principal competing argument. Focusing on the ontological security layer allows an understanding of the role of identity from another angle, one that is different from the one presented by either the constructivist approach or the rationalist-instrumentalist approach to identity. Despite sharing with constructivism the notion that state identities are constructed, a theoretical account that privileges ontological security takes a step further by providing an insight into what motivates states in their actions. Whereas constructivists argue that *interests and identities are co-constituted*, ontological security answers the questions of why they are co-constituted. By addressing the question of why states want to affirm their self-identity, or even why they pursue a foreign policy that conforms to their identity narrative, ontological security provides a more comprehensive analysis. In addition, ontological security shows why and how shared identities can be a source of conflict and enmity, a relationship that has been observed in previous works on Middle East international relations but rarely investigated (Barnett 1998; Kienle 1990; Rubin 2014; Walt 1987).

Furthermore, the argument in this book contributes to the study of sectarianism in the international relations of the Middle East beyond primordial and instrumental approaches. Although instrumental approaches to sectarianism share some elements with this argument, in that elites can manipulate some narratives of sectarian differences. From this instrumentalist perspective, scholars argue that sectarianism is a tool in the hand of authoritarian leaders, who mobilise religious leaders to spread sectarian discourse with the aim to bolster their rule and control over societies, while justifying some foreign policy decisions. Wehrey (2013) illustrates how the ruling elites in the Gulf have used sectarianism to prevent the emergence of broad-based opposition movements. In other words, stocking sectarianism is a strategy to maintain control over societies and strengthen the legitimacy of the ruling elites. Along similar lines, Rubin (2014, 108) argues that sectarian framing can be seen as a strategy of 'ideational balancing', whereby elites manipulate narratives with the purpose of mobilising the masses around the threat of a sectarian other. Through the lens of ontological security, this book provides a third way to examine sectarianism as serving actors' need of distinctiveness and their security-as-being. From this perspective, ontological security is not synonymous to discourses as instruments to serve legitimacy and domestic survival. Instead, ontological security is the 'presence of a stable self-understanding, which can include positive, neutral, and negative components' and a consistent identity and narrative (Mitzen and Larson 2017). Therefore, sectarianism provides stability and continuity in identity narratives for some actors in an uncertain environment, and actors become attached to this sort of stability and distinctiveness. The attachment to this need of stability and distinctiveness is best captured by ontological security. Whereas instrumentalism approaches sectarianism as a rationalist strategy consciously employed by elites for survival, ontological security makes the dynamics attached to the endeavour of maintaining sectarian narratives more visible, such as the need for stability, consistency, and distinctiveness, which would not be otherwise apparent drawing on instrumentalism alone.

Another contribution of ontological security to the debate on sectarianism is related to the level of consciousness in adopting sectarian narratives. The instrumentalist approach assumes elite manipulation of identity and narratives. In other words, elites are fully aware of the security concerns of the masses and deliberately manipulate them to make strategies designed to address material concerns acceptable to the masses. Beyond this discursive consciousness posed by instrumentalist, ontological security approach operates outside of the realm of discursive consciousness. As Giddens puts it: 'On a day-to-day basis identity is not "held in mind"; actors concentrate on the "task at hand" and the need to stabilise one's ends is cognitively set aside' (Giddens 1991, 36). In other words, states and actors maintain certain behaviour and identity-maintaining habits that are unthinking (Mitzen 2006, 346). Also, elites know that it is in their interest to promote behaviour and identity narratives that maintain sectarianism, and yet not understand entirely *why*. Elites may be aware that some identities can be sources of threat to the stability of their identity, but they are not fully conscious of the reason for their discomfort. More importantly, they are unconscious why sectarian narratives can provide more stability over other sources of identity. In other words, elites in the Saudi Kingdom may be aware that Islamic identities promoted by other models in the region can be threatening but they cannot say that the need for their discomfort towards such similarity and the need for distinctiveness is the reason behind maintaining a sectarian narrative and manipulating this narrative to shape the public perception of the sectarian other.

Beyond its theoretical contributions, this book makes important empirical contributions. I have shown that a serious engagement with IR theory can lead to a new understanding of established historical narratives of past events in the international relations of the Middle East. More specifically, the book's argument contributes to the debate on the role of identities in the Middle East, which is divided between primordial and instrumental approaches. This study has presented a middle ground and a novel theoretical entry based on ontological security. First, I counter the primordial approaches that have predominated in the analysis of Middle East alliances, and which portray the Syria–Iran–Hezbollah axis as a 'Shiite axis' and the Egypt–Saudi Arabia–Jordan alliance as a 'Sunni axis'. Instead, I have argued that sectarianism emerged as a defensive mechanism employed by actors whose ontological security was endangered. Second, this analysis in the book also shows that a rationalist–instrumentalist approach to identity obscures those cases where identity is the major driver behind state behaviour. Moreover, the theoretical framework presented can explain other instances in Syrian or Saudi foreign policies. For example, the ontological security lens provides an insight as to why the Kingdom perceived the rise of the Muslim Brotherhood to power in Egypt as a threat (Darwich 2016). In addition, the theoretical framework presented here can inform the study of alliance decisions taken by other Arab states – such as Iraq (pre-2003), Jordan and Egypt – where there is evidence of ideational and material interplay.

Unresolved Anomalies and Avenues for Future Research

The book's argument has notable limitations, some of which suggest areas that deserve further study. Five issues stand out. First, the central argument may be limited in terms of the types of behaviour it explains. It cannot explain all cases of threat perception, as it focuses on those particularly driven by relative power distribution and identity narratives. Moreover, the ideational forces I have considered are mainly limited to regimes' identity and their effect on threat perception. Culture, ideas, and other ideational factors that might contribute to threat perception and state behaviour are not accounted for in this study.

Second, the story in this book tells little about the sources of the replacement identity narratives that are central to restoring or maintaining ontological security. My argument shows how leaders frame and reframe their identity to cope with ontological or physical insecurity, but I have not delved into the sources of these identity narratives or why particular narratives emerge among others. The case of Saudi Arabia is relevant in this respect: namely, why did the ruling elite frame their identity narrative to be distinctive from their Iranian counterparts using a sectarian Sunni–Shiite reference, whereas the Arab versus non-Arab distinction, like the one Saddam Hussein used, could have served the same purpose? I am far from asserting that leaders can enforce any random identity narrative. Instead, this identity narrative should be socially accepted and figure within the existing social and historical structures. That is an important part of the story that takes place in this process of restoring security, and it certainly deserves more attention in future research.

Third, the argument is limited to non-democratic contexts or, in other words, to authoritarian regimes where authority is centralised in the hands of the elite in power. I have told the story of specific elites perceiving threats to the survival of their regimes, while possessing some power to control their societies. From this perspective, some threats might be perceived by the elite but not be understood as such by the subject society. For example, the Saudi people and social groups did not share the regime's perception of Hamas or Hezbollah as threats. A similar situation could be found in Egypt and Jordan. From this perspective, the role of domestic institutions in allowing the regime this sort of independence from domestic forces has not been considered. Also, divided societies, where no one powerful elite is in control, are also outside of the scope of this research. Nevertheless, the book makes a contribution to the dynamics of interplay between ideational and material powers beyond authoritarian regimes. For this framework to be applied in democratic or semi-democratic contexts, a different account of how domestic and regional spheres interact would be necessary. Ideational and material factors interplay is a phenomenon that exists beyond authoritarian regimes and beyond the phenomenon of threat perception. As Risse et al. (1999) show, national identities and interests interacted in European states' decision to join the European Economic and Monetary Union. They examine how the interaction between national identities and interests led to divergent policies in the cases of Germany, France and Great Britain. In other words, the interaction between identity and relative power distribution in this study can inform similar processes in other democratic and autocratic countries. For application to democratic contexts, domestic structures as well as regional interactions might require an adaption of the assumptions underlying the theoretical framework. Moreover, as democratic regimes operate differently, the sources of threats affecting their ontological and physical security can be of different nature.

Fourth, the book's argument does not consider the weight of dynamics at the international level in regimes' threat perception. The Middle East is often referred to as the most 'penetrated' system, as it is deeply influenced by international interventions without being fully subordinated to the international system (Brown 1984, 16–17). Both bipolarity during the Cold War and the Pax Americana after 1991 have influenced regional politics in myriad ways. To examine this influence, Hinnebusch (2003a, chap. 2) distinguishes between interactions at the international system level, or the 'core', and those at the regional level, or the 'periphery'. This study did not, however, make this distinction explicit. International actors and their influence on regimes' threat perception were accounted for only at the empirical level, such as the Saudi–US partnership. The dynamics of the international system and their influence on regional interactions were not theorised. Future studies should explore to what extent this international level of analysis systematically influences regimes' threat perception in Middle Eastern international relations.

Fifth, the research design did not allow for variations in intra-cases comparisons. Although the case studies were chosen based on variation in the dependent variable, intra-case comparisons presented similar cases on the independent variables (ontological and physical security). Syria during the three wars consistently evinced a situation of ontological security and physical insecurity. Meanwhile, Saudi Arabia consistently experienced ontological insecurity and physical security. Further research should examine states that alternate between these situations. Another defect in the research design is the absence of empirical cases that reflect the situation of ontological insecurity and physical insecurity. The argument does not tell us how states would behave in this case or how they would prioritise between different types of threats. Would the state sacrifice ontological security for the physical or the other way around? Ontological security scholars claim that ontological security is far more important, and that states can sacrifice their physical security to satisfy their self-conception (e.g. Steele 2008). In contrast, neorealists argue that leaders' understanding of the danger posed by other actors in the system is primarily the product of relative power distributions. This position can be summarised in Waltz's (1986, 329) claims that material power considerations 'weigh more heavily than ideological preferences or internal political pressures'. In the last few years, scholarship on ontological security has expanded to include cases where physical and ontological security can be reconcilable and are in interaction. Further research could expand to include more cases and provide more depth in this research direction.

While I share Rubin's (2014) assumption that threat perception is a process in Middle Eastern international relations, this study has provided a theoretical model that facilitates the exploration of ideational and material forces and how they are reconcilable in the process of threat perception. By bridging the literature on ontological security, Realism, and self–other relations, this study has prepared the ground for further research. Such research can be developed in two ways.

The first is through widening the scope of the theoretical argument by applying it to other cases. Potential cases may include Jordan, a small state where physical security has been important, but where ideational factors have also been significant in holding together various domestic groups. Jordan could serve as a potential case for examining how states prioritise between ontological insecurity and physical insecurity. Jordan is a case where regime identity has been multi-layered and adapted over time to accommodate physical security needs (Frisch 2002; Layne 1994). The eclectic nature of the regime identity in Jordan has allowed elites to manipulate the ontological foundations of the identity as security concerns changed over the course of state formation processes. Another interesting case to examine is Egypt, where threat perception towards Iran constituted a cornerstone in the country's foreign policy for decades. The examination could involve looking into the factors that led to the regimes' threat perception. Egypt is a rather homogenous country with no Shiite minority. It is puzzling that Iran, a geopolitically distant country, was constantly identified as a threat. Moreover, the Mubarak regime perceived Hamas as threat, while de-emphasising Egyptian animosity towards Israel. Therefore, this book has answered many questions on threat perception in the Middle East but raises many more. A second way to move research beyond the scope of this study is to examine other dimensions in the process of threat perception; how do states prioritise between ontological and physical security and how do they choose among the available possible identities?

The Middle East constitutes an important pool of empirical data for fruitful theoretical frameworks that could be extended to other areas, such as Central Asia and Southeast Asia. Moreover, it is an important repertoire to test and build theoretical arguments that contribute to the development of IR theories. In the previous two decades, many scholars with expertise in Middle East politics have noted the schism between Middle East area studies and mainstream International Relations and Comparative Politics. Nowadays, the common perception that the Middle East is too exceptional to be theory-relevant is diminishing (Haklai 2009; Teti 2007; Valbjørn 2004). During the last decade, scholarly trends have shown that the Middle East is increasingly studied under the lens of theories produced by non-Middle East specialists (Valbjørn 2015). Instead, the Middle East can serve a more important role than theory application. It has the potential to be in itself an invaluable pool of empirical anomalies for both theory development and theory-building efforts.

Bibliography

Abd-Allah, Umar F. 1983. *Islamic Struggle in Syria*. Berkeley, CA: Mizan Press.

Abdelal, Rawi, Yoshiko M. Herrera, Alastair Iain Johnston and Rose Mcdermott. 2006. 'Identity as a Variable'. *Perspectives on Politics* 4 (4): 695–711.

Abdo, Geneive. 2013. 'The New Sectarianism: The Arab Uprisings and the Rebirth of the Shi'a-Sunni Divide'. Analysis Paper 29. Washington, DC: The Saban Center for Middle East Policy at Brookings. www.brookings .edu/research/papers/2013/04/sunni-shia-divide-abdo.

2017. *The New Sectarianism: The Arab Uprisings and the Rebirth of the Shi'a-Sunni Divide*. 1st edn. Oxford: Oxford University Press.

Abir, Mordechai. 1988. *Saudi Arabia in the Oil Era: Regimes and Elites – Conflict and Collaboration*. London: Croom Helm.

1993. *Saudi Arabia: Government, Society, and the Gulf Crisis*. London: Taylor & Francis.

Abu Amer, Adnan. 2013. 'The Regional Powers' Influence on Political Transformation Process in the Palestinian Territories'. Friedrich-Ebert-Stiftung. http://goo.gl/MiQnxv.

ACRPS. 2014. 'Syria on Gaza: Incongruity in the Regime's Resistance Discourse'. Arab Center for Research and Policy Studies. http://goo.gl/ QYeMIB.

Adib-Moghaddam, Arshin. 2006. *The International Politics of the Persian Gulf: A Cultural Genealogy*. London: Routledge.

Adler, Emmanuel. 1997. 'Seizing the Middle Ground: Constructivism in World Politics'. *European Journal of International Relations* 3 (3): 319–63.

Agence France-Presse. 2018. 'Israel Admits 2007 Strike on Syrian Nuclear Site'. *The National*, 21 March 2018. www.thenational.ae/world/mena/ israel-admits-2007-strike-on-syrian-nuclear-site-1.714815.

Agha, Hussein and Ahmed Khalidi. 1995. *Syria and Iran: Rivalry and Cooperation*. London: Chatham House Papers.

'Aḥmad, 'Aḥmad Yusif. 2006. 'Al-Tada'iyyat Al-'arabiyya [Arab Implications]'. In *Al-Ḥarb Al-'Isrā'īliyya 'Alā Lubnān: Al-Tadā'iyyāt Al-Lubnāniyya*

Wa Al-'Isrā'īliyya , Ta'Thīrātihā Al-'arabiyya Wa Al-'Iqlīmiyya Wa Al-Dawliyya [The Israeli War in Lebanon:Lebanese and Israeli Implication and Their Arab, Regional, and International Effects], 245–71. Beirut: Center for Arab Unity Studies.

Ajami, Fouad. 1992. *The Arab Predicament: Arab Political Thought and Practice since 1967*. Updated edn. Cambridge, MA: Cambridge University Press.

2009. *The Dream Palace of the Arabs: A Generation's Odyssey*. New York: Knopf Doubleday Publishing Group.

Al Riyadh. 2006. *Al-Riyadh*, 9 August 2006, sec. www.alriyadh.com/2006/08/09/article178009.html.

Al Saud, Turki Al Faisal bin Abdul Aziz. 2013. 'Saudi Arabia's Foreign Policy'. *Middle East Policy* 20 (4): 37–44.

Alagha, Joseph. 2011. *Hizbullah's Documents: From the 1985 Open Letter to the 2009 Manifesto*. Amsterdam: Amsterdam University Press.

Al-Assad, Bashar. 2006a. 'Bashar Al-Asad's Speech at the Conference of Arab Lawyers in Damascus January 21, 2006'. 2006. http://goo.gl/AiI29x.

2006b. 'Bashar Al-Asad's Speech at the Fourth Conference of the Syrian Journalists' Union in Damascus on August 15, 2006'. 2006. http://goo.gl/heIxID.

2006c. 'Bashar Al-Assad's Speech at the Arab Parties Speech: March 6, 2006'. 6 March 2006. http://goo.gl/d79fRf.

Al-Assad, Hafiz. 1975. 'Speech at the Tobruq Base in Libya'. http://www.presidentassad.net/index.php?option=com_content&view=article&id=650:28-3-1975&catid=208&Itemid=476.

1978. 'President Hafiz Al-Assad's Speech in the Opening of the Third Steadfastness and Confrontation Summit, 20/9/1978'. http://www.presidentassad.net/index.php?option=com_content&view=category&id=211&Itemid=476.

Al-Dakhīl, Khālid. 2007. 'Burūz Al-Dawr Al-Sa'udi Fi "Iṭār Al-Niẓām Al-'Arabī Al-Rāhin [The Emergence of the Saudi Role in the Contemporary Arab System]'. *Majallat Al-Dirasat Al-Falastinyya* 18 (72): 5–14.

Al-Faisal, Turki. 2009. 'Saudi Patience Is Running Out'. *Financial Times*, 22 January 2009. http://goo.gl/6vpA7Q.

Algar, Hamid. 2002. *Wahhabism: A Critical Essay*. North Haledon, NJ: Islamic Publications International.

Al-Harbi, Khalaf. 2009. 'Qasf Al-'Aql Al-'Arabi [The Bombardment of the Arab Mind]'. *Okaz*, 5 January 2009. http://goo.gl/TWXB3d.

Al-Hayat. 2006a. 'Al-Safīr Al-'Irānī: Lā Mu'āhadat Difā' Ma' Lubnān [The Iranian Ambassador: No Defense Treaty with Lebanon]'. *Al-Hayat*, 23 July 2006.

2006b. "Īrān: 'Isrā'īl Kānat Satuhzam Mubakiran Law Kunnā Nad "Am Hizb "Allah 'Askariyyan [Israel Would Be Defeated Earlier If We Supported Hizbullah Militarily]'. *Al-Hayat*, 27 July 2006.

Al-Ifrig, Abdullah. 2009. 'Muftī Al-Mamlaka Li-Okaz: Anṣaḥ Bil-Tajāwub Ma' Al-Aṣwāt Al-Dā'iyya Lahā Bil-Khair [The Mufti of the Kingdom to Okaz: I Advise Hamas to Listen to the Voices Praying for Their Its Good]'. *Okaz*, 2009. http://goo.gl/HfASR9.

Al-Jazeerah. 2015. 'Hamas and Saudi Arabia: Prospects of Future Relations [in Arabic]'. *Al-Jazeerah*, 27 July 2015. www.aljazeera.net/home/Getpage/6c87b8ad-70ec-47d5-b7c4-3aa56fb899e2/2e6937ae-50d1-4152-84d9-f8466a10cd43.

Al-Labbad, Mustafa. 2005. *Ḥadā'iq Al-'Aḥāzān: 'Īrān Wa Wilāyat Al-Faqīh [Gardens of Sorrow: Iran and the Rule of the Leading Jurisprudent]*. Cairo: Dar al-Shorouk.

Al-Mughrabi, Nidal. 2011. 'Foreign Funds for Hamas Hit by Syria Unrest: Diplomats'. *Reuters*, 21 August 2011. http://goo.gl/zsuc52.

2013. 'Cornered Hamas Looks Back at Iran, Hezbollah'. *Reuters*, 20 August 2013. http://goo.gl/UK4H7E.

Al-Rasheed, Madawi. 2006. *Contesting the Saudi State: Islamic Voices from a New Generation*. Cambridge: Cambridge University Press.

2011. 'Sectarianism as Counter-Revolution: Saudi Responses to the Arab Spring'. *Studies in Ethnicity and Nationalism* 11 (3): 513–26.

Al-Rashid, Abdullah. 2013. 'Ta'Āmul Al-'Islāmiyyīn Fī Al-Khalīj Ma' Hizbullah: Qirā'Ah Fī Awrāq Harb 2006 [The Islamists Dealing with Hizbullah in the Gulf: A Reading in the Papers of the 2006 War]'. *Al-Sharq Al-Awsat*, 2 July 2013. www.aawsat.com/details.asp?section=39&article=734662&issueno=12635#.Uz1QKfldVjw.

Altoraifi, Adel. 2012. 'Understanding the Role of State Identity in Foreign Policy Decision-Making: The Rise and Demise of Saudi-Iranian Rapprochement (1997–2009)'. PhD Dissertation. London: London School of Economics and Political Science.

Al-'Ubayykān, 'Abd al-Muḥsin. 2006. 'Wa Lā Tulqū Bi-'Ayydīkum 'Ilā Al-Tahlukah [Do Not Cast Yourselves to Perdition]'. *Al-Sharq Al-Awsat*, 27 July 2006. www.aawsat.com/leader.asp?section=3&article=375028&issueno=10103#.Uynpl6h_sdY.

Al-Yassini, Ayman. 1983. 'Religion and Foreign Policy in Saudi Arabia'. Working Paper. Center for Developing Area Studies, McGill University.

Al-Zahar, Mahmoud. 2009. Interview. http://goo.gl/uw5Emf.

Amba, Faiza Saleh. 2006. 'Arab Leaders, Unlike Much of Public, Uneasy about Hezbollah'. *The Washington Post*, 24 July 2006. http://www.washingtonpost.com/wp-dyn/content/article/2006/07/23/AR2006072300919.html.

Amidror, Yaakov. 2007. 'The Hizballah-Syria-Iran Triangle'. *Middle East Review of International Affairs* 11 (1): 1–5.

Anderson, Lisa. 1986. *The State and Social Transformation in Tunisia and Libya: 1830–1980.* Princeton, NJ: Princeton University Press.

1987. 'The State in the Middle East and North Africa'. *Comparative Politics* 20 (1): 1–18.

Aras, Bülent. 2008. 'Turkey between Syria and Israel: Turkey's Rising Soft Power'. Policy Brief 15. SETA Foundation.

Aras, Bülent and Rabia Karakaya Polat. 2008. 'From Conflict to Cooperation: Desecuritization of Turkey's Relations with Syria and Iran'. *Security Dialogue* 39 (5): 495–515.

Ayoob, Mohammed. 1995. *The Third World Security Predicament: State Making, Regional Conflict and the International System.* London: Lynne Rienner.

Ayoob, Mohammed and Hasan Kosebalaban, eds. 2008. *Religion and Politics in Saudi Arabia: Wahhabism and the State.* Boulder, CO: Lynne Rienner.

Ayubi, Nazih. 1996. *Over-Stating the Arab State: Politics and Society in the Middle East.* London: I.B. Tauris.

Badeeb, Saeed. 1993. *Saudi-Iranian Relations (1932–1982).* London: Centre for Arab and Iranian Studies.

Bahgat, Gawdat. 2009a. 'The Arab Peace Initiative: An Assessment'. *Middle East Policy* 16 (1): 33–9.

2009b. 'Saudi Arabia and the Arab–Israeli Conflict in the Last Years of the Bush Presidency'. *Israel Affairs* 15 (2): 180–9.

Bakr, Amena. 2014. 'Hamas Leader Says Gaza Only a "Milestone to Reaching Our Objective"'. *Reuters*, 28 August 2014. http://goo.gl/r61JDF.

Baldwin, David. 1971. 'Thinking about Threats'. *The Journal of Conflict Resolution* 15 (1): 71–8.

Bank, Andre and Morten Valbjørn. 2010. 'Bringing the Arab Regional Level Back In … – Jordan in the New Arab Cold War'. *Middle East Critique* 19 (3): 303–19.

Baraka, Taher. 2011. 'The Political Memory: With Abdel Halim Khaddam [In Arabic]'. http://goo.gl/PnAEZh.

Baram, Amatzia. 1986. 'Ideology and Power Politics in Syrian-Iraqi Relations 1968–1984'. In *Syria under Assad: Domestic Constraints and Regional Risks*, edited by Moshe Ma'oz and Avner Yaniv, 125–39. London: Croom Helm.

Barkin, J. Samuel. 2010. *Realist Constructivism: Rethinking International Relations Theory.* Cambridge: Cambridge University Press.

Barnett, Michael. 1996. 'Identity and Alliances in the Middle East'. In *The Culture of National Security: Norms and Identity in World Politics*, edited by Peter Katzenstein, 400–47. New York: Columbia University Press.

1998. *Dialogues in Arab Politics: Negotiations in Regional Order*. New York: Columbia University Press.

Barnett, Michael and Jack Levy. 1991. 'Domestic Sources of Alliances and Alignments: The Case of Egypt 1962–1973'. *International Organization* 45 (3): 369–95.

1992. 'Alliance Formation, Domestic, Political Economy and Third World Security'. *The Jerusalem Journal of International Relations* 14 (4): 19–40.

Bar-Simon-Tov, Yaacov. 1983. *Linkage Politics in the Middle East: Syria between Domestic and External Conflict 1961–1970*. Boulder, CO: Westview Press.

'Bashar Al-Assad Speech in the Doha Summit'. 2009. www.youtube.com/watch?v=nltJoXWsx68&feature=youtube_gdata_player.

Bassedas, Pol Morillas. 2009. 'Hezbollah's Identities and Their Relevance for Cultural and Religious IR'. Working Paper. International Catalan Institute for Peace.

Batatu, Hanna. 1999. *Syria's Peasantry, the Descendants of Its Lesser Rural Notables, and Their Politics*. Princeton, NJ: Princeton University Press.

Batrawy, Aya and Abdullah Al-Shihri. 2014. 'Saudi King Condemns Gaza War – But Not Israel'. *The Times of Israel*. 1 August 2014. http://goo.gl/L8uGSh.

BBC. 2009. 'Wide Rifts on Show at Arab Summit'. 19 January 2009. http://goo.gl/EduCX8.

BBC Arabic. 2009. 'Agwā' 'īgābiyya Tuḥīṭ al-Mubāthāt al-Sūriyya al-'Amrīkiyya [A Positive Atmosphere Surrounding the Syrian American Talks]'. 26 July 2009. www.bbc.co.uk/arabic/middleeast/2009/07/090726_aq_syriamitchell_tc2.shtml.

Berti, Benedetta and Jonathan Paris. 2014. 'Beyond Sectarianism: Geopolitics, Fragmentation, and the Syrian Civil War'. *Strategic Assessment* 16 (4): 21–34.

Bilqīz, 'Abd al-'Ilah. 2006. *Ḥizbullah Min Al-Taḥrīr 'Ilā Al-Rad', 1982–2006 [Hizbullah: From Liberation to Deterrence, 1982–2006]*. Beirut: Center for Arab Unity Studies.

Black, Ian. 2009a. 'Saudis Blame Hamas amid Calls for Talks with Fatah'. *The Guardian*. 1 January 2009. www.theguardian.com/world/2009/jan/01/saudi-arabia-hamas-gaza.

2009b. 'Gaza Split Prompts Arab Countries to Boycott Emergency Summit'. *The Guardian*, 15 January 2009, sec. World news. www.theguardian.com/world/2009/jan/15/gaza-egypt-saudi-qatar-summit.

Blyth, Mark. 2003. 'Structures Do Not Come with an Instruction Sheet'. *Perspectives on Politics* 4 (1): 695–706.

Boserup, Rasmus Alenius, Waleed Hazbun, Karim makdisi, Helle Malmvig and Bashir Saade, eds. 2017. 'Hezbollah and Its "Takfiri" Enemy in Syria: Rethinking Relationships between States and Non-State Actors'. In *New Conflict Dynamics: Between Regional Autonomy and Intervention in the Middle East and North Africa*, 81–92. Copenhagen: DIIS – Danish Institute for International Studies/AUB – American University of Beirut.

Bowen, Wayne H. 2008. *The History of Saudi Arabia*. Santa Barbara, CA: Greenwood Publishing Group.

Brand, Laurie. 1994. *Jordan's Inter-Arab Relations: The Political Economy of Alliance Making*. New York: Columbia University Press.

  1999. 'Middle Eastern Alliances: From Neorealism to Political Economy'. In *Area Studies and Social Science: Strategies for Understanding Middle East Politics*, edited by Mark Tessler, Jodi Nachtwey and Anna Banda, 134–47. Bloomington, IN: Indiana University Press.

Brawley, Mark R. 2009. 'Neoclassical Realism and Strategic Calculations: Explaining Divergent British, French, and Soviet Strategies toward Germany between the World Wars (1919–1939)'. In *Neoclassical Realism, the State, and Foreign Policy*, edited by Steven E. Lobell, Norrin M. Ripsman and Jeffrey W. Taliaferro, 75–98. Cambridge: Cambridge University Press.

Brewer, Marilynn. 1991. 'The Social Self: On Being the Same and Different at the Same Time'. *Personality and Social Psychology Bulletin* 17 (5): 475–82.

Bronner, Ethan. 2008. 'Israel Holds Peace Talks With Syria'. *The New York Times*, 22 May 2008, sec. International/Middle East. www.nytimes .com/2008/05/22/world/middleeast/22mideast.html.

Bronson, Rachel. 2000. 'Syria: Hanging Together or Hanging Separately'. *The Washington Quarterly* 23 (4): 91–105.

Brown, L. Carl. 1984. *International Politics and the Middle East: Old Rules, Dangerous Game*. Princeton, NJ: Princeton University Press.

Buchta, Wilfried. 2002. 'The Failed Pan-Islamic Program of the Islamic Republic: Views of the Liberal Reformers on the Religious "Semi Opposition"'. In *Iran and the Surrounding World: Interactions in Culture and Cultural Politics*, edited by Nikki R. Keddie and Rudolph P. Matthee, 281–304. Seattle, WA: University of Washington Press.

Buzan, Barry. 1991. *People, State and Fear: An Agenda for International Security in the Post Cold War Era*. 2nd edn. London: Lynne Rienner.

  2004. *From International to World Society? English School Theory and the Social Structure of Globalization*. Cambridge: Cambridge University Press.

Buzan, Barry and Ana Gonzalez-Pelaez, eds. 2009. *International Society and the Middle East: English School Theory at the Regional Level*. Basingstoke: Palgrave Macmillan.

Buzan, Barry, Ole Wæver and Jaap de Wilde. 1998. *Security: A New Framework for Analysis*. Boulder, CO: Lynne Rienner.

Byman, Daniel. 2006. 'Syria and Iran: What's Behind the Enduring Alliance?' 2006. www.brookings.edu/research/opinions/2006/07/19middleeast-byman.

Campbell, David. 1992. *Writing Security: United States Foreign Policy and the Politics of Identity*. Minneapolis, MN: University of Minnesota Press.

Cardoso, Fernando Henrique. 1980. 'On the Characterization of Authoritarian Regimes in Latin America'. In *The New Authoritarianism in Latin America*, edited by David Collier, 33–58. Princeton, NJ: Princeton University Press.

Carmon, Yigal. 2009. 'An Escalating Regional Cold War – Part 1: The 2009 Gaza War'. Gatestone Institute. 6 February 2009. www.gatestoneinstitute.org/303/an-escalating-regional-cold-war—part-1-the-2009-gaza-war.

Carter, Jimmy. 2009. *We Can Have Peace in the Holy Land: A Plan That Will Work*. New York: Simon and Schuster.

Cashman, Greg and Leonard Robinson. 2007. *An Introduction to the Causes of War: Patterns of Interstate Conflict from World War I to Iraq War*. Lanham, MD: Rowman & Littlefield.

CBS News. 2012. 'Iran Reportedly Admits Helping Gaza Militants Produce Long-Range Missiles'. CBS News. 21 November 2012. www.cbsnews.com/news/iran-reportedly-admits-helping-gaza-militants-produce-long-range-missiles/.

Chalala, B. Y. Elie. 1988. 'Syria's Support of Iran in the Gulf War: The Role of Structural Change and the Emergence of a Relatively Strong State'. *Journal of Arab Affairs* 7 (2): 107–20.

Chubin, Shahram. 2009. 'Iran's Power in Context'. *Survival* 51 (1): 165–90. 2014. 'Is Iran a Military Threat?' *Survival* 56 (2): 65–88.

Chubin, Shahram and Charles Tripp. 1988. *Iran and Iraq at War*. London: I.B. Tauris.

1996. 'Iran-Saudi Arabia Relations and Regional Order'. *Adelphi Papers* 36 (304): 1–120.

Cigar, Norman L. 2016. *Saudi Arabia and Nuclear Weapons: How Do Countries Think about the Bomb?* UCLA Center for Middle East Development (CMED) Series 10. London: Routledge/Taylor & Francis Group.

CNN. 2017. 'Arab League States Condemn Hezbollah as "Terrorist Organization"', 19 November 2017. https://edition.cnn.com/2017/11/19/mid dleeast/saudi-arabia-iran-arab-league/index.html.

Cohen, Raymond. 1978. 'Threat Perception in International Crisis'. *Political Science Quarterly* 93 (1): 93–107.

Cohen, Robin. 1995. 'Fuzzy Frontiers of Identity: The British Case'. *Social Identities* 1 (1): 35–62.

Cole, Juan. 2006. 'A "Shiite Crescent": The Regional Impact of the Iraq War'. *Current History* 105 (687): 20–6.

Cordesman, Anthony. 1994. *Iran and Iraq: The Threat from the Northern Gulf*. Boulder, CO: Westview Press.

2004. *The Military Balance in the Middle East*. Westport, CT: Praeger Publishers.

2006a. 'Iran's Support of the Hezbollah in Lebanon'. Washington, DC. www.ecoi.net/file_upload/145646_en_060715_hezbollah.pdf.

2006b. 'Preliminary "Lessons" of the Israeli-Hezbollah War'. Washington, DC. http://csis.org/files/media/csis/pubs/060817_isr_hez_lessons.pdf.

2014. 'The Gulf and US–Iranian Strategic Competition'. Washington, DC. http://csis.org/program/us-and-iranian-strategic-competition.

Cordesman, Anthony and Arleigh A. Burke. 2008. 'The Israel and Syrian Conventional Military Balance: An Overview'. Working Paper. Center for Strategic and International Studies.

Cordesman, Anthony and Nawaf Obaid. 2005. *National Security in Saudi Arabia: Threats, Responses and Challenges*. London: Praeger Security International.

CounterPunch News Service. 2006. 'The Nasrallah Interview', August 2006. www.counterpunch.org/2006/08/17/the-nasrallah-interview/.

Cox, Robert and Timothy J. Sinclair. 1996. 'Social Forces, States and World Orders: Beyond International Relations Theory'. In *Approaches to World Order*, 85–123. Cambridge: Cambridge University Press.

Cronin, Stephanie. 2014. *Armies and State-Building in the Modern Middle East: Politics, Nationalism and Military Reform*. London: I. B. Tauris.

Currie, Mark. 2004. *Difference*. London: Routledge.

Darwich, May. 2016. 'The Ontological (In)Security of Similarity Wahhabism Versus Islamism in Saudi Foreign Policy'. *Foreign Policy Analysis* 12 (3): 469–88.

2018. 'The Saudi Intervention in Yemen: Struggling for Status'. *Insight Turkey* 20 (2): 125–41.

David, Steven. 1991. *Choosing Sides: Alignment and Realignment in the Third World*. Baltimore, MD: Johns Hopkins University Press.

Davis, Eric. 1991. 'Theorizing Statecraft and Social Change in Arab Oil-Producing Countries'. In *Statecraft in the Middle East: Oil, Historical*

Memory, and Popular Culture, edited by Eric Davis and Nicolas Gavrielides, 1–35. Gainesville, FL: The Florida International University Press.

Dawisha, Adeed. 1990. 'Arab Regimes: Legitimacy and Foreign Policy'. In *The Arab State*, edited by Giacomo Luciani, 284–99. Berkeley, CA: University of California Press.

2003. *Arab Nationalism in the Twentieth Century: From Triumph to Despair*. Princeton, NJ: Princeton University Press.

Drake, Bruce. 2013. 'As It Fights in Syria, Hezbollah Seen Unfavorably in Region'. Pew Research Center (blog). 7 June 2013. www.pewresearch .org/fact-tank/2013/06/07/as-it-fights-in-syria-hezbollah-seen-unfavorably-in-region/.

Drysdale, Alasdair and Raymond Hinnebusch. 1991. *Syria and the Middle East Peace Process*. New York: Council of Foreign Relations Press.

Dueck, Colin. 2005. 'Realism, Culture and Grand Strategy: Explaining America's Peculiar Path to World Power'. *Security Studies* 14 (2): 195–231.

Eckstein, Harry. 1975. 'Case Study and Theory in Political Science'. In *Handbook of Political Science*, edited by Fred Greenstein and Nelson W. Polsby, 79–138. Reading, MA: Addison Wesley.

Ehteshami, Anoushiravan. 1996. 'Defence and Security Policy of Syria in a Changing Regional'. *International Relations* 13 (1): 49–67.

2002. 'Forward'. In *Iran's Rivalry with Saudi Arabia between the Gulf Wars*, edited by Henner Fürtig, i–viii. London/Ithaca, NY: Ithaca Press.

Ehteshami, Anoushiravan and Raymond Hinnebusch. 1997. *Syria and Iran: Middle Powers in a Penetrated Regional System*. London: Routledge.

Eisenstadt, Michael. 1992. 'Arming for Peace? Syria's Elusive Quest for "Strategic Parity"'. 1992. www.washingtoninstitute.org/policy-analysis/view/arming-for-peace-syrias-elusive-quest-for-strategic-parity.

El Husseini, Rola. 2010. 'Hezbollah and the Axis of Refusal: Hamas, Iran and Syria'. *Third World Quarterly* 31 (5): 803–15.

El-Hokayem, Emile. 2007. 'Hizballah and Syria: Outgrowing the Proxy Relationship'. *The Washington Quarterly* 30 (2): 35–52.

El-Khawas, Mohamed. 2011. 'Obama and the Middle East'. In *The Barack Obama Presidency: A Two Year Assessment*, edited by John Davis, 127–64. New York: Palgrave Macmillan.

Erlanger, Steven. 2009a. 'Divisions Deep at Arab League Meeting'. *The New York Times*, 1 January 2009, sec. International/Middle East. www.nytimes.com/2009/01/01/world/middleeast/01arab.html.

2009b. 'Egyptians Blame Hamas, Yet Are Angry at Cairo as Well'. *The New York Times*, 2 January 2009. www.nytimes.com/2009/01/02/world/africa/02iht-egypt.4.19057164.html?pagewanted=all.

Esposito, John L. 1998. *Islam and Politics*. Syracuse, NY: Syracuse University Press.

Fattah, Nabil Abdul. 2006. 'The War of Fatwas about Hezbollah's Resistance'. *Al-Ahram Strategic File*, 2006. http://acpss.ahram.org.eg/eng/ahram/2004/7/5/SFIL12.HTM.

Fawcett, Louise. 2017. 'States and Sovereignty in the Middle East: Myths and Realities'. *International Affairs* 93 (4): 789–807.

Feaver, Peter, Gunther Hellman, Randall Schweller, Jeffrey Taliaferro, William Wohlforth, Jeffrey Legro and Andrew Morascsik. 2000. 'Correspondence: Brother Can You Spare a Paradigm? (Or Was Anybody Ever a Realist?)'. *International Security* 5 (1): 165–93.

Feldman, Shai and Yiftah Shapir, eds. 2001. *The Middle East Military Balance 2000–2001*. Tel-Aviv: Jaffee Center for Strategic Studies.

Finnemore, Martha. 1996. *National Interests in International Society*. Ithaca, NY: Cornell University Press.

Fishman, Robert M. 1990. 'Rethinking State and Regime: Southern Europe's Transition to Democracy'. *World Politics* 42 (3): 422–40.

Frankel, Rafael D. 2012. 'Keeping Hamas and Hezbollah Out of a War with Iran'. *The Washington Quarterly* 35 (4): 53–65.

Frisch, Hillel. 2002. 'Fuzzy Nationalism: The Case of Jordan'. *Nationalism and Ethnic Politics* 8 (4): 86–103.

Fuller, Graham E. 2007. 'The Hizballah-Iran Connection: Model for Sunni Resistance'. *The Washington Quarterly* 30 (1): 139–50.

Fürtig, Henner. 2002. *Iran's Rivalry with Saudi Arabia between the Gulf Wars*. London/Ithaca, NY: Ithaca Press.

2007. 'Conflict and Cooperation in the Persian Gulf: The Interregional Order and US Policy'. *The Middle East Journal* 61 (4): 627–40.

Gause, F. Gregory. 1990. *Saudi–Yemeni Relations: Domestic Structures and Foreign Influences*. New York: Columbia University Press.

1991. 'Revolutionary Fevers and Regional Contagion: Domestic Structures and the "Export" of Revolution in the Middle East'. *Journal of South Asian and Middle Eastern Studies* 14 (3): 1–23.

1999. 'Systemic Approaches to Middle East International Relations'. *International Studies Review* 1 (1): 11–31.

2002. 'Iraq's Decision to Go to War, 1980 and 1990'. *The Middle East Journal* 56 (1): 47–70.

2003. 'Balancing What? Threat Perception and Alliance Choice in the Gulf'. *Security Studies* 13 (2): 273–305.

2007. 'Saudi Arabia: Iraq, Iran, the Regional Power Balance, and the Sectarian Question'. *Strategic Insights* 6 (2). https://core.ac.uk/download/pdf/36704532.pdf

2009. *The International Relations of the Persian Gulf*. Cambridge: Cambridge University Press.

2011. 'Saudi Arabia's Regional Security Strategy'. In *The International Relations of the Persian Gulf*, edited by Mehran Kamrava, 169–83. Syracuse, NY: Syracuse University Press.

2014a. 'Beyond Sectarianism: The New Middle East Cold War'. Analysis Paper 11. Doha: Brooking Doha Institute.

2014b. 'Beyond Sectarianism: The New Middle East Cold War'. Analysis Paper 11. Doha: Brooking Doha Institute. www.brookings.edu/~/media/Research/Files/Papers/2014/07/22%20beyond%20sectarianism%20cold%20war%20gause/English%20PDF.pdf.

George, Alexander. 1979. 'Case Studies and Theory Development: The Method of Structured, Focused Comparison'. In *Diplomacy: New Approaches in History, Theory, and Policy*, edited by Paul Gorden Lauren, 43–68. New York: The Free Press.

George, Alexander and Andrew Bennett. 2005. *Case Studies and Theory Development in the Social Sciences*. Cambridge, MA: MIT Press.

Gerring, John and Jason Seawright. 2007. 'Techniques for Choosing Cases'. In *Case Study Research: Principles and Practices*, 86–150. Cambridge: Cambridge University Press.

Ghadry, Farid. 2009. 'From Hama to Hamas: Syria's Islamist Policies'. *InFocus* 3 (1). www.jewishpolicycenter.org/830/from-hama-to-hamas-syrias-islamist-policies.

Ghattas, Kim. 2017. 'Palestine Is a Victim of the Iranian-Saudi War'. *Foreign Policy* (blog). 2017. https://foreignpolicy.com/2017/12/22/palestine-is-a-victim-of-the-iranian-saudi-war/.

Giddens, Anthony. 1984. *The Constitution of Society: Outline of Theory of Structuration*. Cambridge: Polity Press.

1991. *Modernity and Self-Identity*. Palo Alto, CA: Stanford University Press.

Glaser, Charles and Chaim Kaufmann. 1998. 'What Is the Offense–Defense Balance and How Can We Measure It?' *International Security* 22 (4): 44–82.

Glenn, John. 2009. 'Realism versus Strategic Culture: Competition and Collaboration?' *International Studies Review* 11 (3): 523–51.

Goldberg, Jacob. 1986. 'The Shi'i Minority in Saudi Arabia'. In *Shi'ism and Social Protest*, edited by Juan Ricardo Cole and Nikki R. Keddie, 230–45. New Haven, CT: Yale University Press.

1990. 'Saudi Arabia and the Iranian Revolution: The Religious Dimension'. In *The Iranian Revolution and the Muslim World*, edited by David Menashiri, 155–70. Boulder, CO: Westview Press.

Goldstone, Jack A. 1993. *Revolution and Rebellion in the Early Modern World*. Berkeley, CA: University of California Press.

Goodarzi, Jubin. 2006. *Syria and Iran: Diplomatic Alliance and Power Politics in the Middle East*. London: I.B. Tauris.

2013. 'Syria and Iran: Alliance Cooperation in a Changing Regional Environment'. *Ortadogu Etutleri* 4 (2): 31–54.

Grebe, Jan. 2014. 'The Global Militarization Index 2014'. Annual Report. Bonn: Bonn International Center for Conversation. http://gmi.bicc.de/ index.php?page=gmi-new.

Haaertz. 2006. 'Palestinian FM: Iran Donated $120M to Hamas-Led Government'. Haaretz.Com. 6 November 2006. www.haaretz.com/news/ palestinian-fm-iran-donated-120m-to-hamas-led-government-1.201713.

Haas, Mark L. 2003. 'Ideology and Alliances: British and French External Balancing Decisions in the 1930s'. *Security Studies* 12 (4): 34–79.

2012. *The Clash of Ideologies: Middle Eastern Politics and American Security*. Oxford: Oxford University Press.

Haklai, Oded. 2009. 'Authoritarianism and Islamic Movements in the Middle East: Research and Theory-Building in the Twenty-First Century'. *International Studies Review* 11 (1): 27–45.

Halliday, Fred. 2002. 'The Politics of the Umma: States and Community in Islamic Movements'. *Mediterranean Politics* 7 (3): 20–41.

2005. *The Middle East in International Relations: Power, Politics and Ideology*. Cambridge: Cambridge University Press.

Hamid Al-Din, Abdullah. 2014. 'Saudi National Identity [in Arabic]'. *Al-Hayat*, 22 September 2014. https://goo.gl/7QLEja.

Hamzeh, Ahmad Nizar. 1993. 'Lebanon's Hizbullah: From Islamic Revolution to Parliamentary Accommodation'. *Third World Quarterly* 14 (2): 321–37.

2004. *In the Path of Hizbullah*. Syracuse, NY: Syracuse University Press.

Harel, Amos and Aluf Benn. 2018. 'No Longer a Secret: How Israel Destroyed Syria's Nuclear Reactor'. *Haaretz*, 23 March 2018. www .haaretz.com/world-news/MAGAZINE-no-longer-a-secret-how-israel-destroyed-syria-s-nuclear-reactor-1.5914407.

Ḥasīb, Khayr al-Dīn. 2006. 'Ḥawl Al-Ḥarb Al-'Isrā'īliyya 'alā Lubnān: War-aqat Khalfiyya [On the Israeli War in Lebanon: Background Paper]'. In *Al-Ḥarb Al-'Isrā'īliyya 'alā Lubnān: Al-Tadā'Iyyāt Al-Lubnāniyya Wa Al-'Isrā'īliyya , Ta'Thīrātihā Al-'arabiyya Wa Al-'Iqlīmiyya Wa Al-Dawliyya [The Israeli War in Lebanon: The Lebanese and Israeli Implication and Their Arab, Regional, and International E*, 26–48. Beirut: Center of Arab Unity Studies.

Haugbolle, Sune. 2016. 'In Defense of Ideology: Notes on Experience and Revolution – Project on Middle East Political Science'. *POMPES* (blog). May 2016. https://pomeps.org/2016/05/31/in-defense-of-ideology-notes-on-experience-and-revolution/.

Hegghammer, Thomas. 2010. *Jihad in Saudi Arabia: Violence and Pan-Islamism since 1979*. Cambridge: Cambridge University Press.

Hegghammer, Thomas and Stephane Lacroix. 2007. 'Rejectionist Islamism in Saudi Arabia: The Story of Juhayman Al-'Utaybi Revisited'. *International Journal of Middle East Studies* 39 (1): 103–22.

Hellman, Gunther. 2003. 'In Conclusion: Dialogue and Synthesis in Individual Scholarship and Collective Inquiry'. *International Studies Review* 5 (1): 147–50.

Herb, Michael. 1999. *All in the Family: Absolutism, Revolution and Democracy in the Middle Eastern Monarchies*. Albany, NY: State University of New York Press.

Herrmann, Richard K. 2013. 'Perceptions and image theory in international relations'. In *The Oxford Handbook of Political Psychology*, edited by Leonie Huddy, David O. Sears and Jack S. Levy, 334–63. New York: Oxford University Press.

Herszenhorn, David M. 2012. 'For Syria, Reliant on Russia for Weapons and Food, Old Bonds Run Deep'. *The New York Times*, 18 February 2012. www.nytimes.com/2012/02/19/world/middleeast/for-russia-and-syria-bonds-are-old-and-deep.html.

Hinnebusch, Raymond. 1996. 'Does Syria Want Peace? Syrian Policy in the Syrian-Israeli Peace Negotiations'. *Journal of Palestine Studies* 26 (1): 42–57.

2001. *Syria: Revolution from Above*. London: Routledge.

2003a. *The International Politics of the Middle East*. Manchester: Manchester University Press.

2003b. 'Identity in International Relations: Constructivism versus Materialism, and the Case of the Middle East'. *The Review of International Affairs* 3 (2): 358–62.

2005a. 'Defying the Hegemon: Syria and the Iraq War'. In *The Conference of the European Consortium on Political Research Conference*.

2005b. 'Explaining International Politics in the Middle East: The Struggle of Regional Identity and Systemic Structure'. In *Analyzing Middle East Foreign Policies and the Relationship with Europe*, edited by Gerd Nonneman, 243–56. London: Routledge.

2009. 'Syrian Foreign Policy under Bashar Al-Asad'. *Ortadoğu Etütleri* 1 (1): 7–26.

2010a. 'Syria under Bashar: Between Economic Reforms and Nationalist Realpolitik'. In *Syria Foreign Policy and the United States from Bush to Obama*, edited by Raymond Hinnebusch, Marwan Kabalan, Bassma Kodmani and David Lesch, 5–28. St Andrews: St Andrews Papers on Contemporary Syria.

2010b. 'Toward a Historical Sociology of State Formation in the Middle East'. *Middle East Critique* 19 (3): 201–16.

2013. 'The Politics of Identity in the Middle East International Relations'. In *International Relations of the Middle East*, edited by Louise Fawcett, 148–66. Oxford: Oxford University Press.

2014a. 'The Foreign Policy of Syria'. In *The Foreign Policies of Middle East States*, edited by Raymond Hinnebusch and Anoushiravan Ehetshami, 2nd edn, 207–32. Boulder, CO: Lynne Rienner.

2014b. 'Syria–Iraq Relations: State Construction and Deconstruction and the MENA Region'. *LSE Middle East Centre*, no. 4 (October): 32.

2015. *The International Politics of the Middle East*. 2nd edn. Manchester: Manchester University Press.

Hinnebusch, Raymond and Anoushiravan Ehteshami, eds. 2002. *The Foreign Policies of Middle East States*. London: Lynne Rienner.

Hirschfeld, Yair. 1986. 'The Odd Couple: Ba'thist Syria and Khomeini's Iran'. In *Syria under Assad: Domestic Constraints and Regional Risks*, edited by Avner Yaniv and Moshe Ma'oz, 105–24. London: Croom Helm.

Hobden, Stephen and John M. Hobson. 2002. *Historical Sociology of International Relations*. Cambridge: Cambridge University Press.

Horowitz, Donald L. 1995. *Ethnic Groups in Conflict*. Berkley, CA: University of California Press.

Hollis, Martin and Steve Smith. 1990. *Explaining and Understanding International Relations*. Oxford: Oxford University Press.

Hopf, Ted. 2002. *Social Construction of International Politics: Identities and Foreign Policy, Moscow, 1955 and 1999*. Ithaca, NY: Cornell University Press.

Horowitz, Donald L. 1985. *Ethnic Groups in Conflict*. Berkeley, CA: University of California Press.

Hunter, Shireen. 1993. 'Iran and Syria: From Hostility to Limited Alliance'. In *Iran and the Arab World*, edited by Hooshang Amirahmadi and Nader Entessar, 198–216. New York: St. Martin's Press.

Huntington, Samuel. 1993. 'The Clash of Civilizations?' *Foreign Affairs* 72 (3): 22–49.

Hussein, Abdulrhman. 2012. *So History Doesn't Forget: Alliances in the Foreign Policy of the Kingdom of Saudi Arabia 1979–1990*. Bloomington, IN: Author House.

Huysmans, Jef. 1998. 'Security! What Do You Mean?: From Concept to Thick Signifier'. *European Journal of International Relations* 4 (2): 226–55.

Ibrahim, Fouad. 2006. *The Shi'is of Saudi Arabia*. London: Saqi Books.

Ikenberry, John. 2000. *After Victory: Institutions, Strategic Restraint, and the Rebuilding of Order after Major Wars*. Princeton, NJ: Princeton University Press.

Inbar, Efraim. 2005. 'The Resilience of Israeli–Turkish Relations'. *Israel Affairs* 11 (4): 591–607. https://doi.org/10.1080/13537120500233664.

Islammemo. 2009. 'Mubāthāt Bayn Al-Senator Kerry Wa Al-Ra'īs Al-Sūrī [Talks between Senator Kerry and the Syrian President]'. 21 February 2009. http://islammemo.cc/akhbar/arab/2009/02/21/77528.html.

Ismail, Salwa. 2009. 'Changing Social Structure, Shifting Alliances and Authoritarianism in Syria'. In *Demystifying Syria*, edited by Fred Lawson, 13–28. London: Saqi Books.

Jamus, Abdel Rehim Mahmoud. 2001. *Al-Lijan Al-Sha'biyyah Li Musa'adat Mujahidi Filasteen Fi Al-Mamlakah Al-'Arabiyyah Al-Sa'udiyya [Popular Committee for the Mujahdin of Palestine in the Kingdom of Saudi Arabia]*. Al-Riyadh: Darat Al-Malik Abdel Aziz.

Jensen, Michael Irving. 2008. *The Political Ideology of Hamas: A Grassroots Perspective*. London: I.B. Tauris.

Jepperson, Ronald, Alexander Wendt and Peter J. Katzenstein. 1996. 'Norms, Identity and Culture in National Security'. In *The Culture of National Security: Norms and Identity in World Politics*, edited by Peter J. Katzenstein, 33–75. New York: Columbia University Press.

Jervis, Robert. 1976. *Perception and Misperception in International Politics*. Princeton, NJ: Princeton University Press.

Job, Brian, ed. 1992. *The Insecurity Dilemma: National Security of Third World States*. Boulder, CO: Lynne Rienner.

Jones, Toby Craig. 2007. 'Saudi Arabia's Not So New Anti-Shi'ism'. *Middle East Report*, no. 242: 29–32.

Jouejati, Murhaf. 2005. 'Syrian Motives for Its WMD Programs and What to Do about Them'. *The Middle East Journal* 59 (1): 52–61.

Kabalan, Marwan. 2010. 'Syrian Foreign Policy between Domestic Needs and the External Environment'. In *Syria Foreign Policy and the United States from Bush to Obama*, edited by Raymond Hinnebusch, Marwan Kabalan, Bassma Kodmani and David Lesch, 29–44. St Andrews: St Andrews Papers on Contemporary Syria.

Kam, Ephraim. 2004. 'The Middle East in Transition: An Overview'. In *The Middle East Strategic Balance, 2003–2004*, edited by Shai Feldman and Yiftah Shapir, 5–36. Brighton: Sussex Academic Press.

Kamrava, Mehran. 2013. 'Mediation and Saudi Foreign Policy'. *Orbis* 57 (1): 152–70.

Kandil, Hazem. 2008. 'The Challenge of Restructuring: Syrian Foreign Policy'. In *The Foreign Policies of Arab States: The Challenge of Globalization*, edited by Bahgat Korany and Ali. E. Hillal Dessouki, 421–55. Cairo: Cairo University Press.

Karawan, Ibrahim. 1994. 'Sadat and the Egyptian–Israeli Peace Revisited'. *International Journal of Middle East Studies* 26 (2): 249–66.

2002. 'Identity and Foreign Policy: The Case of Egypt'. In *Identity and Foreign Policy in the Middle East*, edited by Michael Barnett and Shibley Telhami, 155–68. Ithaca, NY: Cornell University Press.

Karmon, Ely. 2008. 'Iran–Syria– Hizbullah–Hamas: A Coalition against Nature: Why Does It Work?' *United Army War College, Proteus Monograph* 1 (3). www.ict.org.il/UserFiles/karmon-iran-syria-hizbollah.pdf.

Kaye, Dalia Dassa and Frederic M. Wehrey. 2007. 'A Nuclear Iran: The Reactions of Neighbours'. *Survival* 49 (2): 111–28.

Kazziha, Walid. 1985. 'The Impact of Palestine on Arab Politics'. *The International Spectator* 20 (2): 11–19.

Kechichian, Joseph A. 1990. 'Islamic Revivalism and Change in Saudi Arabia: Juhayman Al-'Utaybi's "Letters" to the Saudi People'. *The Muslim World* 70 (1): 1–16.

Kedar, Mordechai. 2006. *Asad in Search of Legitimacy: Message and Rhetoric in the Syrian Press under Hafiz and Bashar*. Vol. 2006. Brighton: Sussex Academic Press.

Kedourie, Elie. 1992. *Democracy and Arab Political Culture*. Washington, DC: Washington Institute for Near East Policy.

Kerr, Malcolm. 1971. *The Arab Cold War: Gamal 'Abd Al-Nasir and His Rivals, 1958–1970*. Oxford: Oxford University Press.

Khadduri, Majid. 1988. *The Gulf War: The Origins and Implication of the Iraq-Iran Conflict*. Oxford: Oxford University Press.

Khalidi, Ahmad and Hussein Agha. 1991. 'The Syrian Doctrine of Strategic Parity'. In *The Middle East in Global Perspective*, edited by Judith Kipper and Harold H. Saunders, 186–218. Boulder, CO: Westview Press.

Khalidi, Walid. 1978. 'Thinking the Unthinkable: A Sovereign Palestinian State'. *Foreign Affairs* 56 (4): 695–713.

Khan, M. A. Muqtedar. 2004. *Jihad for Jerusalem: Identity and Strategy in International Relations*. Santa Barbara, CA: Greenwood Publishing Group.

Khashan, Hilal and Ibrahim Mousawi. 2007. 'Hizbullah's Jihad Concept'. *Journal of Religion and Society* 9: 1–19.

Khomeini, Ayathollah. 1980. 'Khomeini: "We Shall Confront the World with Our Ideology"'. *MERIP Reports*, no. 88: 22–25. https://doi.org/10.2307/3011306.

Khomeini, Ruhollah. 1981. *Islam and Revolution: Writings and Declarations of Imam Khomeini*. Edited by H. Algar. Berkeley, CA: Mizan Press.

Khūrī, Yūsif. 1988. *Al-Mashārī' Al-Waḥdawiyya Al-'Arabiyya [Projects of Arab Unity]*. Beirut: Center for Arab Unity Studies.

Kienle, Eberhard. 1990. *Ba'th versus Ba'th: The Conflict between Syria and Iraq 1968–1989*. London: I.B. Tauris.

1994. 'Syria, the Kuwait War, and the New World Order'. In *The Gulf War and the New World Order: International Relations of the Middle East*, edited by Tareq Y. Ismael and Jacqueline S. Ismael, 383–98. Gainesville, FL: University Press of Florida.

1995. 'Arab Unity Schemes Revisited: Interest, Identity, and Policy in Syria and Egypt'. *International Journal of Middle East Studies* 27 (1): 53–71.

Kienle, Eberhard, Derek Hopwood, Habib Ishow and Thomas Koszinowski. 1993. *The Limits of Fertile Crescent Unity: Iraqi Policies towards Syria 1945–1991*. Oxford/Reading, MA: St. Antony's Middle East Monographs/Ithaca Press. https://halshs.archives-ouvertes.fr/halshs-00996815.

Kinnvall, Catarina. 2004. 'Globalization and Religious Nationalism: Self, Identity, and the Search for Ontological Security'. *Political Psychology* 25 (5): 741–67.

Kirkpatrick, David D. 2014. 'Arab Leaders, Viewing Hamas as Worse Than Israel, Stay Silent'. *The New York Times*, 30 July 2014. www.nytimes .com/2014/07/31/world/middleeast/fighting-political-islam-arab-states-find-themselves-allied-with-israel.html.

Kitchen, Nicholas. 2010. 'Systemic Pressures and Domestic Ideas: A Neoclassical Realist Model of Grand Strategy Formation'. *Review of International Studies* 36 (1): 117–43.

Koehler, Kevin. 2018. 'State and Regime Capacity in Authoritarian Elections: Egypt before the Arab Spring'. *International Political Science Review* 39(1): 97–113.

Korany, Bahgat and Ali. E.H Dessouki, eds. 2008. *The Foreign Policies of Arab States: The Challenge of Globalization*. Cairo: Cairo University Press.

Kostiner, Joseph. 1987. 'Shi'i Unrest in the Gulf'. In *Shi'ism, Resistance and Revolution*, edited by Martin Kramer, 172–88. Boulder, CO: Westview Press.

1990. 'Transforming Dualities: Tribes and State Formation in Saudi Arabia'. In *Tribes and State Formation in the Middle East*, edited by Philip Shukry Khoury and Joseph Kostiner, 226–51. Berkeley, CA: University of California Press.

2005. 'Coping with Regional Challenges: A Case of Prince Abdullah's Peace Initiative'. In *Saudi Arabia in the Balance: Political Economy, Society, Foreign Affairs*, edited by Paul Aarts and Gerd Nonneman, 352–71. London: Hurst & Company.

2009. 'Saudi Arabia and the Arab–Israeli Peace Process: The Fluctuation of Regional Coordination'. *British Journal of Middle Eastern Studies* 36 (3): 417–29.

Kostiner, Joseph and Chelsi Mueller. 2010. 'Egyptian and Saudi Intervention in the Israeli-Palestinian Conflict (206-09): Local Powers' Mediation

Compared'. In *International Intervention in Local Conflicts: Crisis Management and Conflict Resolution since the Cold War*, edited by Uzi Rabi, 202–21. London: I.B. Tauris.

Kratochwil, Friedrich and Johan Gerard Ruggie. 1986. 'International Organization: A State of the Art on an Art of the State'. *International Organization* 40 (4): 753–75.

Kuhn, Thomas. 1970. *The Structure of Scientific Revolutions*. 2nd edn. Chicago, IL: Chicago University Press.

Langton, Christopher, ed. 2004. *The Military Balance 2003/2004*. Oxford: Oxford University Press.

Larrabee, F. Stephen and Ian O. Lesser. 2003. *Turkish Foreign Policy in an Age of Uncertainty*. Santa Monica, CA: RAND Corporation.

Lawson, Fred H. 1996. *Why Syria Goes to War: Thirty Years of Confrontation*. London/Ithaca, NY: Cornell University Press.

      2007. 'Syria's Relations with Iran: Managing the Dilemmas of Alliance'. *The Middle East Journal* 61 (1): 29–47.

Layne, Linda L. 1994. *Home and Homeland: The Dialogics of Tribal and National Identities in Jordan*. Princeton, NJ: Princeton University Press.

Legro, Jeffrey. 2005. *Rethinking the World: Great Power Strategies and International Order*. London/Ithaca, NY: Cornell University Press.

Lesch, David W. 2005. *The New Lion of Damascus: Bashar Al-Asad and Modern Syria*. New Haven, CT: Yale University Press.

Levitt, Matthew. 2007. 'Hezbollah Finances: Funding the Party of God'. In *Terrorism Financing and State Responses: A Comparative Perspective*, edited by Jeanne K. Giraldo and Harold A. Trinkunas, 134–51. Stanford, CA: Stanford University Press.

      2008. *Hamas: Politics, Charity, and Terrorism in the Service of Jihad*. New Haven, CT: Yale University Press.

Levy, Jack. 2008. 'Case Studies: Types, Designs, and Logics of Inference'. *Conflict Management and Peace Science* 25 (1): 1–18.

Laitin, David D. 1986. *Hegemony and Culture: Politics and Change among the Yoruba*. Chicago, IL: University of Chicago Press.

Lippman, Thomas W. 2004. *Inside the Mirage: America's Fragile Partnership with Saudi Arabia*. Boulder, CO: Westview Press.

Litvak, Meir. 1998. 'The Islamization of the Palestinian-Israeli Conflict: The Case of Hamas'. *Middle Eastern Studies* 34 (1): 148–63.

Lob, Eric. 2014. 'Is Hezbollah Confronting a Crisis of Popular Legitimacy?' 78. Middle East Brief. Crown Center for Middle East Studies, Brandeis University.

Long, David E. 1986. 'Saudi Foreign Policy and the Arab-Israeli Peace Process: The Fahd (Arab) Peace Plan'. In *The Middle East Peace Plan*, edited by Willard Beling, 54–66. Kent: Croom Helm.

1990. 'The Impact of the Iranian Revolution on the Arabian Peninsula and the Gulf States'. In *The Iranian Revolution: Its Global Impact*, edited by John L. Esposito. Miami, FL: Florida International University Press.

Longva, Ahn Nga. 2000. 'Citizenship in the Gulf States: Conceptualization and Practice'. In *Citizenship and the State in the Middle East: Approaches and Applications*, edited by Nils A. Butenschøn, Uris David and Manuel Hassassian, 179–97. Syracuse, NY: Syracuse University Press.

Lotfian, Saideh. 1997. 'Taking Sides: Regional Powers and the War'. In *Iranian Perspectives on the Iran–Iraq War*, edited by Farhang Rajaee, 13–28. Gainesville, FL: University Press of Florida.

Lupovici, Amir. 2012. 'Ontological Dissonance, Clashing Identities, and Israel's Unilateral Steps towards the Palestinians'. *Review of International Studies* 38 (04): 809–33.

Lynch, Marc. 1999. *State Interests and Public Spheres: The International Politics of Jordan Identities*. New York: Columbia University Press.

2002. 'Jordan's Identity and Interests'. In *Identity and Foreign Policy in the Middle East*, edited by Shibley Telhami and Michael Barnett, 26–57. London/Ithaca, NY: Cornell University Press.

2006. *Voices of the New Arab Public: Iraq, Al-Jazeera and Middle East Politics Today*. New York: Columbia University Press.

2010. 'The Hollow Arab Core'. 2010. www.foreignpolicy.com/posts/2010/06/17/the_hollow_arab_core.

2013. 'The War for the Arab World'. *Foreign Policy* (blog). 23 May 2013. http://foreignpolicy.com/2013/05/23/the-war-for-the-arab-world/.

Mabon, Simon. 2013. *Saudi Arabia and Iran: Soft Power Rivalry in the Middle East*. London: I.B. Tauris.

MacFarquhar, Neil. 2006. 'Tide of Arab Opinion Turns to Support for Hezbollah'. *The New York Times*, 28 July 2006, sec. Middle East. www.nytimes.com/2006/07/28/world/middleeast/28arabs.html.

Mahmoud, Arwa. 2010. *A Battle of Creed: Exploring the Religious Factor in Hizbullah's 2006 Ground Engagements with Israel*. Berlin: Lambert Academic Publishing.

Makinda, Samuel. 2000. 'International Society and Eclecticism in International Relations Theory'. *Conflict and Cooperation* 35 (2): 205–16.

Makovsky, David. 2006. 'Iran's Hand in Lebanon'. *San Diego Union-Tribune*, July 2006. www.washingtoninstitute.org/policy-analysis/view/irans-hand-in-lebanon.

Maltzahn, Nadia von. 2013. *The Syria–Iran Axis: Cultural Diplomacy and International Relations in the Middle East*. London: I.B. Tauris.

Ma'oz, Moshe. 1988. *Asad, the Sphinx of Damascus: A Political Biography*. New York: Gove Weidenfled.

2007a. 'Syria's Role in the Region Mediator, Peacemaker, or Aggressor?' Report. A Century Foundation Report. New York: The Century Foundation.

2007b. 'The "Shi'i Crescent": Myth and Reality', Analysis Paper, no. 15.

Markham, James M. 1979. 'Arafat, in Iran, Reports Khomeini Pledges Aid for Victory Over Israeli'. *The New York Times*, 19 February 1979, sec. Archives. www.nytimes.com/1979/02/19/archives/arafat-in-iran-reports-khomeini-pledges-aid-for-victory-over-israel.html.

Marschall, Christin. 1992. 'Syria-Iran: A Strategic Alliance, 1979–1991'. *Orient* 33 (2): 433–46.

2003. *Iran's Persian Gulf Policy: From Khomeini to Khatami*. London: Routledge.

McSweeney, Bill. 1999. *Security, Identity and Interests: A Sociology of International Relations*. Cambridge: Cambridge University Press.

Mearsheimer, John. 2001. *The Tragedy of Great Powers Politics*. London, New York: Norton.

Menshari, David. 1990. 'Khomeini's Vision: Nationalism or World Order?' In *The Iranian Revolution and the Muslim World*, edited by David Menshari, 40–57. Boulder, CO: Westview Press.

Meyer, Christoph O and Eva Strickmann. 2011. 'Solidifying Constructivism: How Material and Ideational Factors Interact in European Defense'. *Journal of Common Market Studies* 49 (1): 61–81.

Miller, R Reuben. 2000. 'The Israeli-Syrian Negotiations'. *Media, Culture & Society* 11 (4): 117–39.

Milton-Edwards, Beverley. 2013. 'Hamas and the Arab Spring: Strategic Shifts?' *Middle East Policy* 20 (3): 60–72.

Mitzen, Jennifer. 2006. 'Ontological Security in World Politics: State Identity and the Security Dilemma'. *European Journal of International Relations* 12 (3): 341–70.

Mitzen, Jennifer and Kyle Larson. 2017. 'Ontological Security and Foreign Policy'. In *Oxford Research Encyclopedia of Politics*. New York: Oxford University Press.

Moravscsik, Andrew. 2003. 'Theory Synthesis in International Relations: Real Not Metaphysical'. *International Studies Review* 5 (1): 131–6.

Mouzahem, Haytham. 2013. 'Saudi Wahhabi Sheikh Calls On Iraq's Jihadists to Kill Shiites'. Al-Monitor. 28 April 2013. www.al-monitor.com/pulse/originals/2013/04/wahhabi-sheikh-fatwa-iraq-kill-shiites-children-women.html.

Mufti, Malik. 1996. *Sovereign Creations: Pan-Arabism and Political Order in Syria and Iraq*. Ithaca, NY: Cornell University Press.

1998. 'Daring and Caution in Turkish Foreign Policy'. *The Middle East Journal* 52 (1): 32–50.

Mus'ad, Nivīn. 2006. 'Al-Tadā'Iyyāt Al-'Iqlīmiyya: 'Īrān [Regional Implications: Iran]'. In *Al-Ḥarb Al-'Isrā'īliyya 'alā Lubnān: Al-Tadā'Iyyāt Al-Lubnāniyya Wa Al-'Isrā'īliyya , Ta'Thīrātihā Al-'arabiyya Wa Al-'Iqlīmiyya Wa Al-Dawliyya [The Israeli War in Lebanon: Lebanese and Israeli Implications and Their Arab, Regional, and International Effects]*, 297–322. Beirut: Center for Arab Unity Studies.

Myre, Greg. 2005. 'Turkish Leader Visits Israel, Restoring Friendly Ties'. *The New York Times*, 2 May 2005, sec. Middle East. www.nytimes.com/2005/05/02/world/middleeast/turkish-leader-visits-israel-restoring-friendly-ties.html.

Nabers, Dirk. 2009. 'Filling the Void of Meaning: Identity Construction in U.S. Foreign Policy After'. *Foreign Policy Analysis* 5 (2): 191–214.

Nahas, Maridi. 1985. 'State-Systems and Revolutionary Challenge: Nasser, Khomeini and the Middle East'. *International Journal of Middle East Studies* 17 (4): 507–27.

Nakash, Yitzhak. 2011. *Reaching for Power: The Shi'a in the Modern Arab World*. Princeton, NJ: Princeton University Press.

Nakhoul, Samia and Michael Stott. 2012. 'Hamas Says It Will Not Go to War for Iran'. *Reuters*, 10 May 2012. www.reuters.com/article/2012/05/10/us-palestinians-hamas-idUSBRE84917H20120510.

Napolitano, Valentina. 2013. 'Hamas and the Syrian Uprising: A Difficult Choice'. *Middle East Policy* 20 (3): 73–85.

Nasr, Vali. 2006. *The Shia Revival: How Conflicts within Islam Will Shape the Future*. New York: W.W. Norton & Company.

Nau, Henry. 2002. *At Home Abroad: Identity and Power in American Foreign Policy*. Ithaca, NY: Cornell University Press.

Nevo, Joseph. 1998. 'Religion and National Identity in Saudi Arabia'. *Middle Eastern Studies* 34 (3): 34–53.

Niblock, Tim. 2006. *Saudi Arabia: Power, Legitimacy and Survival*. London: Routledge.

Noble, Paul. 2004. 'Systemic Factors Do Matter, But...: Reflections on the Uses and Limitations of Systemic Analysis'. In *Persistent Permeability?: Regionalism, Localism and Globalization*, edited by Rex Brynen and Bassel Salloukh, 29–64. Aldershot: Ashgate.

Nonneman, Gerd. 1986. *Iraq, the Gulf States and the War: A Changing Relationship 1980–1986 and Beyond*. London: Cornell University Press.

2004. 'The Gulf States and the Iran-Iraq War: Pattern Shifts and Continuities'. In *Iran, Iraq, and the Legacies of War*, edited by Lawrence Potter and Gary Sick, 167–92. New York: Palgrave.

Norton, Augustus. 1987. *Amal and the Shia: Struggle for the Soul of Lebanon*. 1st edn. Austin, TX: University of Texas Press.

Norton, Augustus Richard. 1999. *Hizballah of Lebanon: Extremist Ideals vs. Mundane Politics*. New York: Council on Foreign Relations. www.cfr.org/religion/hizballah-lebanon-extremist-ideals-vs-mundane-politics-paper-muslim-politics-project/p8612.

—— 2007. *Hezbollah: A Short History*. Princeton, NJ: Princeton University Press.

O'Brien, Don van Natta Jr and Timothy, L. 2003. 'Flow of Saudis' Cash to Hamas Is Scrutinized'. 17 September 2003. www.nytimes.com/2003/09/17/world/flow-of-saudis-cash-to-hamas-is-scrutinized.html.

Ochsenwald, William. 1981. 'Saudi Arabia and the Islamic Revival'. *International Journal of Middle East Studies* 13 (3): 271–86.

Okruhlik, Gwenn. 2003. 'Saudi Arabian-Iranian Relations: External Rapprochement and Internal Consolidation'. *Middle East Policy* 10 (2): 113–26.

Onuf, Nicholas. 1989. *World of Our Own Making: Rules and Rule in Social Theory and International Relations*. Columbia, SC: University of South California Press.

Owen, Roger. 2004. *State, Power and Politics in the Making of the Modern Middle East*. 3rd edn. New York: Routledge.

—— 2012. *The Rise and Fall of Presidents for Life*. Cambridge, MA: Harvard University Press.

Perthes, Volker. 2001. 'Syrian Regional Policy under Bashar Al-Asad: Realignment or Economic Rationalization'. *Middle East Report* 31 (220): 36–41.

—— 2004. 'Syria under Bashar Al-Asad: Modernization and the Limit of Change'. *Adelphi Papers* 44 (366): 7–26.

—— 2006. 'The Syrian Solution'. *Foreign Affairs* 85 (6): 33–40.

Phillips, Christopher. 2011. 'Turkey's Global Strategy: Turkey and Syria'. SR007. IDEAS Reports. London School of Economics and Political Science.

—— 2012. *Everyday Arab Identity: The Daily Reproduction of the Arab World*. London: Routledge.

Pinto, Paulo G. 2011. '"Oh Syria, God Protects You": Islam as Cultural Idiom under Bashar Al-Asad'. *Middle East Critique* 20 (2): 189–205.

Pipes, Daniel. 1990. *Greater Syria: The History of an Ambition*. New York: Oxford University Press.

Piscatori, James. 1983. 'Islamic Values and National Interest: The Foreign Policy of Saudi Arabia'. In *Islam in Foreign Policy*, edited by Adeed Dawisha, 33–53. Cambridge: Cambridge University Press.

Piven, Ben. 2012. 'Map: US Bases Encircle Iran'. 2012. www.aljazeera.com/indepth/interactive/2012/04/2012417131242767298.html.

Pollock, David. 2009. 'Arab Reaction to Gaza Conflict: Anger at Israel, but Scant Support for Hamas'. The Washington Institute. 9 January 2009.

www.washingtoninstitute.org/policy-analysis/view/arab-reaction-to-gaza-conflict-anger-at-israel-but-scant-support-for-hamas.

Qassem, Naim. 2005. *Hizbullah: The Story from Within*. London: Saqi Books.

2007. 'Al-'Intiṣār Namūdhagan Tatbiqiyyan Lil-Murtakazāt Al-Sulūkiyya 'Ind Hizbullah [Victory as an Applied Model of the Behavioural Pillars of Hizbullah]'. *As-Safir Newspaper*, 14 July 2007. http://assafir.com/Article/217/87892/AuthorArticle.

Qassir, Qassem. 2014. 'Tansiq Maydani Bayn Hamas Wa Hezbollah [Ground Coordination between Hamas and Hezbollah]'. *As-Safir Newspaper*, 12 July 2014. http://assafir.com/article.aspx?articleid=360865.

Quandt, William. 1981a. 'Reactions of the Arab Gulf States'. In *The Iran–Iraq War: Issues of Conflict and Prospects for Settlement (Proceedings of a Seminar)*, edited by Ali E. H. Dessouki, 39–46. Princeton, NJ: Center for International Studies/Woodrow Wilson School for Public and International Affairs.

1981b. *Saudi Arabia in the 1980s: Foreign Policy, Security and Oil*. Washington, DC: The Brookings Institute.

Rabil, Robert G. 2006. *Syria, the United States, and the War on Terror in the Middle East*. Santa Barbara, CA: Greenwood Publishing Group.

2010. 'The Syrian Muslim Brotherhood'. In *The Muslim Brotherhood: The Organization and Policies of a Global Islamist Movement (Middle East in Focus)*, 73–88. New York: Palgrave Macmillan. https://doi.org/10.1057/9780230106871_6.

Rajab, Iman Ahmad. 2010. *Al-Niẓām Al-'Iqlīmī Al-'Arabī Fī Marḥalat Mā Ba'd Al-'Iḥtilāl Al-'Amrīkī Lil-'Irāq [The Arab Regional System Following the American Invasion of Iraq]*. Beirut: Center for Arab Unity Studies.

Ramazani, Ruhollah. 1979. 'Security in the Persian Gulf'. *Foreign Affairs* 57 (4): 821–35.

1986. *Revolutionary Iran: Challenge and Response in the Middle East*. Baltimore, MD: The Johns Hopkins University Press.

Rasid Al-Ikhbariyya. 2006. 'Akbar Shayykh Su'udī Yaftī Ḍid Ḥizbullah [The Most Prominent Saudi Shayykh Issues a Fatwa against Hizbullah]'. *Rasid Al-Ikhbariyya*, 2006. www.rasid.com/?act=artc&id=12035.

Reuters. 2009. 'Egypt's Mubarak: Hamas Invited Israeli Offensive'. Reuters UK. 19 January 2009. http://uk.reuters.com/article/2009/01/19/us-arabs-summit-mubarak-sb-idUKTRE50I2W020090119.

2016. 'Gulf Arab States Label Hezbollah a Terrorist Organization'. *Reuters*, 2 March 2016. www.reuters.com/article/us-gulf-hezbollah/gulf-arab-states-designate-hezbollah-a-terrorist-organization-statement-idUSKCN0W40XF.

Riedel, Bruce. 2014. 'Saudi Arabia and the Third Gaza War – Al-Monitor: The Pulse of the Middle East'. Al-Monitor. 6 August 2014. www.al-monitor.com/pulseen/originals/2014/08/saudi-arabia-gaza-war-egypt-quiet.html.

Rifai, Ola. 2014. 'The Shifting Balance of Identity Politics after the Syrian Uprising'. OpenDemocracy. 28 April 2014. www.opendemocracy.net/arab-awakening/ola-rifai/shifting-balance-of-identity-politics-after-syrian-uprising.

Rinnawi, Khalid. 2006. *Instant Nationalism: McArabism, Al-Jazeera and Translational Media in the Arab World*. Lanham, MD: University Press of America.

Ripsman, Norrin M., Jeffrey W. Taliaferro and Steven E. Lobell. 2016. *Neoclassical Realist Theory of International Politics*. New York: Oxford University Press.

Risse, Thomas, D. Engelmann-Martin, H. J. Knopf and K. Roscher. 1999. 'To Euro or Not to Euro? The EMU and Identity Politics in the European Union'. *European Journal of International Relations* 5 (2): 147–87.

Rousseau, David. 2006. *Identifying Threats and Threatening Identities: The Social Construction of Realism and Liberalism*. Stanford, CA: Stanford University Press.

Rousseau, David and Garcia-Retamero Rocio. 2007. 'Identity, Power and, Threat Perception: A Cross-National Experimental Study'. *Journal of Conflict Resolution* 51 (5): 744–71.

Roy, Olivier. 2007. *The Politics of Chaos in the Middle East*. London: Hurst & Company.

Rubin, Barry. 2000. 'Understanding Syrian Foreign Policy: An Analysis of Foreign Minister Faruq Al-Shara's Explanation'. *Middle East Review of International Affairs* 4 (2): 14–37.

       2007. *The Truth about Syria*. New York: Palgrave Macmillan.

Rubin, Lawrence. 2014. *Islam in the Balance: Ideational Threats in Arab Politics*. Stanford, CA: Stanford University Press.

Rumelili, Bahar. 2015. 'Identity and Desecuritisation: The Pitfalls of Conflating Ontological and Physical Security'. *Journal of International Relations and Development* 18 (1): 52–74.

Saad-Gorayeb, Amal. 2002. *Hizbu'llah: Politics and Religion*. London: Pluto Press.

       2007. 'Questioning the Shia Crescent'. April 2007. http://weekly.ahram.org.eg/2007/841/op122.htm.

Sadiki, Larbi. 2014. 'Huntington in the Middle East: There Is an Escalating Clash within the Abode of Islam'. 16 August 2014. www.aljazeera.com/indepth/opinion/2014/08/huntington-middle-east-2014812112219121218.html.

Sadjadpour, Karim. 2009. 'Iran Supports Hamas, but Hamas Is No Iranian "Puppet"'. Carnegie Endowment for International Peace. 8 January

2009. http://carnegieendowment.org/2009/01/08/iran-supports-hamas-but-hamas-is-no-iranian-puppet/3jq1.

Sadowski, Yahya. 2002. 'The Evolution of Political Identity in Syria'. In *Identity and Foreign Policy in the Middle East*, edited by Michael Barnett and Jack Levy, 137–54. Ithaca, NY: Cornell University Press.

Safran, Nadav. 1988. *Saudi Arabia: The Ceaseless Quest for Security*. Ithaca, NY: Cornell University Press.

Saleh, Alam and Hendrik Kraetzschmar. 2015. 'Politicized Identities, Securitized Politics: Sunni-Shi'a Politics in Egypt'. *The Middle East Journal* 69 (4): 545–62.

Salem, Paul. 1994. *Bitter Legacy: Ideology and Politics in the Arab World*. Syracuse, NY: Syracuse University Press.

Salloukh, Bassel. 2000. 'Organizing Politics in the Arab World: State-Society Relations and Foreign Policy Choices in Jordan and Syria'. PhD Dissertation, Montreal: McGill University.

    2004. 'Regime Autonomy and Regional Foreign Policy Choices in the Middle East: A Theoretical Explanation'. In *Persistent Permeability?: Regionalism, Localism and Globalization*, edited by Rex Brynen and Bassel Salloukh, 81–104. Aldershot: Ashgate.

    2009. 'Demystifying Syrian Foreign Policy under Bashar Al-Asad'. In *Demystifying Syria*, edited by Fred Lawson, 159–79. London: Saqi Books.

Samore, Gary. 1983a. 'Royal Family Politics in Saudi Arabia (1953–1982)'. PhD Dissertation. Boston, MA: Harvard University.

    1983b. 'Royal Family Politics in Saudi Arabia (1953–1982)'. Harvard University.

Saudi Ministry of Foreign Affairs. 2016. 'Kingdom Stance on Palestinian Issue'. 16 February 2016. www.mofa.gov.sa/sites/mofaen/KingdomForeignPolicy/Pages/PalestineCause25461.aspx.

Schmitt, Carl. 1922. *Political Theology: Four Chapters on the Concept of Sovereignty*. Translated by George Schawbe. Chicago, IL: University of Chicago Press.

Schweller, Randall. 1994. 'Bandwagoning for Profit: Bringing the Revisionist State Back In'. *International Security* 19 (1): 72–107.

Seale, Patrick. 1986. *The Struggle for Syria: A Study in Post-War Arab Politics, 1945–1958*. New Haven, CT: Yale University Press.

    1989. *Asad of Syria: The Struggle for the Middle East*. London: I.B. Tauris.

    1992. 'La Syrie et Le Processus de Paix'. *Politique Étrangère* 57 (4): 785–96.

    2003. 'Reflections on Why the United States and Israel Are Threatening Syria'. *Daily Star*, April 2003. www.dailystar.com.lb/Opinion/Commen

tary/2003/Apr-18/103111-reflections-on-why-the-united-states-and-israel-are-threatening-syria.ashx#axzz35610dkTO.

2009. 'Rewards of Syrian Diplomacy'. 2 July 2009. http://gulfnews.com/opinions/columnists/rewards-of-syrian-diplomacy-1.499744.

Segal, Daniel. 1988. 'The Iran-Iraq War: A Military Analysis'. *Foreign Affairs* 66 (5): 946–63.

Sela, Avraham. 1998. *The Decline of the Arab–Israeli Conflict: Middle East Politics and the Quest for Regional Order.* New York: State University of New York Press.

Selden, Zachary and Stuart Strome. 2016. 'Competing Identities and Security Interests in the Indo–US Relationship'. *Foreign Policy Analysis*, 4 May 2016. https://doi.org/10.1093/fpa/orw029.

Serr, Marcel. 2018. 'North Korea Built a Nuclear Reactor for Syria (And Israel Destroyed It)'. The National Interest. January 2018. http://nationalinterest.org/blog/the-buzz/north-korea-built-nuclear-reactor-syria-israel-destroyed-it-23922.

Shama, Nael. 2013. *Egyptian Foreign Policy from Mubarak to Morsi: Against the National Interest.* London, New York: Routledge.

Sherwood, Harriet. 2012. 'Hamas Rules out Military Support for Iran in Any War with Israel'. *The Guardian*, 6 March 2012, sec. World news. www.theguardian.com/world/2012/mar/06/hamas-no-military-aid-for-iran.

Shoham, Dany. 2002. 'Guile, Gas and Germs: Syria's Ultimate Weapons'. *Middle East Quarterly* 9 (3): 53–61.

Sil, Rudra. 2000. 'The Foundations of Eclecticism: The Epistemological Status of Agency, Culture, and Structure in Social Theory'. *Journal of Theoretical Politics* 12 (3): 353–87.

Sil, Rudra and Peter Katzenstein. 2010. *Beyond Paradigms: Analytic Eclecticism in the Study of World Politics.* New York: Palgrave.

2012. 'Analytic Eclecticism in the Study of World Politics: Reconfiguring Problems and Mechanisms across Research Traditions'. *Perspectives on Politics* 8 (2): 411–31.

Simon, Steven and Jonathan Stevenson. 2004. 'The Road to Damascus'. *Foreign Affairs* 83 (3): 110–18.

Sindi, Abdullah. 1986. 'King Faisal and Pan-Islamism'. In *King Faisal and the Modernization of Saudi Arabia*, edited by Willard A. Beling, 184–201. London: Croom Helm.

SIPRI. 2016. 'SIPRI Military Expenditure Database'. 2016. www.sipri.org/databases/milex.

Sirriyeh, Hussein. 1985. 'Development of the Iraqi–Iranian Dispute, 1847–1975'. *Journal of Contemporary History* 20 (3): 483–92.

Skocpol, Theda. 1979. *States and Social Revolutions: A Comparative Analysis of France, Russia and China*. Cambridge: Cambridge University Press.

Sørensen, Georg. 2008. 'The Case for Combining Material Forces and Ideas in the Study of IR'. *European Journal of International Relations* 14 (1): 5–32.

Sottimano, Aurora. 2016. 'Building Authoritarian "Legitimacy": Domestic Compliance and International Standing of Bashar Al-Asad's Syria'. *Global Discourse* 6 (3): 450–66.

Stanely, Bruce. 1990. 'Drawing from the Well: Syria in the Persian Gulf'. *Journal of South Asian and Middle Eastern Studies* 14 (2): 45–64.

Steele, Brent. 2005. 'Ontological Security and the Power of Self-Identity: British Neutrality and the American Civil War'. *Review of International Studies* 31 (3): 519–40.

2008. *Ontological Security in International Relations: Self-Identity and the IR State*. London: Routledge.

Stein, Ewan. 2017. 'Ideological Codependency and Regional Order: Iran, Syria, and the Axis of Refusal'. *PS: Political Science and Politics* 50 (3): 676–80.

Stein, Janice Gross. 2013. 'Threat Perception in International Relations'. In *Oxford Handbook of Political Psychology*, edited by Leonie Huddy, David Sears and Jack Levy, 2nd edn, 365–94. Oxford: Oxford University Press.

Steinberg, Guido. 2005. 'The Wahhabi Ulama and the Saudi State: 1975 to Present'. In *Saudi Arabia in the Balance: Political Economy, Society, Foreign Affairs*, edited by Paul Aarts and Gerd Nonneman, 11–34. London: Hurst & Company.

Stenslie, Stig. 2011. *Regime Stability in Saudi Arabia: The Challenge of Succession*. London: Routledge.

Stephan, Alfred. 1986. 'Paths toward Redemocratization: Theoretical and Comparative Considerations'. In *Transitions from Authoritarian Rule: Comparative Perspectives*, edited by Guillermo O'Donnell, Philippe C. Schmitter and Laurence Whitehead, 64–84. Baltimore, MD: The Johns Hopkins University Press.

Stern, Moran and Dennis Ross. 2013. 'The Role of Syria in Israeli-Turkish Relations'. *Georgetown Journal of International Affairs* 14 (2): 115–28.

Stratfor. 2015. 'Saudi Arabia and Hamas: A Pragmatic Partnership'. Stratfor. 2015. https://worldview.stratfor.com/article/saudi-arabia-and-hamas-pragmatic-partnership.

Sunayama, Sonoko. 2007. *Syria and Saudi Arabia: Collaboration and Conflict in the Oil Era*. London, New York: I.B. Tauris.

Susser, Asher. 2007. 'Iraq, Lebanon and Gaza: Middle Eastern Trends'. *Tel Aviv Notes*, 22 July 2007.

Szorm, Charlie. 2009. 'Iran-Hamas Relationship in 2009'. 27 March 2009. www.irantracker.org/military-activities/iran-hamas-relationship-2008.

Takeyh, Ray. 2009. *Guardians of the Revolution: Iran and the World in the Age of the Ayatollahs*. Oxford: Oxford University Press.

Talhamy, Yvette. 2009. 'The Syrian Muslim Brothers and the Syrian-Iranian Relationship'. *The Middle East Journal* 63 (4): 561–80.

Taylor, Alan. 1982. *The Arab Balance of Power*. Syracuse, NY: Syracuse University Press.

Teitelbaum, Joshua. 2009. *The Arab Peace Initiative: A Primer and Future Prospects*. Jerusalem: Jerusalem Center for Public Affairs. http://jcpa .org/text/Arab-Peace-Initiative.pdf.

Telhami, Shibley. 1999. 'Power, Legitimacy, and Peace-Making in Arab Coalitions: The New Arabism'. In *Ethnic Conflict and International Politics in the Middle East*, edited by Leonard Binder, 43–60. Gaines- ville, FL: University Press of Florida.

 2007. 'Zogby International 2006 Annual Arab Public Opinion Survey Global Perspectives'.

Telhami, Shibley and Michael Barnett, eds. 2002a. *Identity and Foreign Policy in the Middle East*. Ithaca, NY: Cornell University Press.

Telhami, Shibley and Michael Barnett, 2002b. 'Introduction: Identity and Foreign Policy in the Middle East'. In *Identity and Foreign Policy in the Middle East*, 1–25. Ithaca, NY: Cornell University Press.

Teti, Andrea. 2007. 'Bridging the Gap: IR, Middle East Studies and the Disciplinary Politics of the Area Studies Controversy'. *European Jour- nal of International Relations* 13 (1): 117–45.

The International Institute for Strategic Studies (IISS). 1979. 'The Middle East and the Mediterranean'. *The Military Balance* 79 (1): 36–47.

 1980. 'Middle East and North Africa'. *The Military Balance* 80 (1): 39–50.

 2003. 'Middle East and North Africa'. *The Military Balance* 103 (1): 96–125.

 2006. 'Middle East and North Africa'. *The Military Balance* 106 (1): 165–216.

Thompson, Mark. 2014. *Saudi Arabia and the Path to Political Change: National Dialogue and Civil Society*. London: I.B. Tauris.

Trofimov, Yaroslav. 2008. *The Siege of Mecca: The Forgotten Uprising in Islam's Holiest Shrine*. London: Penguin.

Tully, James. 1993. *An Approach to Political Philosophy: Locke in Con- texts*. Cambridge: Cambridge University Press.

Ulrichsen, Kristian Coates. 2013. 'The Gulf States and the Iran-Iraq War: Cooperation and Confusion'. In *The Iran–Iraq War: New International Perspectives*, edited by Nigel Ashton and Bryan Gibson, 109–24. London: Routledge.

Urquhart, Conal. 2007. 'Iran Replaces EU as Top Palestinian Donor'. *The Guardian*, 15 January 2007, sec. World news. www.theguardian.com/world/2007/jan/15/israel.iran.

Uzer, Umut. 2013. 'Turkish–Israeli Relations: Their Rise and Fall'. *Middle East Policy* 20 (1): 97–110. https://doi.org/10.1111/mepo.12007.

Valbjørn, Morten. 2004. 'Toward a "Mesopotamian Turn": Disciplinarity and the Study of the International Relations of the Middle East'. *Journal of Mediterranean Studies* 1 (2): 47–75.

2009. 'Arab Nationalism(s) in Transformation: From Arab Interstate Societies to an Arab-Islamic World Society'. In *International Society and the Middle East: English School Theory at the Regional Level*, edited by Barry Buzan and Ana Gonzalez-Pelaez, 140–69. New York: Palgrave Macmillan.

2015. 'International Relations Theory and the New Middle East: Three Levels of a Debate'. In *Project on Middle East Political Science*, 74–9. POMEPS Studies 16. http://pomeps.org/2015/08/25/international-relations-theory-and-the-new-middle-east-three-clusters-of-a-debate/.

Valbjørn, Morten and André Bank. 2007. 'Signs of a New Arab Cold War'. *Middle East Report* (242): 6–11.

2012. 'The New Arab Cold War: Rediscovering the Arab Dimension of Middle East Regional Politics'. *Review of International Studies* 38 (1): 3–24.

Van Dam, NiKolaos. 1996. *The Struggle for Power in Syria: Politics and Society under Asad and the Ba'th Party*. London: I.B. Tauris.

Van Evera, Stephen. 1997. *Guide to Methods for Students of Political Science*. London/Ithaca, NY: Cornell University Press.

Waever, Ole. 1995. 'Securitization and Desecuritzation'. In *On Security*, edited by Ronnie Lipschutz, 46–86. New York: Columbia University Press.

Walt, Stephen. 1985. 'Alliance Formation and the Balance of World Power'. *International Security* 9 (4): 3–43. https://doi.org/10.2307/2538540.

1987. *The Origins of Alliances*. Ithaca, NY: Cornell University Press.

1996. *Revolution and War*. London/Ithaca, NY: Cornell University Press.

1998. 'International Relations: One World, Many Theories'. *Foreign Policy* (110): 29–46.

Waltz, Kenneth. 1979. *Theory of International Politics*. New York: McGraw-Hill, Inc.

1986. 'Reflections on Theory of International Politics: A Response to My Critics'. In *Neorealism and Its Critics*, edited by Robert O. Keohane, 322–45. New York: Columbia University Press.

Waterbury, John. 1983. *The Egypt of Nasser and Sadat: The Political Economy of Two Regimes*. Princeton, NJ: Princeton University Press.

Wehrey, Frederic. 2011. 'Uprisings Jolt the Saudi Iranian Rivalry'. *Current History* 110 (740): 352–7.

2013. *Sectarian Politics in the Gulf: From the Iraq War to the Arab Uprisings*. New York: Columbia University Press. http://books.google .com/books?id=ZmSsAgAAQBAJ&pgis=1.

Wehrey, Frederic, Theodore W. Karasik, Alireza Nader, Jeremy Ghez, Lydia Hansell and Robert A. Guffey. 2009. *Saudi Iranian Relations since the Fall of Saddam: Rivalry, Cooperation, and Implications for U.S. Policy*. Santa Monica, CA: RAND Corporation.

Wehrey, Frederic M. 2012. 'What's Behind Saudi Arabia's Nuclear Anxiety?' 15. CERI Strategy Papers. Paris: SciencePo. www.sciencespo.fr/ ceri/sites/sciencespo.fr.ceri/files/n15a_17122012.pdf.

Wendt, Alexander. 1992. 'Anarchy Is What States Make of It: The Social Construction of Power Politics'. *International Organization* 46 (2): 391–425.

1999. *Social Theory of International Politics*. Cambridge: Cambridge University Press.

White House. 2006. 'White House Statement on Hizballah Kidnapping of Two Israeli Soldiers'. July 2006. www.freerepublic.com/focus/f-news/ 1664553/posts.

Wikas, Seth. 2006. 'The Damascus-Hizballah Axis: Bashar Al-Asad's Vision of a New Middle East'. *Policy Watch*. http://goo.gl/REgzUs.

Willacy, Mark. 2006. 'Hamas Will Accept Funding from Iran: Meshaal'. *Lateline*. Australian Broadcasting Corporation. www.abc.net.au/late line/content/2006/s1589194.htm.

Wilson, Peter and Douglas Graham. 1994. *Saudi Arabia: The Coming Storm*. New York: M.E. Sharpe.

Wivel, Anders. 2005. 'Explaining Why State X Made a Certain Move Last Tuesday: The Promise and Limitations of Realist Foreign Policy Analysis'. *Journal of International Relations and Development* 8 (4): 355–80.

Wohlforth, William. 1993. *The Elusive Balance: Power and Perceptions during the Cold War*. London/Ithaca, NY: Cornell University Press.

Woods, Kevin M., David D. Palkki and Mark E. Stout. 2011. *The Saddam Tapes: The Inner Workings of a Tyrant's Regime, 1978–2001*. Cambridge: Cambridge University Press.

Yamani, Mai. 2008. 'The Two Faces of Saudi Arabia'. *Survival* 50 (1): 143–56.

Young, Crawford. 1979. *The Politics of Cultural Pluralism*. Madison, WI: University of Wisconsin Press.

York, Valerie. 1988. *Domestic Politics and Regional Security: Jordan, Syria and Israel. The End of an Era?* Aldershot: Gower.

Zādah, 'Alī Nūrī. 2006. 'Ḍābiṭ 'Īrānī: "Ḥizb 'Allah" Ladayyhi Wiḥdat Cumāndūz Baḥariyah [An Iranian Officer: Hizbullah Has a Maritime Commandos Unit]'. *Al-Sharq Al-Awsat*, July 2006.

Zarakol, Ayse. 2010. 'Ontological (In)Security and State Denial of Historical Crimes: Turkey and Japan'. *International Relations* 24 (1): 3–23.

Zartman, I. William. 2017. 'States, Boundaries and Sovereignty in the Middle East: Unsteady but Unchanging'. *International Affairs* 93 (4): 937–48.

Zerden, Alex Benjamin. 2000. 'Syrian Foreign Policy toward Iran: A Strategic Relationship or Tactical Convergence?' *NIMEP Insights* 3 (1): 17–29.

Ziadeh, Radwan.2011. *Power and Policy in Syria: Intelligence Services, Foreign Relations and Democracy in the Modern Middle East*. London: I.B. Tauris.

2019. *Syria's Role in a Changing Middle East: The Syrian-Israeli Peace Talks*. London: I.B. Tauris.

Zisser, Eyal. 2004. 'Syria and the Question of WMD'. *Middle East Review of International Affairs* 8 (3): 1–9.

2006. 'What Does the Future Hold for Syria?' *Middle East Review of International Affairs* 10 (2): 1–26. http://meria.idc.ac.il/journal/2006/issue2/jv10no2a6.html.

2009a. 'Nasrallah's Defeat in the 2006 War'. *Middle East Quarterly*, January 2009. www.meforum.org/2054/nasrallahs-defeat-in-the-2006-war.

2009b. 'Syria's Diplomatic Comeback: What Next?' *Mediterranean Politics* 14 (1): 107–13.

Zubaida, Sami. 2014. 'Sectarian Dimensions'. *The Middle East Journal* 68 (2): 318–22.

Index